The Princess
and the Pheasant

Elisabeth
Luard

THE PRINCESS
AND THE
PHEASANT
and other recipes

BANTAM PRESS

LONDON · NEW YORK · TORONTO · SYDNEY · AUCKLAND

TRANSWORLD PUBLISHERS LTD
61–63 Uxbridge Road, London W5 5SA

TRANSWORLD PUBLISHERS (AUSTRALIA) PTY LTD
15–23 Helles Avenue, Moorebank, NSW 2170

TRANSWORLD PUBLISHERS (NZ) LTD
Cnr Moselle and Waipareira Aves,
Henderson, Auckland

Published 1987 by Bantam Press,
a division of Transworld Publishers Ltd
Copyright © Elisabeth Luard and The Field 1984, 1985, 1986

British Library Cataloguing in Publication Data
Luard, Elisabeth
The princess and the pheasant: and other
writings.
1. Food
641.3   TX353

ISBN 0-593-01440-5

Photoset by Rowland Phototypesetting Ltd
Bury St Edmunds, Suffolk
Printed in Great Britain by
Butler and Tanner Ltd, Frome and London

Contents

FISH

MEAT

POULTRY AND GAME

PUDDINGS AND SWEETS

BREADS AND CAKES

CHUTNEYS, JAMS AND PICKLES

FOREWORD

Simon Courtauld
Editor of *The Field*

I had met Elisabeth Luard several times, usually in Spain, before I came to *The Field*, without being aware of her very special talent for cooking. When Elisabeth told me in 1984 that she had been making notes on food for the past 20 years, and that she was also something of a wildlife artist, her qualifications to write the first regular column on food for *The Field* in its 130-year history seemed sound enough.

Breaking new ground for *The Field*, we decided also that Elisabeth should write *about* food rather than merely contribute a list of recipes. In her first column – which provides the title to this book – we were regaled with a little history, a learned discourse on the characteristics of a pheasant, a practical tip for plucking the bird, and the simplest recipe for roasting it, with bread sauce and game chips – plus the (to me) novel addition of sherry. The accompanying illustration was quite delightful.

The pattern was quickly established, and we were soon learning about the definitive cock-a-leekie; the 17th-century recipes of Sir Kenelm Digby; the perfect fish and chips; the pickled peaches taken by Shackleton to the Antarctic; variations on Irish stew; the best month of the year to eat crab; the French yeast cake, Pompe de Provence, eaten at Christmas after midnight mass; and Spanish soups.

A year in Paris, and later in the Languedoc, together with a much longer period in Spain, had encouraged Elisabeth to extend her gastronomic horizons. More recently she has travelled in northern and eastern Europe, and her book, *European Peasant Cookery*, has been described by Prue Leith, the distinguished cookery teacher and writer, as 'far and away the most interesting book published in 1986, if not for a decade. . . . Not since I first picked up Elizabeth

David's *A Book of Mediterranean Food* 25 years ago has the smell of no-nonsense good food so enveloped every page.'

This collection of Elisabeth's writings from *The Field* is remarkable for several reasons – for the breadth of her knowledge of cooking, both ancient and modern, from different countries; for the easy elegance of her style; and for demonstrating how, in only two years, she came to be compared with the woman who revolutionised our attitudes to food in the 1950s.

It is a matter of no little pride to us at *The Field* that this is where Elisabeth began her literary gastronomic career and where she continues as our regular food columnist, with her articles and recommendations now expanded and her illustrations now in colour.

Soups and Starters

A Taste of Edwardian Soup

The People's Republic of Hungary, cautiously tiptoeing out from under the skirts of the Iron Curtain, has a thriving and profitable tourist trade with both Mother Russia and the West. Budapest, the capital, is no stranger to either colonizers or tourists: the Romans, the Ottoman Turks and the Austrians have all been in residence in their time.

The modern invaders are catered for by a rash of newly built American-franchise hotels such as the Hilton and the Intercontinental, which play host to Loden-coated and -breeched Austrian sportsmen, who drive out every day into the hills behind the city to bag brown bears. The Russian aparatchiks patronize the same luxury hotels, but the boys from Moscow prefer to take their pleasures in more sedentary fashion. They buy the bearskins shot by the Austrian huntsmen, browse among the Japanese new technology on offer in the steel and glass emporiums in Calvin Square, and pay good hard Deutschmarks for Havana cigars (the spoils of a barter deal with Cuba which, on my recent visit, had left Budapest swamped in Monte Cristo no. 2s at the equivalent of 20p apiece).

Both parties share a delightfully Edwardian taste in food. The Austrian huntsmen patronize, after their exertions in the hills, the elegant *fin-de-siècle* tea-rooms attached to the Pâtisserie Gerbaud, where the art of spun-sugar flower-baskets is still practised daily and such delights as *Doobosh Torte* and cold strawberry soup with cream are on offer. The Russians head for the smartest *nouvelle cuisine* restaurants in town where they eat slices of duck breast decorated with kiwi fruit. The Edwardian note is struck by the most popular item on the menu: Consommé Lady Curzon.

How on earth the gourmets of Budapest and their visitors from Moscow came to prize so highly a recipe attributed to the wife of the Marquess of Curzon no one could tell me. The soup is basically a strong consommé topped with a spoonful of whipped cream sprinkled with a little curry powder. A mixture of curiosity and patriotism prompted me to try it, and it is very good indeed. The marquess himself was Viceroy of India from 1898 to 1905, and his chief interest lay in the restoration of the ancient monuments of the subcontinent. Perhaps the Hungarians, busy restoring the ravages of 1945 and 1956 which destroyed much of Buda, found something sympathetic in the blend.

CONSOMMÉ LADY CURZON

For 4, you will need either 3 tins of Campbell's Double Consommé, undiluted. Or make your own strong soup-stock.
Whipped double cream
Curry powder

Soup-Stock for Consommé (serves 6–8)

2 lb shin of beef plus a few bones	*2 small onions unpeeled and stuck*
4 oz sliced lean bacon or ham	*with 2 cloves each*
2 split pig's trotters or 1 cow heel	*2 large old carrots, 2 sticks celery*
	5 pints water

Lay the bacon on the base of the stew-pan. Add the rest of the ingredients rinsed and cut up. Cover and simmer all very slowly for 4 hours. Allow the stock to reduce to 4 pints by removing the lid at the end. Try not to allow it to boil or the soup will be cloudy. Strain out the solids. Clarify if necessary by whisking the whites of two eggs into the hot soup. Simmer for a few moments. Draw to the side of the fire and leave to settle as it cools. Pour all through a jelly-strainer. Colour the soup with a few drops of browning (make your own by heating 1 tablespoon of sugar to a dark caramel in a small pan. Dissolve the caramel with a tablespoon of water and use it when required). Taste and adjust the seasoning.

Reheat or heat the soup and pour it into individual demitasses. Float a tablespoon of cold whipped cream on top of each cupful. Sprinkle the cream with a little curry powder. This soup can be served cold and jellied in the summer – try it with a poached egg per person set into the jelly. Served thus it makes a delicious summery main dish for luncheon if accompanied with a salad. Very Edwardian.

STRAWBERRY SOUP

Serve this sweet 'soup' in demitasses at the beginning or the end of a light lunch. If at the end, accompany with a dish of fresh strawberries, unhulled so that they can be nibbled in the fingers, and perhaps a plate of almond *tuiles*.

TO SERVE 4 PEOPLE

1 lb strawberries (or raspberries or
  any soft fruit)
2 lemons
1 teaspoon cornflour

½ pint water
3–4 oz sugar
¼ pint double cream, whipped

Wipe and hull the strawberries, and then either liquidize or push them through a sieve. Grate the rind of one of the lemons, and then squeeze the juice of both. Mix the cornflour to a paste with the lemon juice. In a small pan heat the water with the sugar and the grated lemon rind until the granules dissolve. Stir in the lemon juice and cornflour and simmer for a moment to thicken. Remove the pan from the heat and allow to cool. Beat in the strawberry pulp. Serve the soup well iced, in individual bowls or cups, with a dollop of whipped cream floating on the surface.

3 May 1986

Instant Soups in Case of Summer

The Duchess of Windsor it was – or maybe some other wittier dame before her – who never served soup to her dinner-party guests. 'One cannot', she opined, 'build a meal on a lake.' In spite of the late duchess's peculiarly silly style in other areas, I am inclined to agree. There is something disappointing about starting a meal on a puddle, however prettily presented. A demitasse of Consommé Lady Curzon to clear the palate between the hors d'oeuvre and the fish – now, that is a different matter. Or a cold creamy soup, served for lunch in the shade of a tulip tree in an English summer garden, accompanied by a fresh-picked salad and something interesting in the way of sandwiches – that also is another kettle.

In anticipation of lazy summer days I keep in my larder various starter-kits for instant soups. That my equally lazy summer children usually get into the cupboard first and leave it bare is a tribute to the ease of preparation of these standbys. You will need a few tins of the necessary and a liquidizer. Serve the same mixtures hot in the winter.

COLD FLAGEOLET SOUP WITH CREAM AND MINT

You will need 1 tin of prepared flageolet beans, the most delicate of all the pulse vegetables, to make soup for 2 people.

1 tin flageolet beans	*Salt and pepper*
½ pint milk	*2 tablespoons double cream*
3–4 sprigs fresh mint	

Drain the beans and put them in a liquidizer with the milk or water, the mint leaves stripped from their stalks, and the roughly chopped onion, the salt and pepper. Process all to a purée. Taste and adjust the seasoning. A pretty pale-green soup with an almost smoky flavour and a slightly gluey texture. Serve in cups, with a tablespoonful of cream floated on the surface of each helping.

Accompany with *Mrs Reginald Hindley's Dandelion Leaves and Worcester Sauce Sandwiches* as offered by Florence White in 1929. Dandelion leaves are just exactly that – all the rest of Europe gathers the whole plants for salad or to use instead of spinach. Pick your dandelion leaves well away from sprayed crops. Wild greens should always be well washed.

'Thin slices of nicely buttered white bread, with just a speck of Worcester sauce spread on them, sprinkled thickly with finely chopped young dandelion leaves, and covered with a thin slice of brown bread and butter.'

13

WHITE BEAN SOUP WITH YOGHURT AND CORIANDER

TO SERVE 2 PEOPLE

1 tin white haricot beans
1/2 pint water
1/2 large sweet onion
Salt and pepper

1/2 small cucumber
1 carton plain yoghurt
1 clove garlic
1 small bunch coriander

Drain the beans and put them in the liquidizer with the water and the roughly chopped onion. Process all to a purée. Taste and add salt and pepper. Grate the cucumber, salt it lightly, and leave it to drain in a colander for ten minutes. Then mix it into the yoghurt, along with the garlic crushed and chopped finely with the coriander. Serve the soup in bowls, with the yoghurt mixture spooned into the middle but not mixed in.

Accompany with *bacon sandwiches*. Do not make these until you are ready to eat. Fry rashers of thin-cut smoked bacon until crisp. Sandwich them between slices of bread spread on one inner surface only with a knife-tip of strong English mustard.

COLD TOMATO AND GARLIC SOUP

TO SERVE 2 PEOPLE

1 tin tomatoes
1 slice stale bread
2 cloves garlic
2 ice cubes
1 small glass cold water

1 tablespoon wine vinegar
1 teaspoon sugar
1 tablespoon olive oil
Salt and pepper

Put all the above ingredients into the liquidizer and process them thoroughly. Serve this instant *gazpacho* very cold with hot croûtons fried in olive oil and garlic.

Accompany with a crisp green salad dressed with basil and *fetta* cheese (or tiny cubes of any strong hard cheese). Have on the table a dish of green olives and another with devilled almonds.

DEVILLED ALMONDS

1/2 lb almonds
1 tablespoon oil
1 teaspoon salt

1 teaspoon cayenne pepper (this is the hot one)

Blanch and pop the almonds out of their skins. Dry them thoroughly. Put the oil into a frying-pan and heat it. When the oil is lightly smoking, toss in the almonds. Fry them gently until they brown. Drain on kitchen paper and then transfer them to a bowl. Toss them with the salt and cayenne pepper. Serve warm.

INSTANT VICHYSSOISE

A soup to make when the children have emptied the storecupboard.

TO SERVE 2–3 PEOPLE

2 large potatoes
3–4 spring onions or 1 large leek or
   ½ Spanish onion
1 bay leaf
½ pint water

¼ pint milk
Salt and pepper
2–3 tablespoons double cream
1 tablespoon chopped chives

Peel and slice the potatoes and the onions quite thin. Put them in a saucepan with the water and the bay leaf. Bring to the boil and cook until soft (about ten minutes). Allow to cool a little, remove the bay leaf and pour the contents of the pan into the liquidizer. Add the milk. Process thoroughly. Taste and add salt and pepper. Serve cold, with cream trickled over the top. Sprinkle with chives. Serve with tiny *croque-monsieur* – cheese and ham sandwiches cut into triangles and fried until golden in half butter, half oil.

21 June 1986

Soups from Spain

Their two thrones united by marriage, Ferdinand of Aragon and Isabella of Castile turned their considerable energies to the reconquest of Spain's southern provinces. The armies of the *Reyes Católicos* entered Granada, pearl of Moorish Spain, in the same year in which Isabella funded Christopher Columbus' expedition to the New World. The year 1492 proved busy and successful for their Catholic Majesties. It was less happy for the Moors – chased, like miscreant Adam and Eve, out of their own particular paradise on earth, the gardens, pools and palaces of the Alhambra. Young Boabdil, last of the caliphs, trudged wearily into exile in the Alpujarra hills. Behind him were the olive groves and almond trees of the fertile Vega, ahead the stony deserts of Africa's Rif mountains. The four-lane highway which connects Granada and Malaga today crosses a pass which gives a last view of the city. Beside the petrol station and cafeteria is the legend 'Sospiro del Moro', the sigh of the Moor.

The Moors had been masters in Spain for eight centuries, and the Spanish propaganda machine had to grind long and hard to erase their traces. The Inquisition was a brutal match for the more obvious nonconformists, but there were little habits that had to be eradicated, too. Pig and goat meat replaced the lamb permitted to Muslims. Lamb-eating became almost an admission of heresy. But memories, particularly culinary ones, are long. No one ripped out the almond trees the Moors had brought from the Jordan valley and tended so carefully through the centuries. The natives had grown too fond of their almond-based nougats and marzipans for that.

Meanwhile Christopher Columbus' labours had borne strange fruit. Instead of spices from the Indies, he brought back outlandish foodstuffs, including the tomato and the capsicum pepper. Both vegetables flourished in the warmth of southern Spain and soon had as strong an influence on Spanish cooking as the skills of the Moors had had in their time.

Two delicious Spanish summer soups embody the two camps. One, child of the elegant Old World, is *ajo blanco*: pale, sophisticated, and based on almond milk, originally cooled with the snow water piped into the Alhambra from the icy ridges of the Sierra Nevada. The other, born of the New World, is far better known: the earthy tomato-and-pepper-thickened *gazpacho*.

AJO BLANCO

TO SERVE 6 PEOPLE

3 oz blanched almonds
4 cloves garlic
2 tablespoons olive oil
2 pints cold water

Salt
1 tablespoon white wine vinegar
Handful of white grapes

Put the almonds, garlic, oil and a pint of the water into the blender to liquidize thoroughly. Add the rest of the water. Season with salt and vinegar. Leave to cool and infuse in the fridge for an hour or so. Peel and pip the grapes. When you are ready to serve, add the grapes and a piece of ice for each serving. No croûtons to mar its pallor – this is a soup for refreshment rather than for nourishment.

GAZPACHO

There is a peasant version of this which is a winter dish, a kind of hot bread soup flavoured with olive oil, tomato and garlic. In the summer it is eaten cold. The recipe has gone through the same sort of gentrification as *bouillabaisse* in France, but is none the less excellent in the grander form which I offer here.

TO SERVE 6 PEOPLE

1 small cucumber
2 lb ripe tomatoes
½ lb green peppers
1 large Spanish onion
2 cloves garlic
3 slices day-old bread

4 tablespoons olive oil
1 tablespoon wine vinegar
½ pint tomato juice
1 pint cold water
Salt and sugar
2 hard-boiled eggs

Reserve a quarter of each of the vegetables (except the garlic) for the garnish. With the remaining vegetables: Peel the tomatoes. Take the seeds out of the green peppers and chop the peppers roughly. Peel the garlic and onion and chop them. Put the chopped vegetables, one slice of bread, two spoonfuls of olive oil, the vinegar and the tomato juice into the blender and liquidize thoroughly. (If you need to keep the *gazpacho*, omit the onion from the soup – it ferments rather easily.) Add water until you have the consistency you like. Season with salt and a little sugar. Put in the fridge for an hour at least. Serve very cold.

Meanwhile cube the reserved vegetables, keeping them separate. Peel and chop the hard-boiled eggs. Cube the remaining two slices of bread and fry in the rest of the oil just before you are ready to serve. Put each garnish into an individual bowl. Hand round with the soup.

6 July 1985

Pumpkin Time

The formidable headmistress of the boarding school in the Malvern Hills which I attended for most of my formative years wore her long grey hair wound round her head in an arrangement like the brim of a governess's hat. She ruled her charges with a rod of iron, with dire penalties for the most minor transgressions. There was but one moment in the year when she descended into the world of mortals, to take shape not as a human being, but as a witch. Each year at Hallowe'en she and the two most senior of our teachers would don black robes, let down their waist-length grey tresses and become the very life and soul of the school's traditional Hallowe'en party. Some of the younger pupils had nightmares for weeks. The central feature of the party, apart from the headmistress's fortune-telling tent (an opportunity for a little bracing propaganda), was the competition for the best-carved pumpkin lantern. Wonderfully ferocious sculptures took shape in the art-room for weeks in advance. For many years I thought that this was the proper treatment for the pumpkin. It was not until long after I had left school that I discovered the delights of this supremely adaptable vegetable.

18

The Gower Peninsula in south Wales seems to have been the only part of the British Isles which took enthusiastically to the pumpkin – like the potato and the marrow, a New World import. 'In Gower,' explained Lady Llanover in her book *The First Principles of Good Cookery* (1867), 'they [pumpkins] are added to hashed meat, made into pies with apples, and put into soup. Pumpkins have one peculiar quality in addition to a good deal of natural sweetness: they will absorb and retain the flavour of whatever they are cooked with. If stewed with plums it tastes exactly like them in puddings and tarts; the same with apples, rhubarb or gooseberries; and for savoury cookery it would be difficult to say in what dish it may not be used with advantage as an addition.'

Pumpkins still appear in our shops to mark the festival of All Hallows Eve – it seems to be the only time these beautiful golden globes are easily available. I particularly like my pumpkin cut into chunks and boiled with an equal quantity of potatoes, then mashed with butter and milk to provide one of the best accompaniments for a winter stew. For those with pumpkins left over from the festival, here are two delicious recipes for pumpkin soup, the perfect way to prepare this neglected vegetable. Don't forget to save the seeds to roast with salt as a delicious nibble for adults and children alike.

GOWER PUMPKIN SOUP

The inhabitants of the Gower Peninsula had strong associations with both Cornwall and Normandy through their sea-routes. Certainly this soup, which my grandmother's Welsh cook used to prepare, makes good use of the rich dairy produce common to both. Adjust the milk–cream ratio to suit your own palate. All-cream is wonderfully luxurious and delicious, but can only be consumed in demitasse quantities.

TO SERVE 6–8 PEOPLE

1 whole pumpkin – a 6–7 pounder	*1 pint milk*
(they come much bigger than that)	*½ pint cream*
	Salt and pepper

Replace the lid on the pumpkin and then put it in a low oven to bake. A medium-sized pumpkin takes three hours at 300°F/gas 3. At the end of that time the pumpkin flesh will be soft, though still in chunks, and the skin will still be whole, though somewhat collapsed and fragile. Scoop out the insides – liquid, flesh and all – taking care not to puncture the pumpkin. Then either push the solids through a vegetable-sieve or process everything in the blender. Return the soup to the pumpkin and carry it to the table.

Serve the soup straight from the pumpkin into bowls. You won't need anything heavy after this – a plain-grilled chop from a year-old mutton from the Welsh hills, perhaps, particularly if you can get some laverbread (Chinese delicatessens stock it as well as health-food stores) to go with it. Soak and then stew the laverbread in a little stock or water for 15–20 minutes, then beat in some butter, or the juices from the grilled chop, and serve the seasoned purée on a slice of fried bread per person.

GERMAN PUMPKIN SOUP

TO SERVE 4–6 PEOPLE

2 lb piece of pumpkin
1 pint water
6 cloves
Small piece of cinnamon stick

2 tablespoons wine vinegar
2 oz butter
Salt, pepper, sugar

Peel the pumpkin and scoop out the seeds and fibrous middle. Cut the flesh into cubes and put them in a saucepan with the water (it looks like too little, but the pumpkin itself is full of water).

Stick the cloves and the stick of cinnamon into a piece of pumpkin flesh so that you can remove them easily. Stew the cubes gently with the spices for 20–30 minutes, until soft. Take out the spices, then purée the pumpkin with its cooking liquid. Stir in the vinegar. Heat again and beat in the butter. Season with salt, plenty of freshly milled black pepper, and a little sugar to bring out the sweetness of the vegetable. This is a very delicate, amber-clear soup. Don't stir in cream or you will alter its nature.

Skip the meat course, and complete the meal with a steamed pudding.

8 November 1986

A Dip by the Sea of Galilee

All summer the Sea of Galilee is ringed with charabancs. The passengers, largely from New York and Philadelphia, inspect the secular Roman town of Tiberias (the only town in Israel with absolutely no Christian tourist draw), and then move round the deep blue water for a group lunch at the kibbutz of En Gev. A mortar-shot away lies the Syrian border. The scream of military jets is particularly deafening when it bounces off the steep mountain slopes which form the lake's basin. The resident population of terns and black-headed gulls scavenges warily round the shore.

The kibbutz restaurant has a limited menu. Its speciality is St Peter's fish, deep-fried and served with chips. Presumably the fish, a species of bream, is the descendant of those which provided a living for the apostle himself. Now it is reared in ponds and comes, like Marks & Spencer underwear, in two sizes – medium or large. Since the restaurant has to serve 200 covers at a time, a machine has been devised which guts, batters and fries the fish on a production-line system of claws, conveyor belts and vats of boiling oil. Large fish down one side and medium down the other: mesmerizing. The loaves – which are equally excellent – are served with the other house speciality, *hummus bi tahini*, a dish which is very popular with the neighbours, Syria, Jordan and the Lebanon – at present on the other side of the barbed wire. *Hummus bi tahini* and *muttabal* are both salad purées, one based on chickpeas, the other on aubergine. The *hummus* is flavoured with *tahini*, a paste made of crushed sesame seeds now quite widely available in British delicatessens. If you can't find it, smooth peanut butter makes a convincing substitute. These

21

purées are served all over the Middle East as hors d'oeuvres (*mezzeh*): in Israel the food is the only thing which has achieved perfect integration.

CHICKPEA SALAD/HUMMUS BI TAHINI

8 oz chickpeas
3 cloves garlic
3 tablespoons tahini paste
Juice of 1 lemon

Salt
Ground cummin
Cayenne pepper

Soak the chickpeas overnight. Throw away the water in which they have been soaking. Put them in a roomy saucepan with plenty of cold unsalted water. Bring to the boil and keep them on the simmer for the whole length of the cooking time: 1–2 hours, depending on the length of their cold-water soaking and the age of the chickpeas. If you need to add more water, let it be boiling. When the chickpeas are soft, drain them, reserving a cupful of the cooking liquor.

Put the chickpeas, with some of their liquor to moisten, into a blender (unquestionably easier than the traditional pestle and mortar) with the peeled cloves of garlic, the *tahini* and the lemon juice. Liquidize thoroughly. Season with salt, cummin and a little cayenne pepper.

AUBERGINE PURÉE/MUTTABAL

2 large aubergines
Juice of 1 lemon
¼ pint olive oil

4 cloves garlic
Salt
Pepper

There is a school which believes aubergines must be salted to extract the bitter juice. I find that if the aubergine is of good quality, firm and fresh, it is never bitter, and this treatment only serves to make the flesh too salty. Make two slashes in each aubergine and press into each pocket a peeled clove of garlic and a trickle of the oil. Put the aubergines, still whole, into a medium oven to bake until soft. This will take about an hour. Take them out and allow to cool. Halve the aubergines and scrape the flesh off the thin skin. (If you leave the skin on, the purée will have little black-purple specks instead of being a pale cream.) Put the flesh with the cloves of garlic in the liquidizer with the lemon juice and the rest of the oil. Liquidize for a few moments until smooth. This makes a delicious smoky-flavoured salad purée.

Serve the two purées together at room temperature, smoothed on to a large flat plate, with the *muttabal* in the centre and the *hummus* round the outside, like a large pale sunflower. Mix a spoonful of oil with a little paprika pepper to colour it red and dribble it over the centre of your flower. Serve hot sesame bread or a baguette to scoop through both purées simultaneously. There should be a bowl of black olives, and at least one other salad of a fresh crisp texture to accompany – perhaps cucumber cut into cubes and mixed with chopped green peppers and walnuts, dressed with yoghurt. Hard-boiled eggs and red peppers softened in oil are the traditional accompaniments. An excellent first course or light luncheon.

1 June 1985

Great Patriarchs from Little Avocados Grow

Buried in the orchid-laden forests around Taxco in central Mexico are caves with sacrificial altar-stones trenched for blood and carved with half-human beasts. The tourists come to see them, and to buy silver mined in nearby Le Borde, worked and set with turquoise in the town. Real Mexican silver.

Outside the town, in the shade of the oldest avocado tree in the world, sits an old man, his face wrinkled like a walnut. A little slant-eyed brown baby crawls among the fallen leaves at his feet. In spite of his great age, the old man is still broad-shouldered and vigorous. The child is his great-great-grandson. The tree itself towers over a two-tier aqueduct which carries water to a rambling stone mansion beyond. The aqueduct provides a convenient ladder

23

to the tree: two of the old man's grandchildren have shinned up the arches to gather fruit from the upper branches.

Tourists are accommodated in the old man's rambling hotel beneath the avocado tree. The old man and the tree have much in common: both are patriarchs. The tree's line of descent is clear: no avocado tree can bear good fruit unless it is grafted with a branch from a fertile tree. Legend and the old man have it that this is the tree from which all the others were born, parent to child from America to Europe to Africa to Asia. As for the patriarch, human affairs are less precise. Legend and the admiring town have it that the old man is the ancestor of everyone who lives and works in his household, around two hundred souls. Estimates of quite how many of these are of his direct fathering vary. Above the blanket upstairs, beneath the blanket below stairs seems to be the rough rule. The hotel is impeccably well run, and avocados are always on the menu. Perhaps this diet accounted for the fecundity and longevity of the patriarch.

An avocado pear, picked rock-hard, wrapped in newspaper and kept in a dry cupboard for exactly fifteen days, will be perfectly ripe and ready to eat. It should not then be filled with prawn cocktail, mayonnaised or otherwise stuffed and sauced. Avocado flesh is very rich, and any addition – apart from a mere trickle of olive oil – which makes it richer is a disaster. Cut the fruit in two, preferably with a silver knife (from the mines at Taxco perhaps), and take out the stone. Put each half on a plate, place beside it a small pile of rock salt, a quarter of lemon or, better still, lime, and a tiny glass of very cold vodka (unless you can find tequila). To eat it, either salt the avocado and squeeze some lemon over it, then crush a little of the spirit into the flesh and eat the whole thing with a spoon; or alternate a suck of lemon, a sip of vodka and a lick of salt with a spoonful of the avocado. By this means the avocado will taste both sweet and fresh, and the strong cold alcohol make it easy to digest.

There are three main varieties of *Persea americana*: the small, thin-skinned and delicious Mexican fruit; the Guatemalan native – a larger, coarser, woody-skinned pear; and the West Indian variety, which is smooth-fleshed, large and good. Imperfect fruit can be made into *guacamole*, an excellent thick sauce-salad which is the glory of Mexican food.

To make *guacamole*, roughly chop the flesh of a ripe avocado in a bowl and then mix into it a chopped onion and a small chopped tomato – the volume of avocado should be double that of the two other vegetables. Then add a spoonful of chopped fresh coriander

24

(which can be grown very easily from seed in a month or two: it has a flavour like the smell of ladybirds and is oddly addictive). Season the mixture with lime or lemon juice, salt and pepper. Absolutely no oil. Eat the *guacamole* scooped up on crisp fried tortillas or chunks of fresh bread, with raw vegetables, as a green chutney with cold meat, or to accompany practically anything Mexican. It's very good with hamburgers too. *Guacamole* is best eaten fresh, but will keep for a day if the stone is left buried in it.

When you have finished your avocado, take the smooth brown stone, place it in a jar just resting the blunt end in water and wait for the tree to sprout. Keep eating the avocados, and by the time you can sit in the shade of your tree you will certainly be as old as the patriarch, and possibly even as fecund.

20 October 1984

A Garlic Touch to a Garden Snail

There is, as every gardener knows, no shortage of snails in Britain, all of which are perfectly edible. The French have no snail problem – they have recently been obliged to declare a closed season on snail-hunting to limit the national appetite for the little hermaphrodites. Some of the British quota are descendants of a batch of *Helix pomatia* imported by the Romans, who used to breed and fatten snails in vivariums. The Romans farmed all varieties of snail, including a giant African *Achatina* species which grew so enormous that the poet Marcus Varro, in *De res rustica*, reported that some of the creatures' shells contained twenty pints. Fortunately, the Romans did not import *Achatina* – it can go through a herbaceous border like a combine harvester.

There is but one caveat to the would-be snail-eater. Although the snail itself will be perfectly wholesome, its diet may not be agreeable

25

to the human digestion. This is the reason for the practice of quarantining (or starving) your snails: after a week or two the creatures will have emptied their digestive systems of any dangerous vegetable matter. In the British countryside this could be anything from hemlock to giant hogweed to lead-painted telegraph poles, so it is well worth being patient. You will have plumper snails if you feed them during the quarantine period – "bolted" vegetables such as lettuce are particularly suitable. Snails which have been farmed and fed on a regulated diet will pose no problem, nor will snails in hibernation which have sealed their shells with a brittle membrane – they have been self-starved. My neighbour in the Languedoc used to fatten his up on young vines. Then he would roast them on the fire like chestnuts.

Roman snails are particularly plentiful on the South Downs and the headlands of Cornwall, where they used to be collected by sailors from French coastal fishing vessels. During the last century both Gloucestershire and Pembrokeshire supplied the factory workers of Bristol with tons of the common British garden variety. The glassblowers and tobacco workers had a strong fancy for them.

Collect your garden snails (the large ones will be *Helix pomatia* or *Helix aspersa*) in a capacious basket with a perforated lid. Or make them a little thrush-proof enclosure on a shaded grassy patch. Feed them up for a week; they like soaked oatmeal and apple peelings as well as vegetables. Ideally you should clean them out, feed them and change their water daily. If all this is too much hard work, perfectly good results will be achieved merely by starving them, although you should clean them out every now and again – the evacuation process is copious.

After a week your charges will be ready for the table. The factory workers of Bristol liked theirs prepared with an onion, bacon and butter sauce, but I think the French way *à la bourguignonne* still has the edge.

ESCARGOTS BOURGUIGNONNE

For the snails

> *A dozen large snails per diner*
> *Salt, peppercorns and bay leaf*
> *1 onion*

> *A handful of fresh herbs*
> *Vinegar*

Put a big pot of water on to boil. Add plenty of salt, peppercorns and the bay leaf. Halve the onion and add that and the herbs to the brew.

Meanwhile wash the snails very thoroughly in several changes of cold fresh water.

When the water in the pot boils, throw in the snails one by one (this guarantees a swift demise). When the water returns to the boil it will foam vigorously. As it does so, stir in a few spoonfuls of vinegar. This will coagulate the mucous froth and it will subside. Simmer for an hour.

Drain the snails. Remove them from their shells with a toothpick or skewer. Pinch off the cloaca (the long black intestine on the end). This is an added precaution against *mauvaises herbes*. Wipe the shells clean – you can polish them with a little oil if you please. They are now ready for stuffing.

Garlic Butter

6 oz butter will stuff 4 dozen snails   *Handful of parsley*
3 large cloves garlic   *Salt and pepper*

Mash the butter with a fork to soften. Chop the parsley and garlic together very finely and then mash them into the butter with plenty of salt and pepper. A dash of *marc de bourgogne* would do no harm.

Push a small knob of the garlic butter into the base of each snail-shell. Press the snail back into its home. Fill up the entrance with another knob of garlic butter. Continue until all the snails are ready. Arrange the shells in a snail-dish if you have one; if not, prop them against each other with the openings skyward.

Turn the oven up to 425°F/gas 7, and give the snails 15 minutes. Serve piping hot with plenty of fresh bread and a good supply of toothpicks to pluck them out of their shells.

28 September 1985

Vegetable Dishes

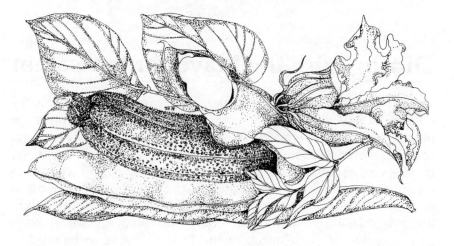

Dining with the Mayor of Jerusalem

Teddy Kolek, the mayor of Jerusalem, is a singular fellow. A stocky politico of the smoke-filled-rooms school, he has occupied the hottest seat in Christendom for a good many years. Surprisingly, considering the passions that surge round the walls of the Holy City, no one yet has lobbed so much as a burnt tyre in his direction. His constituency contains the most quarrelsome rabble of holy men and hooligans in all creation, with the possible exception of the neighbouring township of Bethlehem. There the mob of sectarian monks in possession of the Church of the Nativity came to blows and bloodshed last Easter (spades and broom-handles were the chosen weapons) over demarcation lines in the Stable.

Within Jerusalem's city walls, no farther apart than the arc of a grenade, are the holiest shrines of three of the world's major religions. The Dome of the Rock shelters the imprint of the foot of Mahomet, left when the Prophet sprang into Heaven. The Wailing Wall, relic of King Solomon's Temple, is the divine post-box for all of Jewry. While through the streets of the old city winds the Way of the Cross to Golgotha.

Over all these turbulent factions presides the bulky figure of the mayor. Eating is part of his politics: many non-sectarian dinners have padded his frame. He drives his small white car fast and dangerously through his manor. He goes where he pleases, without bodyguards or motorcycle cops, enjoying his meals all over the city. On Sunday, when the Christian section of Jerusalem is shut down, he will take sesame bread and kebabs in the Arab quarter. On Friday, the Muslim holy day, he might have his lunch at a kosher restaurant in the new town. On Saturday the city's smart set makes its way up the hill in east Jerusalem to the American Colony Hotel for Sabbath lunch. The mayor likes a table in the shade of the flowering tree which shelters the central courtyard. The hotel, in the style of Granada's Alhambra, is considerably prettier than the Odeon/British Museum architecture of the rival King David across the ravine. The food, as befits a former pasha's palace, is also a great deal better.

The American Colony's buffet, in its setting of mosaics, white trellis arches and stucco work, is suitably Moorish and reckoned the best around. Most of the classic Middle Eastern dishes are laid out, including *tabouleh*, a delicious salad based on burghul (cracked wheat). It makes an excellent summer luncheon dish. Cracked wheat is now quite widely available in health stores and delicatessens in Britain. Middle Eastern parsley is the flat-leaved kind, but the British curly parsley will do well enough. *There should be the same volume of herbs as burghul.*

TABOULEH

TO SERVE 6 PEOPLE

4 oz fine burghul (or couscous)
4 oz parsley (young raw spinach is a
  possible substitute)
4 oz mint leaves
1 green pepper
1 onion

½ cucumber
1 lb tomatoes
Juice of 2 large lemons
¼ pint olive oil
Salt

Rinse the burghul (partly cooked wheat which has been dried and ground into coarse, medium or fine grades) in cold water. When the water runs clear, drain the burghul thoroughly and put in a large bowl. If you use couscous, it must be soaked.

Chop the parsley and mint. De-seed the pepper and chop. Chop the onion, the cucumber and the tomatoes. Mix these chopped vegetables and herbs into the burghul. Dress all with lemon juice, olive oil and salt. Leave for half an hour. Then taste and add more lemon, oil and salt if necessary.

Serve with a bowl of lettuce leaves (without dressing) with which to make little parcels of the *tabouleh* – a delicious way to eat it – and bowls of radishes, black olives and quartered hard-boiled eggs.

CUSTARD APPLE SORBET

The dessert-table included an excellent custard apple sorbet, of which the mayor is particularly fond. The custard apple is a large, smooth, soft fruit with a pale green skin and creamy opaque flesh. It is amply equipped for procreation with large black seeds. When ripe it is strongly scented, and has a flavour with echoes of pineapple and banana. Odd – but it makes an excellent sorbet. The fruit can be found at enlightened British greengrocers .

*1 lb custard apples (this might be a
    single fruit)
4 oz caster sugar*

*½ pint water
Juice of 1 lemon*

Peel and de-seed the custard apples. Boil the sugar and water together for five minutes and allow to cool.

Liquidize the flesh of the custard apples with the sugar syrup and the lemon juice. Freeze until quite solid. Turn out and liquidize again. Freeze again. De-freeze for half an hour before serving – this is quite a creamy sorbet with a very subtle flavour and should not be served rock-hard.

Mint tea to finish the meal.

15 June 1985

Acetaria

John Evelyn's *Acetaria, A Discourse of Sallets* rated as a revolutionary tract when it was published in 1699. Its author, more famous as a diarist than as a cook, had the stuff of revolution in his blood anyway: his family fortune was founded on the manufacture of gunpowder. The rich and aristocratic of the time regarded vegetable matter as unwholesome and best left to the peasants; they loaded their own boards with meat and fine white bread. Evelyn prudently prefaced his book with a lengthy dedication to the contemporary great-and-good – the president of the newly formed Royal Society, of which Evelyn, along with his friend Sir Kenelm Digby (of *The Closet Open'd*, see p. 281), was a founding Fellow. The work for which Evelyn is best known, his highly entertaining diary, was discovered in a laundry-basket, along with some dirty linen of a non-literary sort, at the Evelyn mansion of Wotton in 1817, a century after its author's death.

The first section of *Acetaria* (from the Latin meaning 'vegetables prepared with vinegar and oil') is devoted to the proper cultivation of vegetables and their preparation for the table. Artichokes head Evelyn's list: he recommends they should be eaten raw when very young, dipped in oil, vinegar, salt and pepper, and accompanied by a glass of wine. When tender and small, they are to be 'fried in fresh Butter crisp with Parsley'. Delicious. 'In Italy,' he continues, 'they sometimes Broil them' (that is, grill them on the fire) 'and as the scaley Leaves open, baste them with fresh and sweet Oyl, but with Care extraordinary, for if a drop fall upon the Coals, all is marr'd; that hazard escap'd, they eat them with the Juice of Orange and Sugar.'

He includes splendid and exact instructions for the making of salads, and gives a basic recipe for vinaigrette. His proportion of 'Oyl' to vinegar is precisely that offered in the modern *Larousse gastronomique*. Not bad for a seventeenth-century amateur. He also suggests some rather original additions to the salad-bowl: the flowers of rosemary, borage, nasturtium, gillyflower, elder, cowslip and broombuds, as well as a profusion of herb leaves and young vegetables. He advises cucumber 'to sharpen the appetite and calm the Liver', nettle to 'purify the blood', and the taking of lettuce for its 'soporiphorous quality'. Beatrix Potter's Peter Rabbit went to sleep after eating lettuce, too.

TO MAKE A SALLET

Your Herbs being handsomely parsell'd, and spread upon a clean Napkin before you, are to be mingl'd together in one an Earthen glaz'd dishe: Then for the Oxoleon; Take of clean, and perfectly good Oyl-olive, three Parts; of Sharpest Vinegar (sweetest of all condiments), Limon, or Juice of Orange, one Part; and therein let steep some Slices of Horse-radish, with a little Salt: some in a separate Vinegar, gently bruise a Pod of Guinny-Pepper [cayenne pepper], straining both the Vinegars apart, to make use of Either, or one alone, or of both, as they best like; then add as much Tewkesbury, or other dry Mustared grated, as will lie upon a Half-crown Piece: Beat and mingle these all very well together; but pour not on the Oyl and Vinegar, till immediately before the Sallet is ready to be eaten. And then with the Yolk of two new-laid Eggs (boiled and prepared) squash and bruise them all into mash with a Spoon, and lastly pour it all upon the Herbs, stirring and mingling them 'till they are well and thoroughly imbibed; not forgetting the sprinkling of Aromatics and such Flowers as we have already mentioned.

In the final section of the book, a collection of cooked vegetable recipes, Evelyn credits an 'Experienc'd Housewife' as the source. She was clearly a lady of talent and imagination. There are several recipes for vegetable 'puddings' which are not unlike the modern terrine. The 'Carrot Pudding' which follows is the master-recipe for these. Evelyn tells us it can also be made with green herbs such as spinach, or a charming mixture of penny-royal and marigold petals. The result is a sturdy vegetable bread and butter pudding.

PUDDING OF CARROT

Pare off some of the Crust of Manchet-Bread [finest white bread for noblemen], and grate off half as much of the rest as there is of the Root, which must also be grated. Then take half a Pint of fresh Cream or New Milk, half a pound of fresh Butter, six new-laid Eggs (taking out three of the whites), mash and mingle them well with the cream and the butter with half a pound of Sugar [1 oz of sugar is plenty], and a little Salt; some grated Nutmeg and beaten Spice; pour all into a convenient Dish or Pan, butter'd to keep the Ingredients from sticking and burning, set in a quick Oven for about an hour, and so have you a composition for any Root-Pudding.

18 May 1985

Salad Days Are Here Again

Nebuchadnezzar was probably the earliest recorded royal salad enthusiast. He was described in the Book of Daniel as a madman and an eater of grass. Back home in Babylon in the sixth century BC the Chaldean ruler had already demonstrated his interest in matters

horticultural by installing the Hanging Gardens. The pen, however, being mightier than the sword, his conquered subjects in Jerusalem recorded for all time the gardener-king's penchant for greens as a sign not only of insanity but also of the displeasure of the Almighty. Poor Nebuchadnezzar was a long way ahead of his time.

Happily, modern grass-eaters are no longer subject to the same abuse. We can browse on miscellaneous leaves without the slightest doubt being cast on our good sense. The very reverse: thanks to the influence of the *nouvelle cuisine* school, many more salad herbs are now available from the greengrocer, including the fashionable red varieties of lettuce and my own favourite, the tender little leaves of cornsalad, sometimes known as lamb's lettuce, which are available in French markets all year round under the name of *mâche*.

The range available is even wider if you grow your own. Less common leaves range from dandelion (exactly like the wild variety, the plant grows to monster size if free of competition – the taste of the young leaves is surprising mild), Good King Henry, Chinese radish leaves, a dozen or so endives and chicories, salad rape, *mesclun* – a mixture of salad leaves for broadcasting (their variety is the Italian version, *misticanza*) – and lovely old-fashioned leaves such as purslane and rocket. Salads of delicate fresh herbs need no other embellishment than a sprinkle of good oil – olive or nut – the lightest hand with the wine vinegar, a pinch of sea-salt, and a turn of the pepper-mill. With the inclusion of a handful of fresh chopped herbs such as tarragon, chervil, chives or fennel, the mix would please even the discerning Nebuchadnezzar. In honour of the royal gardener you might even include a few of those royal-blue borage flowers which taste of cucumber (be careful to remove their hairy sepals first).

For a main course, make a potato- or bean-based salad to accompany the lightly dressed leaves. Even such sturdy salads as these are best made quite fresh and served at room temperature: they never seem to recover from a night in the refrigerator.

SPANISH POTATO SALAD

A very useful salad which I often make for a Saturday lunch when the weather warms up.

TO SERVE 6 PEOPLE

2 lb new potatoes
3 hard-boiled eggs
1 small tin anchovies
1 small tin tunnyfish in oil
1 onion or 4 spring onions
2 small firm tomatoes (or 1 large one)
1 green or red pepper

Parsley and/or marjoram
1 teaspoon mild mustard
Olive oil and wine vinegar (look for sherry vinegar)
Salt and freshly milled black pepper
1–2 oz black olives

Cook the new potatoes until soft (for 15–20 minutes) in well-salted boiling water. If you use old potatoes, peel them first and start them in cold water. Boil the eggs for 6–7 minutes (I do this in the same water as the potatoes), then rinse them in cold water before peeling and roughly chopping them.

Meanwhile open the tins of tunnyfish and anchovies and drain them. Trim and chop the onion(s). Dice the tomatoes. De-seed and chop the pepper. Chop the herbs. Mix the mustard, 4 tablespoons of olive oil and 1 tablespoon of vinegar together with a fork – they should thicken into an emulsion. As soon as the potatoes have been drained, transfer them to a flat serving-dish and toss them with this vinaigrette and add the chopped onions and green peppers. Allow all to cool. Toss in the herbs, the tomato and the chopped hard-boiled eggs. Season with salt and freshly milled black pepper. Scatter flakes of tunny and fillets of anchovy over the top.

FLAGEOLET SALAD WITH BACON

An elegant pale-green salad for lunch in the garden – accompany with a tankard of Pimms.

TO SERVE 4 PEOPLE

3 tins flageolet beans or 8 oz dried
  flageolet beans
1 small bunch spring onions or
  1 sweet Spanish onion
1 large bunch of parsley
1 large bunch of mint

2 slices of bread
4 oz thin-cut streaky bacon
4 tablespoons olive oil
1 tablespoon vinegar
Salt and pepper

If the flageolets are dried, cook them in water to cover until tender (an hour should be sufficient), and then drain them.

Chop up the onions, the parsley, the mint. Drain the beans. Mix beans, onions, parsley, mint, oil, vinegar in a pretty bowl. Taste and season with salt and freshly milled black pepper.

Dice the bread and the bacon. Put the bacon to fry crisp in a little extra fat in a frying-pan. When the fat has run, add the cubed bread and turn it until it is crisp and golden. Top the salad with the sizzling bacon and croûtons. Serve the salad immediately.

10 May 1986

Returning to Vegetables

My youngest daughter has gone off round Europe on a month-long Interrail ticket with her three best friends, one small bikini and a gigantic tent. She is of course now constantly in my thoughts, viewed with that affection with which only absent teenagers are ever viewed by parents. She did the same thing last year. When the prodigal returned, long-legged and brown and indistinguishable from the three hundred other teenage backpackers disgorged on to Victoria Station that particular midnight, she had (to me) appalling stories of nights spent on railway stations and dramatic encounters on moonlit beaches. After her travels last year, she announced she was considering becoming a vegetarian. Whether this had anything to do with her experiences in the terminals and on the pearly sands of Europe, or whether the decision was dictated simply by economics, I have so far failed to discover.

However, I do worry about it.

VEGETABLE GRATIN

ENOUGH FOR 4 PRODIGAL DAUGHTERS

The Sauce

3 oz butter
3 oz flour
1½ pints milk
1 small onion or 2–3 spring onions
1 teaspoon strong mustard

1 teaspoon Worcester sauce (or
   Pontack sauce; see page 253)
Small bunch of parsley (other fresh
   herbs would be welcome)
2 oz grated cheese
Salt and pepper

The Vegetables

Nicest if you have a mixture. Choose
   about 2 lb – from cauliflower,
   courgettes or a small marrow,
   carrots, leeks, parsnips, broad
   beans, broccoli

1 oz grated cheese and a knob of
   butter to finish

Put all the sauce ingredients in the liquidizer and process them thoroughly. Tip all into a saucepan, bring to the boil and then turn down to simmer until thick.

Prepare the vegetables as suitable – the cauliflower and broccoli should be divided into florets, the courgettes quartered lengthways and halved, the carrots, leeks and parsnips quartered vertically if they are large, and cut into short lengths. Cook your chosen ones in boiling salted water until soft – don't overdo the courgettes.

Arrange the cooked, drained vegetables in a gratin-dish and pour the sauce over them. Sprinkle with cheese and dot with butter. Slip the gratin under the grill until brown and bubbling.

The secret of this dish lies in a *very* strongly flavoured sauce and thorough draining of the vegetables.

RATATOUILLE

Not at all like that wet grey slush which so often masquerades as this beautiful Provençal vegetable stew. The key to the dish is to cook the vegetables *separately* at first.

1 lb aubergines
1 lb onions
2–3 peppers (red, green or yellow)

1 lb tomatoes
1 wine-glass olive oil
Salt and pepper
2 fat cloves garlic

Slice the aubergines into rings, salt them and put them to drain in a colander. Peel and slice the onions finely. Hull, de-seed and cut the peppers into strips lengthways. Scald and peel the tomatoes – discard the pips and chop the flesh.

Put 2 tablespoons of the oil to warm in a saucepan. Add the tomato pulp and leave all to stew gently: 20–25 minutes will reduce all to a rich purée.

Meanwhile, heat another 2 tablespoons of the oil in a frying-pan and cook the onions until they soften. Do not allow them to brown. Take them out and put them aside. Rinse and pat the aubergines dry. Add some more to the oil used for the onions, and put in the aubergines to fry gently until they soften and turn pale gold. Remove and return the aubergines to the colander to drain, taking care to catch the oil. Use this oil to fry the peppers gently until they are soft.

Add all the cooked vegetables to the tomato purée which has been simmering for this past half-hour. Cook all together for another half-hour. Just before you serve, stir in the finely chopped garlic cloves. Makes an excellent first course, or a main dish with an egg or two, fried in olive oil so that the white is frilled with a crisp brown lace and the yolk is still deliciously runny.

NORWEGIAN BREAKFAST

The Scandinavians love soured milk and cream. Since hay for the cows is often the only crop which can be successfully grown in northern Scandinavia, dairy products are very important items of diet. Enough for 4 breakfasting hikers. Good for their bones and teeth.

2 pints milk
1 small carton soured cream
1 pack 'extra-thin' Scandinavian crispbread (supermarkets have it)

Fruit compote: dried or fresh fruit (apples, prunes, blackcurrants or redcurrants or any suitable berries, plums, damsons) simmered until soft with water to cover and a little sugar.

Put the soured cream into a roomy bowl. Heat the milk gently to finger temperature and then pour it over the soured cream. Stir well. Pour into 4 individual half-pint bowls. Cover with a cloth or paper, and put to stand in a warm place until the milk thickens – about 24 hours. Not quite the same as drinking-yoghurt, although it looks rather like it.

Serve with the crispbread – to be crumbled into it (making

particularly healthy cornflakes) – and the bowl of fruit compote. Brown sugar on the side – there's a long Arctic winter ahead.

30 August 1986

Variations on the Pâté Theme

For years I never much liked pâtés – a dislike which in youth extended as far as the rare slice of foie gras which came my way. Anything pink in a block smacked of the Spam fritters which were served up for school dinner on a Tuesday. A year's residence in the Languedoc set me right on the matter of the liver of the Toulouse goose, and since then one thing has led to another. Now I even rather like the showy vegetable terrines and little fish castle-puddings lately introduced by the chefs of *cuisine nouvelle*, *minceur*, *moderne* or whatever it is this year. I do, however, like my pâtés in sufficient quantity and one at a time, not six varieties dealt out round the plate like a pack of tiny playing-cards.

Strictly speaking, *pâtés* are the ones encased in pastry – a group which includes our very own pork pie. *Terrines* are the same kind of mixture baked in an earthenware dish. Then there are *tourtes*, which are shallow pies baked with a top and bottom crust; things *en croûte*, which are usually large pieces of meat – a ham or a piece of beef – enclosed in a dough of some kind; and *timbales*, which are the little castle-puddings mentioned above (the one named after Agnes Sorel, lucky lady, is a wonderful affair with a truffle in the middle). All can be served hot or cold. The cold table also includes the *galantine*, easily recognizable as the one embalmed in aspic (brawn

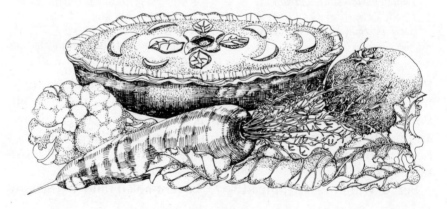

40

comes into this category), not to be confused with the various mousses, a group which embraces that favourite of British caterers, the salmon mousse – a crêpe-de-Chine camiknicker-pink offering of the same school as Tuesday's Spam.

These recipes are for 6–8 servings. No point in going to all that trouble unless there is an audience.

POTATO PIE/TOURTE BERRICHONNE

A closed pie from the sheep country of Berry, from whence come the nut oils. The Berrichonnois grow excellent potatoes. This pie is a useful picnic standby and is equally good made with spinach instead of potatoes.

1 lb puff pastry (or home-made shortcrust will do fine)
2 lb potatoes
Stock or water (not diluted stock cubes)
4 oz streaky bacon
1 oz butter
1 small carton double cream
2 eggs
Salt, pepper, nutmeg

Peel the potatoes and slice them quite thickly. Put them to cook for ten minutes in stock or water with a little salt.

Meanwhile cut the pastry in half and roll it out into two rounds. Use one round to line the base of a shallow ten-inch pie-tin. Put the pastry aside to rest. Preheat the oven to 350°F/gas 4. Beat the eggs up with the cream and season the mixture with freshly milled black pepper, salt and freshly grated nutmeg.

Cut the bacon into dice and fry it gently in the butter.

Drain the potatoes and allow them to cool. Lay them on the pastry-lined tin, scattering in the bacon as you do so, and pour the egg and cream mixture over all. Wet the edges of the pastry and lay on other pastry round as a lid.

Crimp the edges of the pie together and cut a hole in the middle for the steam to escape. Brush on, if you wish, a little egg-and-cream to gloss the top.

Bake the pie for 45–50 minutes. Serve warm with a green salad and perhaps a few slices of Parma ham or salami.

THREE-VEGETABLE TERRINE

A neat trick, this looks rather like a brick of Neapolitan ice-cream but tastes much more delicious. This particular terrine usually figures as

41

one of the aforementioned playing-cards, but is excellent none the less.

1 lb spinach (or broccoli)	*3 large eggs*
1 lb celeriac (or cauliflower)	*½ pint cream*
1 lb carrots (or swede)	*Salt and pepper*

Wash or peel and slice the vegetables as appropriate. Cook each vegetable separately in boiling salted water until soft. Drain and purée them, still keeping them separate. Separate the yolks and the whites of the eggs. Mix the yolks thoroughly into the cream. Season. Beat the whites until fluffy. Mix one-third of the yolk and cream mixture into each vegetable purée. Fold in the whites, equally divided between the three mixtures.

Butter a loaf-tin and spread in the purées in layers – spinach, then celeriac, then carrot. Cover with foil and set the tin in a bain-marie (a roasting-tin with an inch of water in it will do fine). Bake the terrine in a low oven (300°F/gas 2) for an hour.

Unmould the terrine on to a warm plate. It cuts into beautiful three-coloured slices. For a first course, serve with a tomato *coulis* poured round it.

TOMATO COULIS

1 lb tomatoes	*Pepper, salt, sugar*
Juice of a lemon	

Pour boiling water over the tomatoes to loosen the skin, and then peel them, halve them and scoop out the pips. Put the flesh in the liquidizer with the lemon juice and reduce all to a sauce. Season with freshly milled pepper, a little salt and a pinch of sugar if the tomatoes have not been sun-ripened in your garden.

28 June 1986

Irish Suppers

The first time I remember seeing a real red rooster was when I was invited by a schoolfriend to spend the Easter holidays at her family's farm in Ireland. Whether it was north or south of the border I have no memory, but that Irish cockerel lodged for ever in my mind. His

combs were scarlet, his neck-plumes copper, his cascading tail-feathers peacock and kingfisher. He was an absolute monarch on his castle, the farmer's all-important manure-heap. The rooster's scratching-ground was under the big wooden kitchen table, and he wandered in and out of the back door at will. Most of the farm's inhabitants (including the family piglet) enjoyed similar privileges. I had never seen anything like it in all my eleven years. The soft spring days were filled with such delights – lambs to be bottle-fed, cows to be milked, streams to be fished, eggs to be gathered. As evening drew in, the whole household, whether man, woman, child, piglet or rooster, gravitated towards the half-door which separated the cold flagstones of the yard from the warm flagstones of the kitchen. There was never less than a dozen round the kitchen table at meal-times.

On the scrubbed boards there would be a big jug of milk, an iron kettle with the tea already stirred in, soda bread hot from the oven plonked straight on to the table, a big pat of butter and a stone jar of honey. On the side of the kitchen range was the potato-pot – such potatoes as I have never seen since. They were always cooked in their jackets and they were sweet, dry, and as white as snow. Sometimes we would have them plain with eggs, or with a piece of bacon. More often there would be some extraordinary new potato dish that the mother of the house had had from her mother, who had had it from her mother, and so on back to the arrival of Sir Walter Raleigh with the first tuber.

Champ was the most popular of the many recipes. The instrument used in its preparation was a heavy pestle called a beetle, which had pride of place propped up in one corner of the dresser. We had champ made with new peas, with spring onions, with young cabbage greens. Once we had it made with nettle-tops, which we children were delegated to gather, pinching only the top four leaves off with gloved fingers and squealing whenever one of us was stung. We were delighted with our dinner that evening; it had an aura of danger about it which thrilled us. My friend Rita taught me the rhymes to sing when mashing the potatoes. We used them as skipping songs when we were back at school in England.

CHAMP

There was an old woman who lived in a lamp
She had no room to beetle her champ.
She upped with her beetle and broke the lamp
And then she had room to beetle the champ.

2 lb potatoes – large old ones are best	Salt and pepper
1 lb leeks	Plenty of sweet butter
½ pint cream (milk will do at a pinch)	

Scrub the potatoes and put them in a saucepan full of cold salted water. Bring to the boil and cook the potatoes for 20–5 minutes until they are soft. Drain well. Peel them as soon as they are cool enough.

Meanwhile wash the leeks carefully and slice them into rings. Put them to stew in a small pan with the cream or milk until soft – about 6–7 minutes should be enough.

Mash the potatoes with the leeks and their liquid. Beat the mixture over a low heat until it is pale green and fluffy. Champ should not be too sloppy. Add salt and pepper to taste.

Divide the steaming champ between four hot soup-plates. Make a dip in the centre of each helping and put in a large knob of butter to melt. Eat with a spoon. Wonderful for Sunday-night supper.

BOXTY

Boxty on the griddle, Boxty in the pan,
If you don't eat up your Boxty you'll never get a man.

1 lb yesterday's mashed potatoes	2 teaspoons salt
1 lb raw potatoes	1 lb flour
	4 oz butter

Peel and grate the raw potatoes and toss the strands with the salt. Leave to stand for ten minutes and then pour off the water which runs out. Put the butter to melt. Mix in the mashed potato and then sprinkle in the flour. Add the melted butter and work all into a dough. Turn this dough out on to a floured board and knead together until you have a smooth ball.

Cut the dough into four pieces and mould each piece into a flat cake roughly six inches in diameter. Put the cakes on to a well-greased baking-tray and mark them into quarters with a cross.

Put them to bake in a moderate oven (375°F/gas 4) for 35–40 minutes, until they are cooked through. Serve hot, to be split open and spread with butter. Good with a slice of grilled lean bacon for high tea.

12 April 1986

Before and After the Paschal Lamb

The festival of Easter, the breaking of the long Lenten fast, is marked by the eating of lamb with bitter herbs. In the Orthodox Church the feast has considerably more importance and ritual significance than Christmas. The celebration takes place on a different date (this year it is 4 May) from the Church's brethren in the West. The two churches have been unable to reach a compromise for the last ten centuries – a disagreement which has endured since Pope Leo IX excommunicated the patriarchs of Constantinople. In Greece whole lambs are roasted, basted with plenty of fennel, in each household's courtyard – rich and poor alike – and the day starts as early as 4 a.m. when the barbecue fires must be laid and lit. From then on it is one long street-party, in the smallest village as in the grand suburbs of Athens itself.

For your own Easter lunch choose a leg, loin or shoulder of lamb for roasting. Rub it well with salt and pepper and crushed thyme, and leave it in the larder overnight – all roasting joints are improved by this mild marination. Before you put the meat to roast, baste it well with butter. Put it on a grid above a baking-tray in a pre-heated oven. Cooking time is 20 minutes per pound, starting in a high heat

at 450°F/gas 8, to seal the crust, and reducing after the first 15 minutes to 350°F/gas 4. Froth with more butter and a light dusting of flour 20 minutes before the end of the cooking time. Give the meat 10 minutes or so to rest after it comes out of the oven so that it firms up for carving. Serve with new potatoes and new peas. Accompany with mint sauce – plenty of the year's first tender leaves of mint chopped up, infused in a splash of boiling water (enough to cover) for ten minutes, then mixed with as much again of cider or wine vinegar. Only a suspicion of sugar to soften the harshness. No sweet redcurrant jelly today: this is the day for bitter herbs.

When the early Christian missionaries arrived in pagan Britain, the festival of Easter was tactfully named after the Anglo-Saxon goddess of spring, Eastre, and its date was established according to the phases of the moon. As for the celebration meal, the last bit of winter bacon and the first salad herbs of the year broke most people's long fast. Dame Alice de Bryene's household book of 1413 records the purchase of 200 eggs for an Easter feast in which the traditional Easter dish of boiled eggs with green sauce was eaten. Such a menu makes for a rather dull Sunday lunch. However, I can report an excellent Provençal dish of eggs and vegetables which follows the spirit closely. Serve it for your Easter Saturday supper.

SPRING VEGETABLE TIAN

The recipe will feed 4–5 as a main dish.

2 lb spring vegetables. Choose 3–4 different varieties among: young broad beans (pods and all), new peas, baby green beans, spinach, Swiss chard, new baby carrots, and tender baby artichokes – the really small ones. Best of all, those spindly bright-green thin asparagus which are often sold cheaply by weight; or they can be found under wild asparagus bushes at this time of year (look for those fronds which fringe wedding-buttonholes). They are the sweetest and best flavoured of all asparagus.

2 cloves garlic
8 eggs
½ pint single cream
2 oz grated cheese – Parmesan is good, Cheddar is fine
1 teaspoon salt and plenty of freshly milled pepper

Put on a saucepan of salted water to boil.

Prepare the vegetables. String and chop the whole broad bean pods into lengths. Pod the peas. Top and tail the little beans. Rinse the spinach well and remove the tough stalks. Slice up the Swiss chard. Cut the artichokes into fine strips. Wash and slice the carrots. Wash and cut the asparagus into short lengths – discard any stalk-ends which feel stringy to the knife.

By now the water in the saucepan will be boiling, so plunge in the vegetables, boil them for one minute, and then drain them immediately. Leave them aside while you make the custard.

Peel and crush the garlic with a little of the salt. Don't use one of those garlic-crushers; they produce a bitter juice. Use a small mortar or a sharp blow with the flat of a heavy knife. Mix the garlic, the eggs, the cream, the cheese and the seasoning. You can if you like put the whole mixture, including the peeled garlic, into the liquidizer and let the machine do the job for you.

Mix the now-cooled vegetables into the custard. Pour the mixture into a round shallow earthenware dish: a Provençal *tian*. Or use your favourite gratin-dish.

Bake the *tian* in a gentle oven for 1 hour at 325°F/gas 3 until the custard is set but still tender. Plenty of fresh bread and a cool bottle of a sparkling white wine to accompany, such as a chalky dry Blanquette de Limoux from the plains below Carcassonne.

29 March 1986

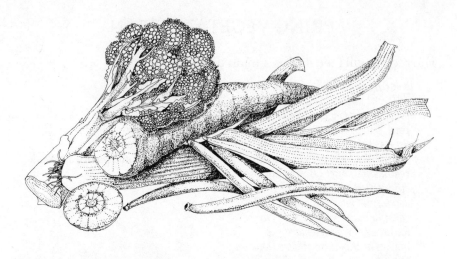

Roll Up for a Vegetable Strudel

The Austrians learnt to make their strudel pastry from the sybaritic Ottoman Turks. The almonds and spices which the Turks loved to layer into their pastries were not so easily available in the fertile but chilly mountains and valleys, and it was not long before some inspired cook wrapped up the old apple-dumpling filling in the new Turkish filo pastry. The apple strudel was born.

Herr Heinrich Wittman makes strudel pastry daily in the *pâtisserie* of the Vienna Hilton. He spins through the air circles of transparent dough, kneading them in full flight, catching them on the knuckles of his fist, delicate porcelain plates spun by a master conjuror. He is not satisfied until they are as fine as tissue paper. His skill is such that it becomes a kind of performance art.

A fine pastry-maker needs the complement of an inspired chef. Enter now Herr Wittman's *alter ego*, Herr Werner Matt, Austria's star exponent of *cuisine moderne*. Austrian appetites do not take kindly to one mangetout and a sliver of duck breast, and Herr Matt's version of new-wave cooking is by no means *minceur*. No Austrian chef worth his salt would want his customers to leave hungry. But he is at his best when he joins company with his master strudel-maker. Here is one of their particular brainwaves.

VEGETABLE STRUDEL

TO SERVE 4–6 PEOPLE

1 packet ready-made filo or strudel
  pastry; unless, of course, you can
  make your own
or 8 oz puff pastry
2 lb vegetables (a mixture of at least
  two: carrots, celery, broccoli,
  beans, courgettes, leeks)

Small carton double cream
3 egg yolks
Salt and pepper
4 oz fresh breadcrumbs
4 oz butter

Prepare all the vegetables and cut them into fat matchsticks.

Take 4 oz of the prepared vegetables and cook them with very little water until they are soft. Purée them in the liquidizer, or through a sieve, with the eggs and cream.

Blanch the remaining vegetables: plunge them into boiling salted water, bring the water back to the boil and then drain immediately. Mix them with the purée. Salt and pepper generously.

Fry the breadcrumbs in 3 oz of the butter. Melt the last ounce of butter in a small pan and place it ready with a pastry-brush.

If you are using bought strudel, put a clean linen cloth on the table and flour it. Then take four sheets of the pastry (work quickly, because they dry out and become brittle) and overlap them to give you a sheet of pastry about 18 inches square. Brush with melted butter and sprinkle with the fried breadcrumbs.

Spread the vegetable mixture over two-thirds of the sheet of strudel to within an inch of the sides. Fold two inch-wide edges of the pastry over the filling. Pick up the nearest two corners of the cloth and roll the strudel over itself away from you, like a Swiss roll. Pick the strudel up in its cloth and roll it into a buttered baking-tray. Brush the top of the pastry with melted butter. (At this point you can freeze the strudel for storage.)

If you are using puff pastry, roll it out on a floured board to an oblong about ¼ inch thick. Lift it on to a baking-tray. Arrange the vegetable mixture in a long sausage in the middle of the oblong of pastry. Fold the edges of the short sides over the filling to close the ends. Brush the edges of the pastry with water, then bring up the long sides to meet over the top. You should now have a long sausage-roll shape with closed ends. Pinch the edges together to make a wavy pattern like a Cornish pasty. Glaze the top with milk or milk-and-egg.

Bake in a *pre-heated* hot oven at 425°F/gas 7 for 45–55 minutes until the pastry is crisp and golden. Brush the top of the strudel pastry with melted butter. Serve hot accompanied by a *beurre blanc*. Perfect with a green salad as a luncheon or light supper dish. In winter, for a more substantial meal, serve a thick vegetable soup or a strong consommé before the strudel.

Beurre blanc

6 oz butter	Peppercorns
1 shallot or a slice of onion	1 tablespoon wine vinegar
Bay leaf	Water

Chop the butter into 1 oz pieces. Peel and slice the onion. Put it in a small saucepan with the vinegar, the peppercorns, bay leaf and two tablespoons of water. Simmer until you have about a teaspoon of liquid left. Take off the heat, remove the onion, peppercorns and bay leaf, and mix a spoonful of cold water into the liquid in the pan. Put in an ounce of butter. Return the pan to the stove, and over a gentle heat stir with a wire whisk until the butter melts to a cream. Add another ounce of butter and whisk that in. And so on until the butter is all used up. Be careful not to overheat and thus oil the butter – if you do, whisk in a teaspoonful of iced water quickly. The sauce should have the consistency of thin cream. Waiters in restaurants tend to be very mean with it – which is an excellent reason to make your own.

11 January 1986

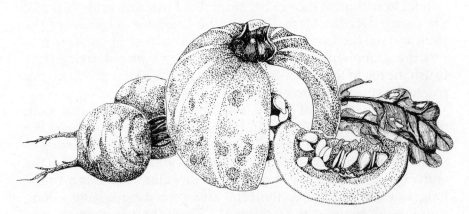

Game Tricks with Vegetables

Young game birds simply roasted in what the French would call the English style are at their best when accompanied by one or two interesting vegetable dishes. These recipes should make a welcome change from game chips and Brussels sprouts. They even conform to the most traditional chauvinist sportsman's demand for crisp potatoes and soft vegetables.

POTATO GALETTE

My favourite potato dish, this is delicious with stewed game.

TO SERVE 4–5 PEOPLE

3 lb potatoes	1 large frying-pan with a lid
Oil and butter for frying	Salt and pepper

Peel and slice the potatoes very fine, as for game chips. Don't rinse them – they need the starch to hold the galette together.

Heat a thin layer of vegetable oil with a knob of butter in the frying-pan (the butter enhances the flavour and the oil prevents burning). When it is hot, spread in all the potatoes in a thick layer. Turn down the heat and put on the lid. Leave to cook for 15–20 minutes, checking every now and again that the base is not burning; if the bottom cooks too quickly, slip the crisp bits out and on to the top. When the whole galette is soft right through and the bottom is golden brown, turn it over and brown the other side (this time do not lid it).

Two vegetables which go particularly well with game, since they are both earthy and sweet, are pumpkin and swede. This year seems to have been an especially good pumpkin year, perhaps because of the late summer.

PUMPKIN PURÉE

Pumpkins, like water-melons, are very heavy. For four you will need half a small pumpkin (one with an eight-inch diameter weighs about 5 lb).

Cut the pumpkin into slices, as for a melon, peel the slices and take out the woolly middle and the seeds. (Children love the seeds dried and lightly roasted.)

Cut the flesh into chunks and put the pieces into a lidded saucepan with a very little water. Stew gently for 20 minutes or so until soft. When cooked, drain the pumpkin very thoroughly, pressing out the water. Put back into the pan and mash vigorously,

51

shaking the purée over a gentle heat to dry it as much as possible. Stir into it the contents of a small carton of double cream (milk and a knob of butter would do at a pinch). Beat the purée over the heat and season it with freshly ground pepper, salt and a little ground allspice.

SWEDE SOUFFLÉ

Swedes can evoke memories of horrible school dinners, but served like this they are unrecognizable.

TO SERVE 4 PEOPLE

2½ lb swede (can be a single large root)

1 large egg
2 oz butter

Peel the swedes and cut into large chunks – unlike turnips, swedes rarely go woody. (The Swedish turnip or swede, a hybrid turnip crossed with wild cabbage which was developed in the early nineteenth century, is yellow-fleshed and sweet.) Boil the pieces in plenty of salted water until soft, about 20 minutes.

Separate the eggs and beat the whites until fluffy.

Drain the swedes thoroughly and then put them in a liquidizer with the butter. Purée. As the mixture cools add the yolks of the eggs. Fold in the whites. If you have no liquidizer, push the swedes through a sieve and then beat in the butter and eggs. Season with salt and pepper.

Butter a soufflé-dish and fill nearly to the top with the mixture. Bake in a hot oven for 15–20 minutes, until well risen. A light and delicious accompaniment to any roast bird.

BEETROOT AND CREAM

This is the best of all foils for little birds like woodcock and snipe.

For 4, grate 1½ lb cooked and peeled beetroot, using a coarse cheese-grater. A few moments before you are ready to serve, heat a small carton of thick cream with a little grated fresh horseradish and a teaspoon of English mustard. When the mixture is boiling, stir in the beetroot. Season with salt and pepper. Serve piping hot.

Mallard and teal have rich dark meat and are at their best in the company of some sharp flavour – which accounts for the popularity of duck and orange. I like my aquatic birds served with lightly cooked tart apples.

For 4–5 people, you will need 2 lb plain boiled potatoes and 2 lb Bramleys or some other sour hard apple. Peel and quarter the apples and cut the potatoes into similar pieces. Heat a mixture of oil and butter in a frying-pan and sauté first the potatoes (gently) and then the apples (swiftly, so that they brown lightly and do not fall apart). Serve the apples and potatoes mixed together, so that your guests do not know what they have until they bite into it.

16 November 1985

Noodles across the Seas

Whether Marco Polo brought the secret of noodle-making back to his native Venice from his travels in China, or whether it was the Italians themselves who taught the Chinese how to make their flour-and-water paste edible, it would be churlish not to acknowledge the role of Renaissance Italy in the kitchens of Europe, including those of France.

It is as masters of the art of saucing dishes that the Italians have excelled since Roman times. This natural skill may well explain their fondness for pasta – the perfect plain foil for the national culinary strength. Roman habits died hard all over Europe and, until the end of the fifteenth century, the tables of the rich were laden with dishes sauced with the most exotic and expensive ingredients possible, chosen for show rather than for any gastronomic consideration. Things changed perforce during the troubles of the Middle Ages, which brought the closing of overland trade routes with the East and the transference of the sea-based spice trade to Portugal. Spices and exotic foods could no longer be easily obtained. The resourceful Italians adapted swiftly.

Necessity became virtue and, by the time the two Medici princesses moved to France, Italian cuisine was the best and most sophisticated in Europe. The princesses – first Catherine, wife to Henry II, followed by Marie, betrothed to the future Henry IV –

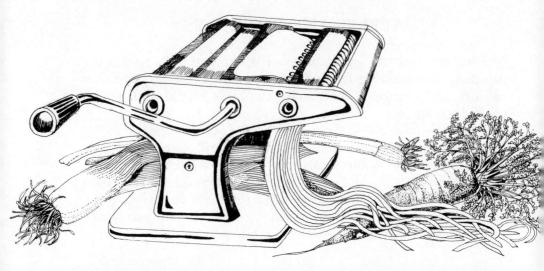

took their servants with them in their bridal suites. The Italians taught the French their skills, and the French were undoubtedly the best of pupils.

Noodle-making is not a difficult skill to master. It is made much easier by the ownership of a pasta-rolling device which works like a miniature mangle. This recipe continues the collaboration between the two great noodle-eating nations of the world: Chinese vegetables to sauce Italian pasta.

TAGLIATELLE WITH VEGETABLES

TO SERVE 4 PEOPLE

The Pasta
1 lb strong flour   *4–5 eggs (size determines)*
1 teaspoon salt   *3–4 tablespoons water*

Put the flour and salt into a roomy bowl and make a well in the middle of the flour. Mix the eggs together with the water and pour them into the well. Work the flour and the liquid together with your hands, to form a soft ball. You may need a little more or less liquid – it depends on the flour and the size of the eggs. Knead thoroughly for ten minutes to develop and stretch the flour. At the end of this pummelling, the dough should be smooth and elastic. The job can be started in a mixer with a dough-hook, but it will be better if you finish it by hand. Put the dough aside to rest for 15–20 minutes while you prepare the vegetables.

The Vegetables

2 leeks or a bunch of spring onions
½ lb young carrots
½ lb courgettes
1 clove garlic

4 oz lean bacon or gammon
4 oz peeled shrimps
4–5 tablespoons light oil (sunflower
   or soya)
Salt and pepper

Trim and slice the leeks or onions into long matchsticks. Scrub the carrots and hull the courgettes and do the same for them. Peel and slice the garlic. Trim the rind off the bacon and dice it small. If the shrimps have been frozen, drain them well.

Back to the pasta: Cut the dough into six pieces and roll each piece out on a floured board until it is nearly thin enough to read a newspaper through. Sprinkle the rolled-out dough with fine semolina or flour and then leave it to rest again for another 15–20 minutes.

Roll each piece of pasta up loosely as you would a carpet for storage, and slice across into quarter-inch strips. Loosen the strips and toss them lightly on to a board well dusted with fine semolina or flour. If you prefer, hang the long ribbons over a washing-line or airing-horse for 10 minutes. At this point the ingredients can wait to be assembled until just before you are ready to serve.

If you have a pasta-rolling machine, use that to roll out the dough. Good kitchenware stores such as David Mellor have the hand-operated version for the price of one dinner in a fashionable Italian restaurant.

Put on a big pan of salted water to boil. Pasta needs plenty of water: 10 pints for this quantity of noodles.

When the water boils, drop in the tagliatelle by the loose handful. Try not to let the water go off the boil. Give the pasta a quick stir with a wooden fork to make sure it has not stuck together. Cook for no more than a minute or two – test by nibbling it before you take it out. Drain the tagliatelle well and toss them with a tablespoon of oil.

Warm the rest of the oil in a large frying-pan or Chinese wok. Stir in the chopped bacon, then the garlic, and the shrimps. Turn them in the oil for a moment, and then add the leeks and carrots. After another minute add the courgettes. Turn the vegetables in the hot oil for another moment. The vegetables should still be crisp. Tip in the noodles and turn all together for a moment over the heat. Season with plenty of freshly milled black pepper and a little salt Lovely for a lunch in the garden in the first warm days of spring.

5 April 1986

Venus in the Kitchen

The year that the Mrs Beeton facsimile edition was published I received five variously gift-wrapped copies for Christmas. My good friend Edith, a vigorously liberated American several summers older than I, received that same Christmas five beribboned copies of a reprinted edition of Stephen Viscenzki's erotic tribute *In Praise of Older Women*. Mulling over the implications with her in the hangover-time of early January, she offered a blanket explanation for the success of Joan Collins, Sophia Loren and herself.

'Today,' said Edith, 'it's the judgement of Venus that counts. Forget about Paris and his apple. There's plenty more in the orchard.' Confronted with an apple, my own instincts are to peel it, sugar it and bake it in a pie. Edith would never do anything so foolish. She is, on the other hand, a terrible cook. When she decided to give a spring dinner-party and invited me, I volunteered, in self-defence, to take charge of the catering. Paris was to be there, of course, not to mention Adonis, Apollo and all the rest of the gang.

The following recipe uses nettles and was specially composed for Edith. I feel it strikes a blow (albeit below the belt) for us apple-pie makers. There's something about eating nettles that worries the uninitiated. Use only the top four leaves of young nettles – pick them with gloves because they will indeed sting, young as they are. The sting vanishes with the cooking of course. Nettles were always the first green vegetables of the year in the medieval kitchen garden, and much prized after the deprivations of winter. The local butterfly population depends on your nettle-patch, so there is an added incentive to keep it going.

NETTLE PANCAKES

TO SERVE 8–10 PEOPLE

The pancakes:

3 eggs	1 tablespoon oil
5 oz plain flour	½ teaspoon salt
½ pint milk	Butter for frying

Put the flour and salt into a basin and break the eggs into the middle. Mix the eggs into the edge of the flour. Add the milk gradually and beat until you have a smooth batter the consistency of pouring cream. Beat it some more. The more you beat, the lighter the pancakes. The mixture should be cool when you fry it. (If you make it in winter, a spoonful of snow works wonders.)

Heat a heavy frying-pan or griddle. Melt a nugget of butter to grease the pan. When it is smoking, pour on a couple of tablespoons of the pancake mixture. Tip it round the pan to cover the surface and give you a delicate lacy pancake. Cook until the edges dry and curl. Flip over and fry on the other side. Continue until you have used up all the batter.

Nettle Filling

1 lb nettle-tops (failing these, use spinach)	4 oz grated cheese
	Salt and pepper
3 oz butter	1 egg
3 oz plain flour	A large flat round baking-dish
1½ pints milk	

Wash the nettle-tops or picked-over spinach in cold water. Put the leaves with the water that clings to them in a saucepan with a lid. Stew in their own juices for 5 minutes to soften. Chop the leaves. Make a thick white sauce: fry the flour in the butter until it is sandy but still pale. Add the milk – heated if you find that easier – and beat the sauce smooth as you bring it back to the boil. Cook for a few minutes after it thickens to take the raw taste from the flour. Beat in 3 oz cheese. Season. Stir the cooked nettles into half the sauce. Leave the rest plain.

1 tablespoon oil	¼ lb mushrooms
1 onion	2 tins tomatoes
1 lb mince	2 tablespoons tomato purée

Chop the onions and soften them in the oil. Add the mince and fry lightly. Slice the mushrooms and add to the mixture. Cook for a moment, then add the tomatoes and tomato purée. Boil to reduce and thicken. Pour half the plain sauce into the bottom of the baking-dish. Place a single layer of pancakes on top. Spread the pancakes with the nettle mixture. Put another layer of pancakes on top of that. Now spread on a layer of the tomato-and-meat mixture. Then a layer of nettle. Continue until there are no more ingredients for layers – the last layer should be pancake.

Beat the egg into the remaining half of plain sauce. Spread it over the pancake layer. Sprinkle the last 2 oz of grated cheese over all. Bake in a medium-hot oven (375°F/gas 5) for 30–40 minutes to heat the layers together and brown the top. Wait until all your guests have finished and are congratulating you on the dish. Then tell them about the nettles. Apples to complete the meal, naturally.

4 May 1985

In Praise of Chanterelles

Lisa is a plump pretty girl from Cracow. She struggled into a pair of green rubber dungarees and waded waist-deep into the icy water of the Spey. The noble river had not been generous to the rest of us. A rusty oil-can and a waterlogged squirrel made up the day's haul, even though we had some serious fly-artists among us, men who could land a Hairy Mary on the nose at thirty paces. But Lisa hauled out salmon after twenty-pound salmon. Her skill was informed by passion. Not for abstract concepts like perfect technique, or the romance of the chase of the king of fish, or even the beauty of the most famous water in Scotland. Lisa was, quite simply, crazy about food. The trophies which sportsmen elect to have stuffed and cased and glazed for the display cabinet interested her not at all. Not even the monster which took the year's record for the beat received anything but a culinary appraisal. Lisa supervised its smoking and had the salmon sent south.

The rest of the party, disconsolate, set off for the trout-stocked lakes above the river, hoping the half-tamed would be easier to deceive than the wild. Lisa, her triumph on the water now complete, turned her attention instead to the hazel wood which fringed the lake. Recognizing a punter on a winning streak, I took my chances with her. There, almost hidden under the bronze leaf-carpet, she uncovered skein after skein of brilliant yellow mushrooms. 'Pierprznik – chanterelles,' she said happily. 'Pass the basket.'

Gathering wild mushrooms is not without its hazards, as the unwary have discovered across the centuries. Today careful checking in one of the field-guides available can eliminate most of the dangers. But for the beginner far and away the best advice is the oldest: learn in the field from someone who knows. Stick to the species you are sure of until, one by one, you can add others to your list. Chanterelles, girolles or egg-mushrooms as they are also called, are very distinctive: they are apricot both in colour and in scent, shaped like baroque trumpets, curled and curved at the edges; the stalk has no ring; instead of gills, there are fluted folds like fine-ribbed buttressing. I know of no poisonous variety with which they could be confused. The *Collins Guide to Mushrooms and Toadstools* suggests the orange-yellow *Hygrophoropsis aurantiaca* as the only possible look-alike, but this grows on heaths and in pinewoods, and is in any event edible – although not particularly good. Once you have the measure of chanterelles, you will not confuse them with anything else. At any meal and as any course they are one of the supreme delicacies of the mushroom world.

Chanterelles grow all over Britain, but in my experience are most prolific in Scotland – German tourists come over especially to pick them. The species particularly likes beech or hazel woods, and the season runs from July to December. Even the smallest lip curling from beneath a leaf shines like a flash of sunlight. And one chanterelle always leads to another. I have found them growing in company with wood-bluets and the extraordinary wood-hedgehog (which has tiny vertical spines instead of gills). Any fungi at all in a wood usually means there's an edible variety around. Pick all mushrooms gently by twisting them loose from their base, like picking an apple from a branch. The fungus plant they grow from – the mycelium, a network of fine threads spreading from the base – can then remain to fruit again.

Wild mushrooms need no fancy treatment in the kitchen, apart from the pleasure of piling them on the kitchen table first to admire their beauty. Chanterelles should be eaten as fresh from the woods as possible: they have a remarkable knack of growing a crop of all-devouring grubs if left lying around for a day or two, particularly in a plastic bag in August. Their flesh tends to be chewy, particularly the stalk, which gets tougher if cooked for more than 10 minutes. They also produce a great deal of watery juice if they have been picked on a damp day. To prepare them, cut off the earthy base and shake any loose bits of leaf or grit out of the 'gills'. They cannot be peeled, so wipe their tops, but avoid washing them, which only adds to the water problem. Then cook them lightly in butter, raising the heat if necessary to evaporate any extra moisture. Finely chopped garlic and parsley can be added at the end, or just a screw of black pepper and a little salt. Eat them with fresh bread. Or stir some cream into them and have them with toast. Or scramble them with eggs when their bright flesh makes a perfect match with the yellow of the yolks.

Lisa and I picked pounds of chanterelles that day, a golden scented basketful speckled with bright green moss. Lisa dried the best in the airing cupboard, strung on cotton threads. Then she packed them in brown paper bags and they, too, went south with the salmon.

13 October 1984

Pick of the Penny Buns

Last year was a particularly good year for the penny bun, *Boletus edulis*, most delicious of its tribe and a three-star item in any fungi manual. 'Edible and excellent,' enthuses the *Collins Guide to Mushrooms and Toadstools*. The year 1984 was also a fine one for toadstools, the beautiful shiny red ones with white spots which have served so many generations of gnomes. *Amanita muscaria* does not get such a good press from *Collins*: 'Fly agaric – poisonous and dangerous.' Last autumn the Hebridean woods positively glowed with the risky scarlet globes. Oddly for something so inedible, many had had large bites taken out of them – not the frilly nibbles of grubs or worms, not even gnome-sized mouthfuls, but great human-teeth-shaped crescents. Enquiries among the locals produced an explanation: sheep, I was told, have always had a taste for a scarlet toadstool. As far as sheep are concerned, you can keep your penny buns.

The early Finns, according to some Finnish historians, felt much the same. Searching for diversion during the long and boring six-month Arctic night, they hit upon a new amusement – lunching off the landscape. The particular piece chosen happened to be embellished with a fine crop of *Amanita muscaria*.

60

After their unusual hors d'oeuvre the picnickers were lying around on the sphagnum moss blinking at the northern lights, when they found they had been joined by a short fat old gentleman in a red and white knickerbocker suit. No one was in the least surprised when the old boy did a vertical take-off in a sledge hooked up to some flying reindeer. Word spread, and the toadstool festival became an annual event. Soon Santa Claus and his little tricks were a national institution: much more fun than aurora borealis.

Trouble really started when the Vikings collected a basketful of the toadstools to take on one of their rape-and-pillage sorties. A handful of *Amanita muscaria*, they discovered, sent the longship men, never noted for mildness of manner or gentleness of soul, off their rockers. They invented the word 'berserk' to describe the effect and from then on took a supply on every raid. Imagine what it does to Hebridean sheep.

But to return to safer ground and the penny bun. Most members of the *Boletus* genus make excellent eating. The French give them top billing and scour their native woods for *cèpes* from the end of August until the first frosts. The French family I picked with avoided those which turned blue after cutting – but I have since discovered several perfectly good ones with this characteristic. The Italians call them *porcini*, piglets, and like to dry them for use in winter sauces. In Britain we tend to be nervous of all but the field-mushroom, *Agaricus campestris*, false security since it can be confused with truly poisonous fungi such as the Death Cap, *Amanita phalloides*, or the Destroying Angel, *Amanita virosa*.

I like to add at least one new species of fungus to my repertoire every year. The amiable *Boletus* has no fatal members in its fifteen-strong British family, although they do include one or two which can thoroughly upset the human digestion. The specimens to avoid in the early stages of collecting are those with a red tinge about the stalk or pores. Not even they can cause serious harm – and there are some perfectly good ones with this coloration, too. In fact the group is probably the safest for the beginner to concentrate on. Take a good identification manual with you.

Boletus are common in woodland, and several types have a particular liking for pinewoods. The *Boletus* family has large round brown or golden caps and spongy (usually yellow) pores underneath, quite distinct from the mushroom's radiating gills. If you are worried about identification (and everyone is when trying a new species), cut a small piece from the cap and put it on the tip of your tongue. If it tastes at all bitter or unpleasant, reject it. You will soon get your confidence. In Bordeaux they like their *cèpes* fried in olive oil with garlic and parsley – *Boletus* have a gelatinous texture and strong flavour which respond well to such robust treatment. If you pick yours in Scotland, try them gently stewed in butter and then stirred into haddock simmered in cream.

TO DRY BOLETUS FOR STORAGE

Choose large and maggot-free specimens (*luteus*, very yellow and perishable, is the only edible *Boletus* not suitable for drying). Do your picking on a dry day. Wipe the caps and cut off the stalks. Pull off the spongy pores underneath; they will come off quite easily. Cut the caps into slices. Thread the slices on to button twist and hang the strings in an airing cupboard or in a warm current of air to dry thoroughly. Store in airtight jars until you need them. Soak in a little hot water before using both the fungi and the soaking liquid in recipes for soups, sauces or stews.

31 August 1985

Swiss Passion for Mushrooms

The Swiss, denizens of the most sought-after tax-haven in the world, take the allocation of their foreign residents' permits very seriously indeed. They do of course take most things quite seriously, including nuclear shelters and statutory supplies of three months' non-perishable food for each household. Come the nuclear holo-

caust, it is probable that the last human breeding pair left on the planet will be Swiss: Family Robinson revisited. Meanwhile, those seekers-after-tax-havens who wish to be awarded their *permit de séjour* have to satisfy the inspectors in various exclusively Swiss, somewhat personal ways. One gentleman who recently applied for his naturalization papers was rejected on the grounds that he was cohabiting with a young Swedish lady. The decision was not (as one might suppose of the land which sponsored Calvin) ethical; it was purely ethnological. Had the young lady been Swiss, the matter would have had quite a different complexion.

Not only the bedroom but also the kitchen comes under the inspectors' scrutiny, and the officials have been known to sneak up to the candidate's back door for a spot-check on the contents of his cooking-pots. Woe betide the sheikh who has a sheep's eye simmering. Enquiries of a Swiss friend reveal a passionately nationalist view of the Swiss culinary traditions – a little confused, naturally, by the diverse leanings of the three nationalities who make up the populations of the cantons. Swiss cooking is by no means all *fondue* and *raclette*. The Swiss are among the most enthusiastic fungusgatherers of Europe – they have done some pretty scary medical studies of the effects of picking the wrong ones, too. This autumn should, after all the wet weather and the sunshine, yield a particularly generous harvest of mushrooms, and anyone contemplating applying for tax asylum would be well advised to start picking. Otherwise, there are plenty of dishes the Swiss claim as their own. There is even a perfectly Swiss fish – freshwater of course – the *omble chevalier*. I am assured the government inspectors would be quite satisfied with any of the recipes which follow.

63

GRATIN AUX BOLETS

A main dish for 4–5 people. *Bolets* to the Swiss, *cèpes* to the French, accurately called *porcini* (little pigs) in Italy, these large brown fungi, whose common characteristic is a spongy yellow underside, are known as 'penny buns' to those British mycologists brave enough to gather them.

*1 lb Boletus mushrooms or large
    cultivated mushrooms
2 lb potatoes
8 oz cheese (Gruyère or Cheddar)
1 oz butter*

*1 pint good stock (not cubes – use
    water and a glass of white wine
    instead)
Salt and pepper*

Wipe the shiny brown caps of the bolets and brush off any dirt which clings to their spongy undersides. Cut them vertically in slices ¼ inch thick. Peel and slice the potatoes to the same thickness as the mushrooms.

Grate the cheese. Butter an oven-proof casserole. Put in a layer of potatoes, then a layer of the sliced mushrooms, sprinkling on cheese, salt and pepper as you go. Continue with the layers until all is used up, finishing with potato and a topping of cheese. Dot with a little more butter and put to bake in a hot oven 450°F/gas 8. After 20 minutes, pour in a glass of the stock and turn the heat down to 400°F/gas 6. Leave to cook for another 50 minutes or so, adding more stock as the previous lot dries out. Serve, say the Swiss, as the *plat de résistance*, accompanied by plenty of dry white wine and a green salad.

CHANTERELLES À LA POULETTE

This is a light supper or a delicious first course for 4 people. Chanterelles are those beautiful apricot-yellow fungi, which hide under moss and leaves in the autumn woods. Sometimes only the edge of one is visible, like the frill round a yellow petticoat.

*1 lb chanterelle mushrooms (or 1 lb
    cultivated button mushrooms)
1½ pints milk*

*2 oz butter
1 small carton double cream
2 egg yolks
Salt and pepper*

Clean the chanterelles carefully. Little bits of grit and leaf-mould lodge stubbornly in their elegant curves. Blanch them for 5 minutes in boiling water (this is not necessary with cultivated mushrooms).

Drain and dry them well in a cloth. Put them in a bowl and cover them with the milk. Leave to soak for an hour and then drain them well (save the milk as a basis for a mushroom soup).

Melt the butter in a shallow pan and add the mushrooms. Add salt and pepper and leave the mushrooms to stew gently in their own juices for 20 minutes. Stir from time to time to make sure they are not sticking. Add a little of the milk if they dry out too much. Beat the egg yolks with the cream and stir it in off the fire just before you are ready to eat.

Serve in vol-au-vent cases, or on slices of bread fried golden in butter. Follow with a salad and cheese if the mushrooms are the main dish.

23 August 1986

St George's Mushroom Pie

St George's mushroom is one of the most delicious edible species and is a much-favoured market mushroom throughout Europe in the spring. It has firm white flesh with a strong and pleasant scent of fresh flour. St George's is one of those fungi it is really only safe to pick when you have been out with an expert. Two species in particular when young can be confused with it: the extremely poisonous Red-Staining Innocybe and the poisonous but not fatal *Rhodophyllus sinuatus*. Once you have taken guidance, however, the mushroom is a culinary delight.

ST GEORGE'S PIE

TO SERVE 4–6 PEOPLE

1 lb bought flaky pastry (or your own
rough-puff would be best of all)
4 thin slices raw ham or gammon
1–2 lb St George's mushrooms
3 oz butter

1 oz flour
¼ pint milk
¼ pint double cream
1 heaped tablespoon chopped parsley
2 chopped hard-boiled eggs
1 raw egg
Salt and pepper

Roll out two-thirds of the pastry into a circle and lay it in the base of a pie-dish. Lay over it two of the slices of ham or gammon. Roll out the other third of the pastry into a lid. Set the pastry aside to rest while you prepare the filling.

Clean, wipe and trim the stalks of the mushrooms. Slice the flesh. Put the butter to melt in a small pan. When it is frothing, add the mushrooms and cook them gently for 5 minutes. Sprinkle in the flour and turn it in the butter. Add the milk gradually, stirring as the sauce thickens. Stir in the cream and bubble up for a moment. Take the pan off the heat and stir in the chopped parsley and hard-boiled egg. Allow the mixture to cool. Stir in the raw egg, add ½ teaspoon of salt and freshly milled black pepper. Pour all into the lined pie-dish. Lay the rest of the ham or gammon over the top of the filling, wet the edge of the pastry, and put on the lid. Cut a hole in the top for the steam. Bake the pie in a hot oven (400°F/gas 6) for 45–50 minutes, until the pastry is well risen and golden. Serve warm, with a spring salad.

GOUGÈRE AUX MORILLES

TO SERVE 4–6 GATHERERS

The Gougère

¼ pint water
2 oz butter
4 oz flour

3 eggs
4 oz cheese
Salt and pepper

The Filling

1 lb morels
3–4 oz butter
1 teaspoon flour

1 glass of white wine
½ pint double cream
Salt and pepper

Make the *gougère* first. Put the water to boil in the saucepan with the butter. When the butter has melted, beat in the flour. Put the pan back on the heat, and beat the mixture until it leaves the sides of the pan clean.

Remove it from the heat, and allow the dough to cool for a moment while you grate the cheese. The dough should now be cool enough to allow you to beat in the eggs one by one. You may not need all the eggs – the mixture should be firm but soft, so that it holds its shape but drops from a spoon. Beat two-thirds of the grated cheese in with ½ teaspoon of salt and plenty of freshly ground black pepper.

Butter a baking-tray, and use two tablespoons to drop egg-shaped (and -sized) dollops of the pastry on to it in a circle, each dollop to overlap the other. Smooth the top so that you have a round ring. Sprinkle with the rest of the cheese. Put the pastry to bake in a moderate oven (350°F/gas 4) for 35–40 minutes.

Meanwhile make the filling: clean the morels carefully – they catch earth and sand in their rough caps and hollow stems, and you may have to rinse them. Trim the bases of the stalks, leaving the morels whole if possible. Melt the butter in a saucepan and add the morels. Cook them gently for 5 minutes, then sprinkle in the flour. Pour in the wine and stir while you allow the mixture to bubble for another 5 minutes. Stir in the cream and then turn the heat down. Simmer all uncovered for 10 minutes. Taste and add salt and plenty of freshly milled black pepper.

Transfer the by now well-risen *gougère* to a warm serving-dish and pour the creamed morels into the well in the middle. Enjoy the fruits of your gathering.

19 April 1986

Morels are a much more easily identified species for the spring fungi cook. All the *Morchella* have a dark crinkly cap and pale stem, are edible and good, and it is difficult to mistake them for anything else. Dry or fresh, the morel has a great affinity with cream. My favourite way to eat them is as prepared at the Auberge du Poids Public of St-Félix Lauragais near Toulouse. M. Augé the chef-proprietor gathers his *morilles* and serves them in cream with lightly sautéd slices of fresh foie gras. Ah, me: it's just as well the 'Poids Public' refers to passing lorries rather than to the customers.

For a less financially demanding dish, make a *gougère* to enclose your cream-sauced crop.

Fish

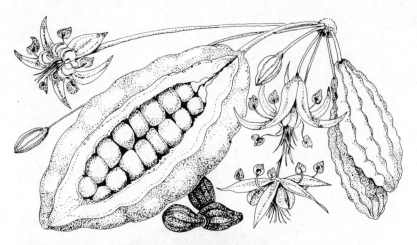

Thomas Gage in the New World

Thomas Gage, reprobate son of the Gage family of Firle in Sussex, traveller, epicure and seventeenth-century supergrass, was a rogue in the mould of his contemporary, the Vicar of Bray. Young Thomas, disinherited by his father after a quarrel with his Jesuit schoolmasters, served as a Spanish Dominican friar for the first sixteen years of his adult life. As such he travelled to the New World as a missionary monk with the Dons, the first Englishman to do so. Appropriately for a young man of his culinary interests, Brother Thomas joined the expedition to New Hispania by stowing away in a biscuit-barrel aboard a galleon in the Spanish port of Sanlúcar de Barrameda. Once in Mexico, he developed a passion for the drink of chocolate, and the preparation features regularly in his topographical writings.

> This chocolate is an Indian name, and is compounded from the *atle* which in the Mexican language signified 'water', and from the sound which the water, wherein is put the chocolate, makes, as *choco choco choco*, when it is stirred in a cup by an instrument called a molinet, or molinillo, until it bubble and rise into a froth. The chief ingredient, without which it cannot be made, is called cacao, a kind of nut or kernel bigger than a great almond which grows upon a tree called the tree of cacao, and ripens in a great husk. . . .

The last fourteen years of Thomas's life, after his return to the land of his birth, were spent as an anti-Papist Puritan minister. As the author of *The Tyranny of Satan – Discovered by the Tears of a Converted*

Sinner Thomas had, it was said, the ear of Lord Protector Cromwell himself, particularly since the turncoat was more than willing to name and give evidence against his former co-religionaries, including three priests and his own brother. The publication in 1648 of his *magnum opus*, *The English-American*, was intended both as an exposure of Spanish colonial misdeeds and as an encouragement to his own countrymen to take over the Conquistadores' territories. 'It is perhaps somewhat unusual', writes Eric Thompson in his preface to a modern edition of the work, 'for an editor of a book to point out in the first paragraphs of his introduction that the author was a scoundrel. . . .' Indeed, but he was a thoroughly entertaining scoundrel, and an accurate observer with a keen interest in the table.

On the voyage to the New World, the company ate salted shark, which the young monk said tasted just like tortoise. He also had occasion to sample the tortoise itself: 'All the ships make their provision for Spain of tortoise meat. They cut the tortoise in long thin slices, and dry it in the wind after they have well salted it, and so it serveth the mariners in all their voyage to Spain, and they eat it boiled with a little garlic, and I have heard them say that it tasted as well as any veal.'

Thomas recommended the Indians' favourite meat, hedgehog: 'Of these the Indians eat much, the flesh being white and sweet as a rabbit, and as fat as a January hen kept up and fatted in a coop. I have also eaten of this meat, and confess it a dainty dish. . . .'

One dainty dish which Thomas must certainly have enjoyed is the Hispano-Mexican *Seviche*. Sir Kenelm Digby, born, as was Gage, in 1603, included in his cookery-book, *The Closet Open'd* (see page 281) a Spanish recipe for 'Ceveach'. This method of pickling raw fish so successfully transported to the New World that it is now Mexican street-food. Today small boys carry jars of it for sale by the ladleful to the sunbathers on Mexico's beaches, which is where I first tasted it. It makes a delicious light summer lunch or a first course for dinner. Here is the Acapulco version.

SEVICHE

2 lb haddock, skinned and filleted (or any other firm white fish)
4–5 limes (limes are best, but lemons will do)
1 fresh green chilli (or a shake from the tabasco bottle)

1 onion
2 tomatoes
4 oz green olives
1 large firm avocado (ripe but not mushy)
Small bunch coriander
Salt

Cut the fish into pieces ½ inch square and put the pieces into a bowl. Sprinkle the fish with the juice of two of the limes. Put the fish in the fridge to pickle in the juice for 3–4 hours – it will turn opaque and virtually cook.

De-seed and slice the chilli finely. Peel and chop the onion. Chop the tomatoes. Pip and slice the olives. Peel and chop the avocado (don't mash it). All the vegetable pieces should be roughly the same shape as the fish pieces. Chop the coriander. Squeeze the rest of the limes.

Drain the fish. Combine it with the chopped raw vegetables. Sprinkle in the coriander and the freshly squeezed lime juice. Toss all gently and add a little salt. Serve cool in small glass dishes, with crisp-fried tortillas or French bread (a crisp element is required) and lettuce leaves.

19 July 1986

Gros Soupa

It was around the year AD 40 that Mary the Mother of God and her companion Mary Magdalene, attended by their black servant Sarah, fled, according to Provençal legend, from the Holy Land and crossed the Mediterranean to beach their coracle on the French shore at Les Saintes-Maries-de-la-Mer. Three weary women, muffled in the dark cloaks of the East, stole up the pale sand and found sanctuary at last in the gentle hills behind. There each year they continued to celebrate the Saviour's birthday. Dusk falls early on Christmas Eve in Provence. Christians draw their curtains to keep in the warmth, but leave a lighted candle glowing on the window-sill to welcome the passing stranger, perhaps even three

bowed figures in salt-stained clothing. Tomorrow there will be turkeys and tinsel, but tonight is the meal of fasting, the *Gros soupa* – the festival of renewal before the Christmas Mass.

Naturally, in this stronghold of good things, fasting is a relative term, and on Christmas Eve the Provençal kitchen is filled with the fruits of the earth and the sea. The symbolism of the *Gros soupa* has not been shaped by Christian hands alone: a pagan Yule log, cut from a fruiting tree which died during the year, blazes in the hearth. The fire is lit from kindling carefully saved from last year's log and must glow nightly until the new year. By the fire the children arrange a crib. Tiny clay *santons* of the Holy Family crowd a little bark stable while an audience of Provençal figurines – lacemakers, fishermen, woodmen, musicians – watch from without. The manger itself is empty. At the table's centre, in honour of Ceres, stands a saucer in which a miniature field of young wheat-shoots has sprouted on the window-sill in the weak winter sunshine. Three cloths for the Trinity cover the table, and three candles, which must burn throughout the vigil, surround the wheat. Beside them rests a basket garlanded with myrtle and piled with twelve small round loaves for the apostles, together with a thirteenth, much larger and marked with a cross, for the Saviour.

On the table throughout the meal are thirteen desserts, which cannot be eaten until after Midnight Mass. These are our own familiar mixture of fruit and nuts, but in Provence each has a special significance. There are four fruits of the orchard – apples, plums, grapes and roast chestnuts – for the year's four seasons. The four mendicant orders of monks are represented by wrinkled walnuts for the Augustans, dried figs for the Franciscans, pale almonds for the Carmelites, and plump raisins for the Dominicans. Then there is black and white honey nougat for the bad and good days of the year. Dates and oranges – rare in the old days – are a reminder of the flight into Egypt. Preserved melon or quince paste symbolizes eternity.

With the table ceremoniously prepared, the celebration of the Great Vigil begins – and the best place nearest the fire's glow will always be left empty for the unexpected guest. The meal may start with an *anchoiade*, a paste of salt-pickled anchovies pounded with garlic and olive oil, to be eaten with the loaves. Then follows one of the traditional Mediterranean salt cod dishes – a *brandade de morue* or an *aioli* accompanied by fresh vegetables and perhaps a plate of winter snails dug from hibernation to be stewed with an onion and herbs. Afterwards the edges of the tablecloth are folded back so the souls of the departed may feed off the crumbs.

When the family returns from Mass, the adults mull wine with sugar and spices. The children gather round the crib to tuck the infant Jesus into his manger. Beside him they place the saucer of young wheat. From the kitchen wafts the delicious scent of new bread. It is time to bring in the shepherds' traditional gift to the newborn Child: a yeast cake called the *Pompe*, which is baked with olive oil and marked with the Star of Bethlehem.

THE POMPE OF PROVENCE

1 oz fresh yeast (½ oz dry)
2 lb plain flour
6 oz brown sugar
4 tablespoons good olive oil

1 egg
Grated rind of 1 lemon and 1 orange

Dissolve the yeast in half a cup of warm water. Mix it and all the other ingredients together in a large basin. Knead until you have a soft elastic dough – a little more water may be necessary. Form the dough into a large round flat cake and make deep slashes on the top in the shape of a star. Put to rise for three hours in a warm place, or an unlit oven with a dish of boiling water on the base – the richer the dough, the longer it takes to rise. When doubled in bulk, bake in a hot oven (400°F/gas 6) for 40 minutes. This produces a light and scented brioche which is wonderful with mulled wine. It's pretty good toasted for breakfast on Christmas morning, too.

22 December 1984

Twelve Aphrodisiac Oysters

Samuel Pepys, seventeenth-century diarist and rake, recommended a barrel of oysters as a New Year feast, and very good advice it is, too. In France lorry-loads of the succulent bivalves are sold for the Nouvelle Année in every market-place and outside every supermarket. They go like hot cakes – not in piddling singles or sixes, but by the crate. As for their well-known aphrodisiac qualities, you have only to look at one, smell one, taste one to understand their fame; their status as hermaphrodites has something to do with it, too. Oysters have been eaten with relish since prehistoric days – their shells have been unearthed in many an ancient camp. The Chinese were the first to farm them. The pillaging Romans shipped barrels of them back to Italy. By the seventeenth century palates were getting thoroughly refined: Essex oysters were found to be feeding on an algae which turned them green and gave them a superb flavour (the oysters of Marenne are green and prized to this day). However, things have not been the same anywhere in Europe since the mid-nineteenth century when the oyster-beds succumbed to over-fishing and pollution, and oysters ceased to be the food of the poor and became the pleasure of the rich.

To return to the matter in hand: choosing your oysters. Buy them from a responsible fishmonger who can guarantee their freshness. Count your guests with care. For a proper celebration there must be a dozen molluscs apiece – one for each month of the new year. Even, for the profligate and brave, one to be swallowed on each stroke of the midnight chimes. Wild oysters of the species *Ostrea edulis* are the

75

best. They have a stronger sea-flavour than the cultivated, which are fattened in river mouths where they are washed with alternate tides of sea and fresh water. Otherwise, differences depend on size and source. Portuguese oysters are the long and narrow ones. Cheaper and not as finely flavoured, they are a different species, *Crassostrea angulata*, and although they can change sex at will they are not hermaphrodites. Oysters out of season (the months without an *r*) are perfectly edible, but will be breeding – this gives them a milky appearance which the French call *laiteuse* – and should be allowed to get on with it in peace.

Having selected your oysters, check that their shells are firmly clamped shut – a relaxed oyster is a dangerous oyster. Now you need an oyster-knife, a squat dagger-shaped instrument with a hilt to protect your fist. An ordinary short strong kitchen knife will do at a pinch, but in that case lay in a small supply of Elastoplast. Other equipment: clean cloths, large plates, some cracked ice. Rinse your oysters in cold water to remove loose sand and grit from the shells. Gripping the mollusc firmly in a cloth, carefully push the point of your knife into any gap in the side of the oyster and lever the two halves apart. If all else fails, try going in through the hinge. Once you have forced your way through, wriggle the blade round inside against the flat shell to detach the flesh. Take care not to spill any of the delicious liquor. If there's a whiskery black beard, trim it off. Put the oyster, still in the deep half of the shell, in a bed of cracked ice on a plate. Continue until each plate contains twelve oysters. Serve with quartered lemons, tabasco, and plenty of thin-cut sweet-buttered brown bread. If you are fortunate enough to have a few oysters left in the bottom of the barrel, here's what to do with them.

ANGELS ON HORSEBACK

Wrap each oyster, seasoned with a squeeze of lemon, in a thin strip of smoked bacon. Fry in butter for exactly two minutes, turning once. The oyster should be just warmed. Serve on rounds of bread fried crisp in butter.

OYSTER BUNS

Hollow out small day-old bread rolls – one for each two or three oysters. Toast the buns in a slow oven until crisp and golden. Take

¼ pint of double cream for each dozen oysters, season it with pepper and Worcester sauce. Bring the cream to the boil and add the oyster liquor. Reduce to thicken again. Tuck the oysters into each baked bun, pour the cream into the buns, and bake them in a hot oven for a further five minutes. Serve piping hot with quartered lemons and very cold Muscadet.

If, like me, you have never thought it essential to join a Rugby scrum of near-strangers to welcome the New Year, a dozen raw bisexual bivalves is quite enough of a crowd. To drink, a tankard of Black Velvet – equal quantities of champagne and Guinness – provides a suitably rich foil for Sam Weller's companion to poverty. Two is the perfect number for the feast: a dozen aphrodisiac oysters apiece guarantees a happy New Year.

29 December 1984

Perfect Fish and Chips

The Holiday Inn in Gaborone, Botswana, is an unexpected place to find a vanload of fish and chips pre-frozen and wrapped in last year's *Daily Mirror*. Not least because this southern African republic, formerly the British Protectorate of Bechuanaland, consists of little apart from the Kalahari Desert – a huge land-locked space of open sand whose few bronzed inhabitants are not noted for their appetite for ocean delicacies.

The fish and chips were not unaccompanied. They were present as the obligatory garnish to the elderly British comic, Mr Tommy Trinder, the Holiday Inn comedian-of-the-month. The whole package had been delivered to the tiny capital in a refrigerated truck with a Union Jack painted on the side.

Having just returned myself to Gaborone after a 2,000-mile jaunt round the Kalahari, I entered the cool un-sandy dining-room in pleasurable anticipation of a slice of iced papaya. The heady scent of vinegar and damp newsprint assailed my nostrils. The room itself was packed with the local Tswana citizenry, its collective fingers playing lightly among the soggy chips, dark shining faces eagerly raised towards the barely defrosted Mr Trinder.

'And now, ladies and gentleman,' rasped the cockney entertainer from beneath his titfer. 'Which of you supports Fulham?'

Well, he *was* nearly eighty. There was less excuse for the fish and chips. Certainly the gourmets of Gaborone didn't think much of the lumpy batter, over-cooked cod, and soggy potatoes. Even after my six weeks on an expedition diet of baked beans and elderly guinea-fowl I couldn't manage it, either.

Fish and chips were a Victorian innovation. The first fried-fish cookshop opened in London in 1851 in indirect response to the building of the railways. For the first time the northern fishing fleets were able to send their catches fresh to the hungry southern markets. The idea of selling the fish ready-battered and ready-fried developed naturally in a society accustomed to buying meat pies and pasties from cookshops. The chips were a contribution from the French and were added some twenty years later. Fish and chips, deep-fried in beef dripping, seasoned with salt and vinegar, soon became the favourite fast food of the Victorian urban poor. It is excellent nourishment and, if eaten with a pickled onion and a hefty dollop of tomato sauce, a well-balanced meal – almost as good nutritionally as peanut-butter-and-jelly sandwiches.

Today good fish and chips are hard to come by. Sometimes, travelling through a city or town at midday, you may pass a long and patient queue leading into a small white-painted shop, its open doorway gently puffing aromatic steam into the street. Stop immediately and join the line. You have found one of the last of the Perfect Fish and Chip Shops. Failing such good fortune, you had better make it at home.

PERFECT FISH AND CHIPS

The fish: Use a fillet of a large white-fleshed fish such as haddock, cod or coley. Modern fishmongers never seem to have whole fish of this size, so to test for freshness use your nose. Sole or a fillet of plaice also makes good fish-and-chip material.

The batter: For 4 fillets of fish, you need 4 oz flour, a pinch of salt, 3 tablespoons of oil, a bare ¼ pint of water, and the white only of one egg. Mix the oil into the flour with a wooden spoon and then beat in the water until the batter is smooth and liquid, but will still coat the back of the spoon thickly. Leave to rest for a while. When you are ready to fry, whisk the egg white to a firm snow and fold it into the batter with a metal spoon. Dry the fish fillets and dip them into the batter.

The potatoes: Choose a 'waxy' variety, easier to obtain in the north, such as Golden Wonder (as used by Messrs Smith of crisp fame), Kerr's Pink, Red King or the creamy-fleshed Duke of York. (The ubiquitous King Edwards and Maris Pipers sold in the south are 'floury' and suitable for mash.) Peel the potatoes, rinse the residual dirt off, and then cut and slice lengthways into fat chips. Don't soak them in water after you have chipped them and don't salt them.

The oil: Pure beef dripping gives an authentic East End flavour, but may be a little heavy on your cholesterol levels. Use a good vegetable oil such as sunflower, soya or, best of all, pure olive oil. Fifty-fifty soya and olive gives good results.

The cooking: Heat the oil in a heavy pan until a faint blue haze rises from the surface. Fry the chips until they are soft but only just beginning to take colour. Take out and drain on newspaper. Heat the oil again and fry the battered fish. Take out and drain on newspaper. Heat the oil for the third time and give the chips their second fry. Now you can salt them.

Serve all together, *on* newspaper if you like but not soggily wrapped *in* it, accompanied by tomato ketchup, pickled onions, quartered lemons, and a small bottle of malt vinegar.

2 March 1985

Rainy-Day Crab

The trickle of spring rain down the kitchen windows is the perfect accompaniment to the patient business of picking out the little bits of meat from the shell. Even children can be persuaded to help if the alternative is a soggy walk.

If possible, crabs should be bought alive straight from the creel. Failing that, they should come still warm from the fishmonger's boiler. Dressed crab will not do: it might have breadcrumbs to bulk it out or, worse, permitted additives. Above all, avoid those obscene pink fingers that have crept on to the fishmonger's slab recently under the name of crab sticks. They belong to a tube-squirted family called 'extruded food' and are close cousins of those limp motorway-chips which appear to be made of reconstituted mashed potato.

There's nothing extruded about a live crab, although it does present one with the problem of how to kill it. The official advice from the Universities Federation for Animal Welfare is to stab the creature with a skewer through the back of the head, and plunge it straight into boiling water. If you opt for that, hold the crab under for two minutes after you put it in. However, I'm far from sure the Federation has got it right. I prefer to fill a large saucepan with heavily salted water (6 oz salt to 4 pints water), put the crab in, with its claws tied, while the water is still cold, and then bring it gently to the boil. Hold it under for the statutory two minutes. I hope this lulls the crab to sleep, like boiled missionary. Either way keep the water just on the boil for 15 minutes for the first pound and 10 minutes for each subsequent pound.

The common British crab is *Cancer pagarus*, a fine meaty fellow which is fished in British waters all year round. Like the lobster it is a scavenger and enjoys a good sea-coast rubbish-dump. Female crabs are considered the sweeter. You can tell the sex by looking at the tail-flap which is tucked under the body: the male's is much narrower than the female's, who needs the extra width to protect her eggs. When cooked, the crab should feel heavy for its size. To prepare, pull the body from the shell, remove the ring of feathery grey 'dead man's fingers', and snap off the mouthpart. Everything else is edible. A good 2½ lb crab will give 1 lb of meat, enough for four. Poke out the meat from the body, the claws and the legs, keeping the brown and white meat separate. Pile the meat back into the shell, with the brown down the middle in a stripe. Serve with a home-made mayonnaise, quartered lemons, lettuce hearts with no dressing, and thin slices of brown bread and butter.

The spider crab, *Maja squinado*, a spiky scarlet creature which drapes itself with a camouflage of seaweed, is fished off the Atlantic coasts of France and Spain. Spider crabs make excellent eating and can sometimes be found in British fishmongers'. I first came across them in a fisherman's bar in Tarifa, a former Phoenician customs post which guards the pillars of Hercules at the entrance to the Mediterranean. Every Tarifa barman is an expert in preparing them. Pull the body from the shell and trim off the 'fingers'. Then chop each leg division towards the centre so that the crab is divided into ten lollipops, each with a chunk of white meat on the end of a leg. The crab is served with the dark body meat mixed with a little brandy in the shell, accompanied by a fresh bread roll, half a lemon, and a small glass of toothpicks. To drink: a glass of pale dry sherry.

Both species can be potted with butter, or mixed with cream and a pinch of paprika to make a delicate sauce for tagliatelle or fresh noodles. There is also this more robust Spanish–Moorish recipe of which I am particularly fond.

CRAB PIL-PIL

TO SERVE 4–6 PEOPLE

4 fat cloves garlic
¼ pint olive oil
4 small, dried, de-seeded chillies or
   one fresh green

1 lb crab meat
1 tablespoon brandy
Salt

Peel and roughly chop the garlic. Put the olive oil to heat in a shallow pan. When a faint blue haze rises from the hot oil, throw in the garlic and let it soften, then add the chillies. Turn up the heat and quickly stir in the crab meat and brandy. Sprinkle with a little salt and bring the mixture to a rapid boil. The crab should be in the pan for as little time as possible so that its fresh flavour is unimpaired. Serve very hot as soon as the alcohol has evaporated, with quartered lemons and rough chunks of bread to sop up the juices.

30 March 1985

Other People's Salmon

Some of us are fishermen. Some of us are wet-bread artists. I belong irrevocably to the second group. It is not for want of patience and stamina. I will gladly straddle the Spey from dawn to dusk and count the time well spent. It is merely that the king of fish has no interest in my fly. Other people have to catch my salmon for me, if, on the other hand, those others care to accompany me down the estuary to a likely patch of sea, preferably lapping the harbour of a populous seaport, I will show them how to catch a very sweet supper indeed. The skilled wet-bread artist – that is, a person dependent on the success of the day's fishing for the day's meal, where failure is unthinkable – must load the dice. This I learnt on the waterfront of a small seaport on the Atlantic coast of Uruguay in South America. My parents were there on a diplomatic posting and

I, eight years old at the time, spent a glorious summer of freedom. I had for company a one-year-older brother and a bicycle. The brother gave me credibility and the bicycle mobility. It wasn't long before I found my vocation. The dice were loaded at the outlet of the town sewer. There it was that the sardines came to feed. The local inshore fishermen were a motley crew: two very old gentlemen of the kind my mother told me never to consort with, several unemployed youths in tattered shorts, and my hero and mentor, our cook's infinitely knowledgeable young son, Sebastian.

My brother and I took up our positions in the long-established pecking order: last in the line perched, like a juvenile fish-eagle, on the large boulders which formed the breakwater. Pole position was occupied by the old men. We all had the same equipment: a bucketful of stale bread soaked in sea-water, a short length of fishing line, a small bag of raw meat (provided by the cook) and a stock of pins. The drill was simple enough. Tie three pins bent into hooks on the line – Sebastian was the acknowledged expert. Fix a sliver of meat on to each hook. Dump a spoonful of wet bread on the water, drop the baited line into the cloud it forms, and watch for the silver flash of sardine flank. Yank as soon as you get a nibble. Easy. When you have enough fish to replace the wet bread in the bucket, light a small driftwood fire, gut the sardines, spit them on a sharpened stick, salt them and grill them. Sebastian's mother never had to cook for us.

But if salmon is on the menu it is a different story. I have mastered a neat Speyside cast, the envy of many a watcher. Yet the king of fish has never so much as flicked an experimental lip in my direction. Nor am I resentful: like any good half-back, I am only too grateful when the centre three-quarter touches down from my pass. I am then free to scramble up the bank and repair to the kitchen, there to dig out the fish-kettle and await the rewards of other people's scores.

POACHED SALMON WITH HOLLANDAISE SAUCE

If the salmon is to be eaten cold, put the fish, scaled and gutted (with half a quartered lemon in the cavity), into a fish-kettle. Cover with cold water and spice with peppercorns, bay leaf, salt and half an onion. Bring to the boil. Give it three or four rolling belches and then remove from the heat. Leave the fish in its water. When it is cool it will be perfectly cooked. Serve at room temperature, with quartered lemons and a home-made mayonnaise.

If the salmon is to be eaten hot, or if you have no fish-kettle large enough to accommodate it, you can bake it, prepared as above, in buttered foil, at 300°F/gas 2, for one hour if the fish weighs 5 lb, and adding 10 minutes for each extra pound. Allow the fish to settle for ten minutes before you serve it.

To accompany, a Hollandaise sauce: Tip the juices from the salmon into a small saucepan. Bring to the boil and reduce the liquid to a couple of tablespoonfuls. Allow the base of the pan to cool for a moment. Then whisk in four raw egg yolks, previously beaten with a little water. The residual heat will thicken the yolks. At the same time melt ¾ lb of butter. When the yolks and the butter are at the same temperature, proceed to add the butter to the yolks as for a mayonnaise. It will thicken: you will not need to cook it any more. Finish with a squeeze of lemon. Serve warm – do not try to serve it hot and you will be in no danger of turning it into scrambled eggs.

11 May 1985

Scottish Skate to a French Tune

As is inevitable after a long day spent in a small boat with a couple of eager young novice anglers trawling for mackerel off the coast of Mull, the shoal showed up just as the sun dipped down. At the moment of maximum excitement, with six fat fish flopping beneath the thwarts and a couple more on the line, the engine propeller churned into a patch of weed. Preliminary investigations indicated the machinery was as thoroughly entwined with watery fronds as a Neapolitan's fork with his lunchtime spaghetti.

An in-depth in-board post-mortem confirmed the grim diagnosis: something structural had come adrift. The propeller would clearly turn no more until it had received the attentions of the local mechanic. The light from his cottage window winked at my small barque through the dusk across the bay, where he was distantly and obliviously tucking into his tea-time pieces by the warmth of his peat fire.

The shoal of mackerel shoved off, leaving a round dozen of their number carpeting the wet duckboards. Gloomily we shipped the engine, fitted the rowlocks and slipped in the oars. It would be a good two-hour heave against the tide and the evening wind back to our berth. We pulled on our anoraks and set to.

At that moment salvation puttered over the horizon: miraculously, for once the seaborne school-run was an hour behind schedule. At the head of sea-loch where we fish for mackerel is the hamlet of Ulva Ferry. The tiny Ulva Ferry community maintains an even tinier primary school – two of whose pupils are fetched daily and carried by boat to the isolated little island of Gometra at the other end of the loch. Their father and mother had put out nets on the way to collect them, and had found the shoals. Their good fortune, which had caused the delay, proved to be ours, too.

Gratefully we clambered aboard. Our little boat was taken in tow and we headed back for Ulva Ferry. Our hosts' offspring were twins – small, red-headed and sturdy little nine-year-olds, their faces freckled by sun and wind. They hung over the side, scanning the darkening waters for signs of the shoal we had struck into. We were halfway back before I realized what the children were using as a footstool. Propped against the side of the boat was part of the catch: the largest skate I have ever seen. From snout to tail it measured a full ten feet, and the wings must have been nearly that across. Yes, indeed, said the fisherman's wife in reply to my query as to its edibility, it would make excellent eating. But not for a couple of days, until it had lost its harsh ammoniac smell.

Ray and skate all develop this pungent smell within an hour or two of being caught. It is caused by a chemical (urea – a component of urine, and hence the ammoniac smell) manufactured by the fish. It takes two days to disperse. The smell disappears in the cooking anyway, and some fishmongers recommend eating skate perfectly fresh. So you may make your own choice.

Ray is one of my favourite fish. It has, as well as an exquisite flavour, a most delicate and interesting texture of flesh and bone, both of which are formed of long strands, as if stroked by a comb. The bones are supple, gelatinous and semi-transparent, jointed like long fingers: there are no sharp spikes to get stuck in your throat. When you have poached your skate wing, you can peel off the skin like a thick soft blanket and lift the long pearly strips of flesh clean off the bones in a single layer.

So gelatinous a fish needs a sharp sour sauce to enhance the flavour and balance the texture. This can be provided by a simple squeeze of lemon, but to my mind the best way of all to eat skate is with black butter spiked with vinegar and capers – *au beurre noir*, as the French love to serve it.

Legend has it that the skate is a music-lover, and can be enticed to the hook by a fiddler playing him a melody.

SKATE WITH BLACK BUTTER

TO SERVE 4 PEOPLE

2 lb skate on the bone	*Onion, 2 bay leaves, 1 teaspoon salt,* *1 teaspoon peppercorns,* *1 tablespoon vinegar*

Beurre noir

4 oz unsalted butter	*2 teaspoons capers*
2 tablespoons wine vinegar	

Wipe the skate.

Put 2 pints of water in a large saucepan and bring to the boil with the onion sliced, bay leaves, salt, peppercorns and vinegar. Allow to cool.

Put in the skate wing and bring it to the boil. Turn the heat right down and simmer for 15 minutes. Remove, drain and fillet the fish.

Heat the butter. As soon as it turns nut-brown throw in the vinegar and the capers and boil fiercely for a moment or two. Pour over the filleted fish. Forget not the violins to accompany.

21 September 1985

The Herring's Return

Amsterdam, say the Dutch, is built on herring bones. Many a Netherlander has made his fortune from the silver fish – salted, pickled or just plain fried. The Sea-Fish Marketing Board of Great Britain is currently campaigning to bring the herring back on to the plates of Britain; this traditional staple of our sea-going nation has been frozen out these many years by the all-conquering fish-finger. The Sea-Fish Marketing Board deserves every encouragement: a fat fresh herring is a very fine thing. If we all took their advice, and then took our herring-bone mountain to the M1 and donated it to the contractor in charge of rebuilding the motorway's crumbling found-

ations, we might get a road system as durable as old Amsterdam.

The best British herrings come from Loch Fyne, and the Clydeside method of cooking them fresh is excellent.

GRILLED HERRINGS

2 herrings per person   Salt and pepper
½ oz butter per pair of herrings

Make sure the fish are gutted and scaled. Wipe them inside and out. Cut off the heads and clip the fins and tails. Split the herrings down the back (kipper fashion) and remove the backbone. Dot the flesh with bits of butter and sprinkle with salt and pepper. Sandwich the opened fish together, skin-side out. Skewer them in place,and then grill or fry them in a lightly greased frying-pan (herrings have plenty of their own fat and need no extra in the pan). Serve with floury boiled potatoes, well drained and shaken over the heat to dry.

OATMEALED HERRINGS WITH MUSTARD SAUCE

1 herring per person   Small bit of bacon fat (or butter) per
Pepper and salt   fish
1 spoonful oatmeal per fish

Scale, gut and wipe the fish. Split them in half down the back and lift out the backbone. Sprinkle with salt and pepper. Roll each fish thoroughly in oatmeal. Dot with bacon fat or butter and grill on each side for five minutes a side. You could also fry them. The oatmeal coating is delicious and filling. Serve with mustard sauce and brown bread and butter for high tea.

Mustard Sauce

TO SERVE 6 PEOPLE

2 oz butter
2 oz flour
½ pint milk
Small carton double cream

3 teaspoons English mustard
  (already made – not powder)
Salt, pepper

Melt the butter in a small saucepan and add the flour. Fry together until the mixture looks sandy but has not browned. Add the milk slowly, beating well, and bring all to the boil. Boil for at least 5 minutes to cook the flour, still stirring so that the sauce does not stick. Add the cream and bring the sauce back to the boil. Stir in the mustard and add salt and pepper.

SALT-COOKED HERRINGS

A lovely recipe given by Dorothy Hartley in *Food in England*, published in 1954 when herrings were still a popular dish. She says the method was taught her by the ship's cook on her ferry-crossing, with blue sky overhead and the salt spray flying.

> Take an iron pan and put in a pinch of salt for each fish, and gut and trim the fish, taking off the fins and head; wipe them *bone dry* with a cloth dipped in fine oatmeal and put them in the pan on to the *hot* salt, and keep shaking the pan so that they do not stick.
>
> Cook till they are done one side, and then turn over with a knife and do the other side; when cooked through, and crisp outside, slide out of the pan on to a hot plate, put a lump of butter and a dash of pepper inside each, and eat with a slab of buttered oatcake.

SOUSED HERRINGS

The classic way of preparing fresh herrings. Each person can usually manage two.

TO SERVE 4 PEOPLE

8 herrings
Salt
1 onion

Peppercorns and a bay leaf
½ pint wine vinegar
½ pint water

Scale, gut, behead and trim the herrings. Split open and remove the backbones. Salt the fish and roll them up into little bolsters. Slice the onion finely and make a bed of it on the base of an oven-proof dish. Pack all the fish-bolsters on top in a single layer. Tuck in the bay leaf, scatter over a few peppercorns and pour the vinegar and water over all. Cover and bake at 400°F/gas 6, for half an hour. Allow to cool in their own liquid and serve with hot boiled potatoes dressed with chopped raw onion. A bowl of sour cream or yoghurt goes well with the dish.

SOFT ROES

If you are fortunate, your herrings will yield a few roes. They are delicate and delicious and make an excellent simple savoury. Perhaps you might serve them hot alongside the cooled soused herrings and enjoy a mouthful of each in turn.

Mix a little flour with salt and pepper and dust the herring roes lightly. Melt butter in a frying-pan, and when it is hot lay the floured herring roes gently in it. Fry for a few minutes, turning once, until the roes are cooked through. Serve immediately on fingers of hot toast, with the cooking butter poured over, sprinkled with more freshly ground pepper and accompanied by quarters of lemon.

5 October 1985

Life and Sole of Picardy

The little fishing village of Le Crotoy stands guard over the coast of Picardy at the mouth of the River Somme. Before the gunpowder and shells of both world wars flattened every edifice for a hundred miles, the stone cottages of Le Crotoy nestled under the battlements of a fine medieval fortress. In its dungeon the Maid of Orleans was imprisoned before her transfer to Rouen.

Just across the estuary lies the port of St-Valéry, from whose shores Duke William of Normandy embarked in 1066. Then, as now, the Crotellois earned their living as inshore fishermen.

Today's invaders are the summer tourists, mainly those Parisians who have not joined the annual stampede to the overcrowded beaches of the Mediterranean. For the months of July and August

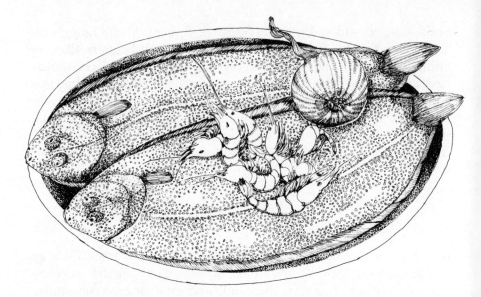

the bucket-and-spade brigade takes over the tidal flats which are usually the domain of the whelk- and cockle-gatherers.

The town's fishermen moor their small sturdy wooden smacks to the bollards which line one side of the Place Jeanne d'Arc. The tides at the end of April were running high at midday, and the real business of the town was over in a flash. The little fleet numbers no more than six vessels at full strength, and they had rounded the harbour wall and tucked in beneath the shelter of the quay before the few tourists, who had settled in the midday sun, had even noticed their arrival.

But the rhythm of local life is governed by the tides, and the little port suddenly came alive. Swiftly a flock of *camionette* vans backed up dangerously close to the edge of the steep drop of the quay. A small knot of housewives, retired fishermen and assorted children and dogs gathered as soon as the mooring ropes were thrown over the bollards. Perhaps the Maid herself had been afforded a similar sight as her captors hurried her away to face her inquisitors.

The catch had been a respectable one that morning: the fishermen in their *bleu-de-travail* slung the crates out of the holds and into the waiting arms above. The catch from five of the boats disappeared immediately into the open rear doors of the vans. Within a few moments motors were revving and the fish was on its way to the markets of Rouen and Caen, Lyons and Paris. There remained the catch from the last vessel, reserved for the local inhabitants.

Set out by the fisherman himself were trays of herrings flashing silver flanks; sand-speckled soles with asymmetrical eyes still bright; trays laden with turbot and brill, the sea-bloom veiling their patterned skins; and, most dramatic of all, crates of small grey shrimps, the last caught jumping among their fellows like fleas. The bargaining was swift and sure: 50 francs a kilo for fine fat turbot, 35 francs for sole as thick as a thumb. The spoils vanished rapidly up the narrow alleyways in the bulging string-bags and buckets of the shoppers, to join the small sweet local mussels, butter and cream from the rich pastures of nearby Normandy on the kitchen tables of Le Crotoy.

FILETS DE SOLE CROTELLOIS

TO SERVE 5–6 PEOPLE

3 large soles weighing about 1 lb each	1 glass dry white wine
2 carrots	4 oz small shrimps
1 small onion	2 oz butter
Parsley, bay leaf, thyme, chervil	¼ pint thick cream
Salt and pepper	2 shallots or spring onions
1 pint mussels	1 oz butter worked with 1 oz flour

Skin and fillet the soles. If you have this done by the fishmonger, make sure he gives you the heads and bones as well. Put these trimmings into a small saucepan with the peeled and quartered onion, the carrots, scraped and cut into chunks, the herbs, a little salt and 3–4 peppercorns. Cover with ½ pint water, put on the lid and leave to simmer on a low heat for 25–30 minutes. Strain out the solids.

Meanwhile clean the mussels and put them to open in a little of the wine in a lidded shallow pan over a high heat. As soon as the shells are open, remove the pan from the heat, take the mussels out of their shells and reserve them. Strain and keep the liquor (watch out for the sandy deposit).

If the shrimps are raw, cook them for a few moments in enough boiling salted water to cover; drain and peel them. Peel and chop finely the shallots or spring onions (use only the white part). Butter a shallow casserole and lay the fillets of sole in it. Cover them with the fish liquid from the trimmings, the rest of the white wine, and the strained mussel-juice. Dot with butter and cover with foil. Cook either in a hot oven or on direct heat for 10 minutes, until the fish is cooked through.

Take off the foil and pour the juice into a small pan. Leave the sole in a very low oven to keep warm. Boil the juices fiercely to evaporate the quantity down to ½ pint. Stir in the butter-and-flour and

91

allow the mixture to simmer until it thickens. Remove from the heat and stir in the shallots, mussels and shrimps. Stir in the cream.

Pour the sauce over the fish and serve with new potatoes and tiny spring vegetables.

17 May 1986

Pilgrim Shells

The scallop, emblem of pilgrims, is the most versatile of shellfish. It provides both dish and dinner. The dinner is delicious, the dish beautiful, tough, re-usable and impeccably designed. Artists draw inspiration from it: the curve of the scallop shell decorates many an architect's grand portico. Botticelli raised Venus from the sea in it. Infants are baptized from a silver replica of it. In short, the scallop is a bargain at any price. It is available fresh in the shell during the same period as the oyster. In so far as the old adage about an *r* in the month holds good in these days of refrigerated transport, that means from September to April.

When you have located a reliable purveyor of scallops, you can look forward to eight months in which to enjoy them. They are sold either unopened (you will have to scrub off the mud and rinse them thoroughly) or opened and cleaned (not so good – they will not taste of the sea, and in this case make sure you are given the *deep* shell and not just the flat one).

If your scallops are not opened, leave them in a pan of cold water after you have scrubbed them. They will open and allow you to get your knife in. Alternatively, put them (round side down to cup the juices) in a shallow pan of boiling water or into a low oven. After a few moments they will open.

The scallop has a curious anatomy. The round white piece in the middle is the adductor muscle, which enables the fish to open and close its shell and propel itself through the water. The cream and orange-red tongue-shape which curves round the muscle is the reproductive organ. The creature is a hermaphrodite: the creamy part is the male gland while the coral-coloured tip is the female. The frill round the outside contains little pin-point eyes which peer backwards, checking for pursuing predators, and the dark frill which skirts the coral is the gills. Remove the frills and the little sandy sac of intestine. Rinse the scallops.

SCALLOPS IN GARLIC BUTTER

8 scallops	1 oz butter
Few sprigs of parsley	1 tablespoon oil
1 clove garlic	Salt and pepper
1 oz fresh breadcrumbs	1 lemon

Clean and trim the scallops and pat dry. Slice the white part horizontally into three or four medallions. Scrub the curved shells and put them to warm in the oven. Chop the parsley and garlic very finely and mix them into the breadcrumbs.

Melt the butter and oil in a frying-pan. When they are hot but not smoking, put in the scallops and fry them gently for five minutes, turning once. Put the scallops back into their warm shells.

Reheat the butter and oil and throw in the minced garlic and parsley. Fry for a moment, and then add the breadcrumbs. Fry until golden, then scatter them over the scallops.

Serve piping hot with wedges of lemon.

Vary the recipe by adding a little white wine to the scallops when they are in the frying-pan. Boil rapidly to evaporate the alcohol. Transfer the scallops and their sauce to the shells, scatter bread-crumbs over, dot with butter, and brown under the grill. Delicious.

POACHED SCALLOPS WITH SPINACH

This is a rich but delicate supper dish to serve as a main course. The colours – orange, bright green and ivory – are particularly pretty.

1 lb leaf spinach	½ glass dry white wine
4 oz butter	1 glass water
½ pint cream	Slice of onion
2 oz flour	Bay leaf
8 scallops	

Pick over and wash the spinach, then cook it in the water which clings to its leaves. Drain thoroughly and chop. Fry the flour gently in 2 oz of the butter. Add the cream and bring to the boil, stirring as it cooks and thickens. Mix half of this rich cream sauce into the spinach. Put aside to keep warm.

Make a court bouillon with the wine, water, onion and bay leaves. Prepare the scallops as for the previous recipe. Poach the scallops in the court bouillon. Remove and put aside.

Boil down the court bouillon rapidly until it is reduced to 2 tablespoons of liquid and stir into the remaining cream sauce. Bring all back to the boil and then beat in the remaining butter. Stir in the scallops. Serve in a bed of the creamed spinach. White fluffy rice to accompany.

Use your empty scallop shells to make Aberfrau cakes for tea. Aberfrau is a small fishing village in Anglesey, and the fishermen's wives are clearly inventive and frugal cooks. Children love these little cakes.

SCALLOP-SHELL CAKES

½ lb butter   ½ lb self-raising flour
½ lb sugar

Beat the butter and sugar together until light and fluffy. Fold in the flour. Butter a dozen of the deep scallop shells and divide the mixture among them. Bake at 350°F/gas 4 for 20 minutes.

30 November 1985

Maître d'hôtel Vatel and M. Paul Bocuse

The father of the theatre of the kitchen – which has nothing in common with kitchen-sink drama – M. Vatel, celebrated major-domo to the prince de Condé, achieved immortality on 24 April 1671. His final act on the stage of life, as recorded by Madame de Sévigné in a letter to her friend Madame de Grignan, took place in the early hours of the second morning of the grand entertainment being offered by his master to the Sun King himself, Louis XIV.

The previous evening had not been a happy one for the Swiss-born maître d'hôtel. Two of the tables had been short of the roast, and the fireworks, even though they had cost full 16,000 francs, had gone off like the damp squibs they were. The following morning the troubled major-domo rose early to supervise in person the arrival of the fresh produce for that day's banquet. The household slept. Only M. Vatel was there to greet the messenger who appeared post-haste from the coast with the fish. There were but two packets. Two packets to feed the King, the Court and the prince de Condé's

94

household. Two packets of fish and no turbot at all. There was only one course open to an honourable man. M. Vatel returned to his quarters and fell on his sword. Racine could not have improved on the drama. Cookery had its first martyr. The theatre of the kitchen was born of tragedy, and it has taken itself seriously ever since.

M. Paul Bocuse, France's current star of the culinary stage, is a man in the traditional dramatic mould. He and the near-equally famous M. Gaston Lenôtre were in London in March for a culinary demonstration (not the full three-acter, you understand, just a brief two-handed prologue) to promote French goods in that contemporary palace of opulence, Harrods department store. The two stars chose, perhaps in homage to their illustrious predecessor, to perform their art in the fish hall under the watchful eye not of a turbot but of a magnificent sturgeon. The space, however, was by no means adequate to their thespian might. When both men got weaving with the skillet, they had the air (and indeed the bulk) of Elizabeth Taylor and Richard Burton crammed into a Punch-and-Judy show. Almost as little went right as for poor M. Vatel. The British scallops were underweight. The microphone crackled like a breakfast cereal. The gas wouldn't light. Neither gentleman chose to emulate the great Swiss. None of the audience cared much anyway, since the sponsor was a maker of very good champagne whose wares we had all been encouraged to sample. By this time the ladies and gentlemen of the press had toasted (under direction from the Harrods toastmaster) the sponsor, the sponsor's wife, the manager, the manager's wife, the new owner of Harrods, and a dusky Serene (but Unidentified) Highness.

As with all good chefs, however, the day was finally won. I tasted M. Lenôtre's scallops – and they were excellent, underweight or no. Here is the recipe as provided.

SCALLOPS IN CHAMPAGNE

Vegetables

1 lb carrots
½ lb leeks
4 oz celeriac
4 oz button mushrooms

1 oz butter
Salt and pepper
1 shallot or 2 spring onions

Scallops

10 scallops (plus the shells, top and
*   bottom)*

½ lb puff pastry, rolled
*   thin and cut in strips*

1 bunch of tarragon
1 oz butter

Beurre blanc au champagne

1–2 shallots or spring onions
¼ bottle champagne
6 tablespoons white wine
*   vinegar*

¼ pint double cream
1 lb butter
Salt and pepper
1 small bouquet garni

Method

Peel the vegetables. Cut them into matchsticks. Trim and matchstick the shallots, then sweat them in a touch of butter. Add the vegetables gradually. Keep the vegetables crispy and then let them cool. Mix the vegetables with a little hopped-up tarragon. Clean the scallop shells carefully and butter their insides and lids with a pastry-brush. Place a little of the finely sliced vegetables in the bottom of the scallops. Place the scallops, sliced horizontally and seasoned, on top of the vegetables. Add a little more of the finely sliced vegetables, tarragon, etc. Add a coffee-spoonful of champagne and a nut of butter. Place the lid on top. Cover the whole with strips of puff pastry to keep it tightly shut. Glaze the puff pastry. Cook in a hot oven for about 10–12 minutes. Make the *beurre blanc* as for the vegetable strudel on page 50 and serve it separately.

Bon appétit.

26 April 1986

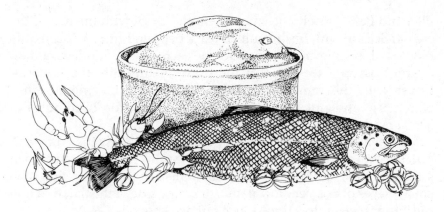

Pâtés for the Sportsman

The recent popularity of delicate *nouvelle cuisine* fish pâtés has opened a new area of gastronomic interest, particularly to the keen fisherman. In the following recipe wild mushrooms such as chanterelles (which very often grow in the birch thickets beside trout streams) can be substituted for the smoked trout – the gatherer often has more luck than the hunter. Clean your wild mushrooms first, slice them and then sauté them lightly in butter.

SALMON AND SMOKED TROUT TIMBALES

This is to salmon mousse as Châteauneuf du Pape to Bulgarian red. If you would like to be really grand, garnish each *timbale* with a couple of scarlet freshwater crayfish, which can be caught by trailing a string baited with raw (and by no means fresh) meat in a clean upland stream. If your fishmonger has live crayfish, they have probably been imported from Turkey. A good harvest of crayfish can be substituted (poached, peeled and cut into short lengths) for the smoked trout.

1 lb raw salmon, skinned and boned
1 pint single cream
4 egg whites
Salt and pepper
1 smoked trout (or cooked crayfish or chanterelles)

2 shallots or 1 small onion
6 tablespoons white wine vinegar
½ lb butter

Pound up the salmon in the food processor with half the cream and all the egg whites; it would take a long time by hand. Season. Skin, fillet and flake loosely the smoked trout. Toss it with the rest of the cream. Season with freshly milled black pepper. Butter a dozen little moulds. Line the base and sides of each with pounded salmon mixture. Drop a teaspoon of the trout mixture into the hollows. Cover with the remainder of the salmon. Set the moulds in a bain-marie and put them to cook in the oven for 25 minutes at 325°F/gas 3.

Meanwhile make a *beurre blanc*. Peel and chop finely the onion and put it to cook with the vinegar in a small pan. When it has reduced to 4 tablespoons, strain out the onion. Whisk in the butter slowly in small pieces over a very low flame, or by the side of the flame so that the butter melts into a thick sauce but does not oil.

Unmould the *timbales* on to warm plates. Pour the *beurre blanc* round the unmoulded castles. Heaven. Make a rabbit terrine tomorrow to bring you back to earth.

RABBIT AND GOOSEBERRY TERRINE

MAKES ENOUGH FOR 8–10 HELPINGS

1 *large hutch-bred rabbit or 2 little wild ones*	1 *teaspoon salt*
	1 *teaspoon peppercorns*
1 *lb lean pork (shoulder off the bone is good)*	1 *teaspoon juniper berries*
	2 *onions*
1 *lb pork belly*	2 *carrots*
½ *lb pork back fat (or good, properly cured streaky bacon)*	2 *bay leaves*
	½ *lb gooseberries*
1 *small glass gin*	

Skin and bone the rabbit(s). Save the bones. Pound the salt, halve the peppercorns and the juniper berries up together. Put the saddle fillets of the rabbit, the liver and the little kidneys into a dish, and sprinkle them with the gin and half the pounded aromatics. Leave aside to take the marinade.

Cut the skin off the pork belly. Put the meat aside, and roll up the skin and secure it with string. Put it in a large saucepan with the rabbit bones, including the head, the washed and roughly chopped carrots, the onions quartered but not peeled, the bay leaves and the rest of the peppercorns. Cover all with water (1½ pints should be ample), bring to the boil, skim and cover and then leave to simmer for an hour. Strain the stock and bring it back to the boil. Let it boil ferociously uncovered until it has reduced to ⅓ pint. Taste and add salt, and leave it aside to cool.

Meanwhile chop up very thoroughly the belly pork with the lean pork and the rest of the rabbit meat. Season with the remaining salt and aromatics.

Top-and-tail the gooseberries.

Mix the gooseberries, the reduced stock and the marinade from the rabbit fillets into the chopped pork and rabbit meats. Work all well together with your hands.

Line a loaf-shaped mould with thin slices of back fat or rashers of bacon. Pack in half the chopped-meat mixture. Lay over it the rabbit fillets, the liver and kidneys. Cover with the rest of the chopped-meat mixture. Finish with a layer of back fat or bacon. Place the mould in a bain-marie and put to cook in a low oven (300°F/gas 2) for 1 hour 15 minutes. Test by running a skewer into the centre; if the juice runs clear, it is done. Leave overnight under a weight if you would like to serve it cold.

Accompany with a gooseberry sauce made by stewing another pound of gooseberries in enough water to cover, sweetened with a little sugar and then sieved or liquidized. Or delicious with some of last year's well-matured chutney.

5 July 1986

Meat

The King's Bag-Pudding

When old King Arthur ruled this land
    He was a thieving king,
He stole three bolls of barley-meal
    To make a bag-pudding.

The pudding it was sweet and good
    And storéd well with plums.
The lumps o' suet into it
    Were big as both my thumbs.

Nursery rhymes may be the oldest form of propaganda, but bag-pudding, cloutie-dumpling, whatever you care to call it, is indeed good – and as British as Arthur himself. Furthermore suet pastry is the easiest of all pastries to make. A light hand with the mixing (Arthur clearly hadn't got the hang of suet – his lumps are far too big) and a vigilant eye on the boiling are all that are required. So turn down the central heating and set to work, for nothing becomes a northern winter better than a suet dumpling.

SUET PASTRY

8 oz suet　　　　　　　　　　　　　*½ teaspoon salt*
1 lb self-raising flour　　　　　　　*½ pint cold water*

Suet is the fat which encases a beef kidney, and can be obtained from your butcher. Preparing your own is easy and cheap, and the flavour will be fresher than the ready-processed variety. Peel off the transparent skin and slice the suet with a sharp knife. Dip your fingers in flour and work the pearls of white fat free from their fibre casings. Chop the suet thoroughly, then mix into the salted flour. (If you have a wonderfully light hand with pastry, you can use plain flour.) Add cold water slowly to make a smooth firm dough which leaves the sides of the bowl clean. This is the basic suet pastry and can also be used to make delicious little soup dumplings.

Halve the above quantities to line a two-pint pudding-bowl (to feed 4). Prepare the filling, which can be sweet or savoury; see below. Butter the bowl thoroughly. Save a quarter of the pastry for the lid and roll out the rest lightly into a circle big enough to line the bowl. Drop the pastry in and ease into the corners. Layer your chosen filling to within a finger's breadth of the top, then wet the rim of the pastry and cap with the rolled-out lid. Pinch the edges together to seal. Cover either with a round of greaseproof paper and a clean white cloth, both pleated in the middle to allow room for rising and tied with string below the bowl's lip, or a similarly pleated and tied sheet of silver foil. Stretch a string handle across the bowl for lifting it in and out of the boiling water. The pudding can be cooked in a steamer, or in a saucepan with the water reaching two-thirds of the way up. If the latter, use a tripod to protect the base of the bowl from direct heat. Bring the water to the boil before you put the pudding in and make sure it never boils dry. Cover with a well-fitting lid. The pudding must not be allowed to come off the boil at any time or the pastry will be heavy and grey as a school dinner. Always top up with *boiling* water. Serve a suet pudding without delay – it gets heavier as it cools, although an extra half-hour's boiling will do it no harm. The pudding can be made in advance and then reboiled for at least an hour to return it to its former lightness.

Meat puddings: Traditional recipes give very long cooking times – from 7 to 14 hours. The pastry has little chance of surviving this without getting soggy, so I suggest cooking a meat filling first, as for an ordinary pie. Allow the filling to cool before you arrange it in the pastry. The pudding will then only need four hours' boiling, and the crust will stay light and slightly crisp. As for the fillings, Eliza Acton, who loved a suet pudding, had a wealth of suggestions in 1856. Neck of venison with perhaps a truffle or two, sweetbreads sliced with button mushrooms, a mixed bag of woodcock, snipe, plover and partridge – all to be seasoned with onions and herbs and moistened with good stock. And the chief glory of the genre, John Bull's Pudding: rump steak layered with juicy oysters and gravied with a glass of good claret. Perfection.

Sweet puddings: Fill the dumpling with apples spiced with cinnamon and honey, or with blackberries, cherries, damsons, plums. An ounce or two of butter buried in the fruit, a spoonful of orange marmalade, or a little glass of *eau de vie* can do no harm on a cold day. Most elegant of all: Jane Grigson's recipe for Sussex Pond Pudding in her excellent *English Food* (1974). This is a simple suet pudding containing a whole lemon, well pricked, the remaining space to be packed with butter and brown sugar. When the pudding is un-moulded, the sauce runs out to form a delicious scented buttery moat.

As for Arthur and his plum pudding, Queen Guinevere even has a nice line with the leftovers:

> The King and Queen did eat thereof,
>   And noblemen beside;
> And what they could not eat that night
>   The Queen next morning fried.

12 January 1985

Burns Night

January 25th, as every Scot well knows, is Burns Night, an occasion to be celebrated from Potters Bar to Valparaiso with piping, poetry, haggis and good malt whisky. So raise a glass to the health of HM Customs and Excise, who around 1790 were far-sighted enough to give employment to Scotland's favourite prodigal poet. If poor old Robbie had had a penny of the duty payable on every bottle drunk in his honour since then, he would never have died with a pair of begging letters dropping from the tip of his pen. The bard made his

feelings about his native tipple clear in an early poem, 'Scotch Drink'. Written shortly after a New Year carouse in which the party premises were burnt to a cinder, my favourite stanza goes robustly as follows:

> O Whisky! Soul o' plays an' pranks!
>   Accept a Bardie's gratefu' thanks!
> When wanting thee, what tuneless cranks
>   Are my poor verses!
> Thou comes – they rattle in their ranks
>   At ither's airses!

That'll do for the verse and the whisky. Your Burns Night party may now proceed to table. Shortly before you will have delegated one of your more extrovert guests to read (or possibly recite) the whole of the rather more delicate 'The Cotter's Saturday Night'. This will not only create an atmosphere proper to the haggis's arrival, but take long enough (10 minutes 32 seconds on my stopwatch) to allow the cook to get into the kitchen, kick the piper awake, dish up the bard's 'great chieftain o' the pudding race', and bash the neeps and tatties – turnips and potatoes to the Sassenachs.

It is not impossible to make your own haggis. It is after all merely a large sausage stuffed with oats and sheep's innards. Do not be intimidated. The only ingredient difficult to obtain is the sheep's stomach for the skin. Bully your butcher to bully his slaughterhouse or wholesaler to provide one. A lamb or even a veal caul will do at a pinch. Failing this, F. Marion McNeill allows in her excellent book, *The Scots Kitchen* (1929), that a haggis may be boiled for four hours in a buttered jar or basin instead of a stomach-bag. *In extremis* it can even, if kept moist and stirred, be cooked like a stew in a saucepan, although it will lack that delicious, slightly sour rennet flavour imparted by a caul.

The classic haggis recipe was given by Mistress Margaret Dods, whose pudding – according to the tangled mythology that surrounds Sir Walter Scott's Cleikum Inn – was awarded first prize in Edinburgh's great Haggis Festival of 1830. Here, with my own observations, it is.

THE CLEIKUM HAGGIS

1 sheep's (or lamb's) stomach
1 ditto 'pluck' (the liver, heart and
*   lungs)*
6 oz coarse oatmeal

1 lb onions
1 lb beef suet
Pepper, salt, cayenne, 1 lemon

Tackle the stomach-bag first. Turn it inside out, then scrub and scrape it in several changes of cold water. Scald it and leave it to soak for a few hours in water and salt. Put the oatmeal to toast to a golden brown in a slow oven.

Wash the pluck. Drain the liver and heart of its blood (your butcher will probably already have done this). If you cannot get the lungs, the kidneys and tongue will do. Put the pluck into cold water and bring to the boil. Simmer for an hour at least. If you are using the lungs, make sure the windpipe hangs over the side of the pan to empty.

Drain the pluck and check it over, removing the black bits and veins. Grate the liver and chop the rest of the meat. (You may not need all the liver – half is usually enough.) Chop the suet. Chop the onions and scald them. Mix the meat, suet and onions together, and spread them out on the table. Sprinkle the oatmeal over the top. Season well with the salt, cayenne, lemon juice, and a heavy hand on the pepper-mill. The secret lies in the proportions, and you will soon establish your own preference. Mix the whole lot together and stuff it into the clean stomach-bag, which should be a little over half-full to allow room for the oatmeal to swell. Moisten with good stock – enough to make the mixture look juicy. Press out the air and sew up the bag. Put the haggis on an upturned saucer in a pan of boiling water or stock. Prick the bag with a needle when it first

106

swells. Simmer without allowing it to boil for three hours if the haggis is a large one. When you want to reheat it, simmer for an hour.

Serve the haggis with *Clapshot*: equal quantities of boiled potatoes and turnips (the Scots prefer the yellow Swedish variety), well seasoned and mashed together with good dripping or butter. And Rob's your uncle. Keep the fire blazing in the hearth and restrain yourself from pouring whisky on the pudding. Save the precious dram to toast the bard himself.

19 January 1985

The White Feast of Marco Polo

Marco Polo, traveller extraordinary and citizen of Venice in its prime, was born in 1254. He was a young lad of some eighteen summers when he accompanied his father and uncle to Cathay to visit the splendid court of Kublai Khan, mightiest of the kings of the earth, ruler of innumerable cities, infinite gardens and numberless fish-pools in the sands of the desert; keeper of the Tree of the Sun, on whose dry branches hung the apples of the sun and the moon, in whose shadow fought Darius and Alexander. Such a demigod as the Khan could afford to be generous – even to the three tattered dusty foreigners who arrived penniless at his gates. The Venetians remained in the King's employment for seventeen years, but it was the youngest of them who served the Khan so well as his chronicler. Like all the best travel-writers, young Marco had a good eye for detail and a fine taste for luxury.

Recounting the splendours of Genghis Khan's Great White Feast 'held on the first day of the month of February, being the commencement of their year', the chronicler describes the snowy clothing, smooth bleached linen, pure white horses, presents of pale pearls and diamonds and silver, all furnished in the amount of nine times nine and designed to promote good fortune in the coming year. 'The tables', he tells us, 'are now prepared for the feast, and the company, women as well as men, arrange themselves there.'

No menu – and that from a man who is widely believed in his native land to have transported the noodle from China and turned the Italians into a nation of pasta-eaters. He can only be excused on the grounds of extreme youth. 'Upon the removal of the victuals, the musicians and theatrical performers exhibit for the amusement of the court.' Then, says Marco, they all went home. Not a mention of the liqueurs and speeches, let alone the after-dinner mints.

The victuals must have included a selection of the Khan's spoils of the hunt: wild boars, stags, fallow deer, roebucks and bears (the paw being particularly prized as a titbit). Wild asses and oxen were hunted by the royal pack of lynxes, leopards and lions. These 'lions', Marco assures his Italian readership, were particularly fine beasts and larger than the Babylonian lions, with fine coats streaked lengthways with white, black and red stripes. The taking of storks, swans, herons and all feathered game his Majesty reserved for his own gyrfalcons and hawks. Closed season on all game was declared between between the months of March and October, thus assuring the Khan's position as one of the earliest gamekeepers.

Young Marco observed the royal cellar with equal curiosity. 'The greater part of the inhabitants of Cathay drink a sort of wine made from rice mixed with a variety of spices and drugs. This beverage, or wine as it may be termed, is so good and well flavoured that they do not wish for better. It is clear, bright and pleasant to the taste, and being made very hot, has the quality of inebriating sooner than any other.'

The fuel for the stove is not unfamiliar: 'Throughout this province there is found a sort of black stone, which they dig out of the mountains, where it runs in veins. When lighted, it burns like charcoal, and retains the fire much better than wood. . . .'

Seven centuries have passed since the Great Khan welcomed young Master Polo to his Court. Here is a very small White Feast of good fortune to commemorate their encounter.

WHITE FEAST FOR TWO

Sweetbreads in Cream

2 fine veal or lamb sweetbreads. These delicate little white meats are the pancreas (elongated in shape and to be found near the stomach) and the thymus glands (rounded in shape and found in the animal's throat).

2 oz butter　　　　　　　　　　*1 small carton thick cream*
1 small glass brandy (or, better still,
　　Chinese Mao Tai)

Soak the sweetbreads for at least two hours in salted water to soak out any traces of blood. Clean and wipe. Then put them into boiling water with peppercorns and a tablespoonful of vinegar. Bring back to the boil and simmer for 15 minutes. Drain and remove all traces of skin and sinew. Press between two weighted plates until cold and firm. Cut into squares.

Melt the butter in a small casserole and put the sweetbreads in. Stew them gently for 15 minutes. Pour in the brandy and allow it to warm for a moment. Flame it. Then add the cream. Simmer for another 10 minutes, uncovered, to thicken the sauce. Season with mustard, pepper, salt and a teaspoon of lemon juice.

Serve with fresh egg noodles. Warm Chinese rice wine or *sake* to accompany of course.

˙1 February 1986

Out of the Frying-Pan into a Stew

Giraldus Cambrensis, twelfth-century Welsh cleric, chronicler of Henry II's conquest of Ireland and author of the *Topographica hibernica*, was a keen student of Hibernian natural history. He observed that the denizens of Irish roosts are not as other roosters. 'Cocks at roost in Ireland', he notes, 'do not, as in other countries, divide the third and last watches of the night by crowing at three successive periods in the interval. Nor is it to be supposed that they have here a different nature from those in other countries, for cocks which are brought over to the island from other parts crow here at these Irish periods.'

Last week I discovered that Irish stews are also not as other stews.

I was queuing in the butcher's shop for a shoulder of spring lamb. The elderly lady at the front had decided on several pounds of neck of lamb to make an Irish stew for her grandson's football team. The butcher threw the discussion of its preparation open to the gathering. Cooking methods, it emerged, varied as widely as the ingredients. To fry or not to fry the meat? Were carrots or leeks or turnips to be featured? Above all, what about the inclusion of barley? Opinions divided so sharply that when I returned home, having firmly given my opinion on the controversy, I set out to find the genuine recipe. It turns out I have been making Irish stew the wrong way all my life. It's not so surprising, of course: no one ever gets the answer to the Irish problem right.

The Irish stew is a white stew. All authorities are quite clear on that: the meat and onions are not to be fried first. No hint of gold is to mar the virginity of its composition. Theodora Fitzgibbon, in her recent book *Irish Traditional Food* (1968), gives proportions of (for 4 persons) 3 lb neck of lamb, to 2 lb potatoes, to 1 lb onions and 1 pint of stock. Parsley and thyme to flavour. All to be layered in a deep covered pan and cooked on top of the stove or in a slow oven for 2 hours. Notice the absence of vegetables and barley. Its Irish name is *stobhach gaelach*. A 'hotpot', on the other hand, she says, is an Irish stew with the lamb's kidneys in as well, and the lid taken off at the end to allow the top to brown. Eliza Acton, although she suggests using a brown, upright, somewhat un-Irish Nottingham jar as a cooking-pot, also thinks it a good idea to take the lid off to allow the stew to brown.

E. S. Dallas, unacknowledged (at the time) author of *Kettner's Book of the Table* (1877), has words on the matter:

The Irish are not cooks. They have done nothing to furnish the table except in the way of Usquebaugh – water of life – which, however, it must be admitted is an immense achievement, worthy of the magicians, and proving beyond a doubt that in the older time Ireland was an abode of giants.

Irish stew is a white ragout of mutton with potatoes for the chief garnish. . . . The beautiful symplicity would be lost if it were allowed in any way to brown. . . . The potatoes are so important in it that they are always double the weight of the meat. . . . In the true Irish stew, too, both potatoes and onions are exceedingly well done, so that they are half reduced to a mash.

Let us leave the problem cloaked in a soft Irish mist. Here is my own version, as given to the grandmother in the queue, of a lamb stew for a windy March day.

LAMB STEW

TO SERVE 6 PEOPLE

2 lb neck of lamb	4 oz barley
1 oz dripping	2 bay leaves
1 lb carrots	Salt and pepper
1 lb onions	2 lb potatoes
1 lb turnips and parsnips	1 earthenware casserole with a lid
2 fat leeks	

Fry the neck chops lightly in the dripping. Take out the meat and save the frying fat. Prepare the carrots, turnips and parsnips and leeks in roughly equal chunks. Slice the onions into rings. Layer the meat, onions and vegetables into the earthenware pot. Sprinkle in the barley and season the layers as you go, and tuck in the bay leaves. Peel and slice the potatoes and lay them over all. Pour in enough boiling stock or water to come halfway up the layers. Sprinkle the reserved dripping over the layer of potatoes, put the lid on the dish and bake at 350°F/gas 4 for two hours. Take the lid off for the potatoes to brown for the last half-hour. Serve it in its dish with good brown bread to mop up the barley-thickened gravy. If it wasn't for the initial frying, you could call it a *stobhach uaineola no cuioreola* and be done with it.

16 March 1985

111

Thumbs Up for a Carpet-Bag Steak

Some of Hong Kong's more sentimental citizens are planning a Colonial Week – a delightful idea guaranteed, I would have thought, to upset all sorts of people – to be marked by a series of colonial menus in one of the major hotels. I learnt this when a request for colonial recipes for the celebration was passed my way, with a particular plea for something from Australia. Australia, it appears, is not strong on indigenous cuisine. On the other hand, a country which pioneers dwarf-chucking and sheila-in-a-wet-T-shirt competitions is clearly not raising its offspring on purées and paps.

Recipes which nurtured the infant fantasies of such robust entertainers as Clive James and Dame Edna Everidge, to say nothing of a revolutionary philosopher of the calibre of Germaine Greer, must be sturdy fare indeed. Researching the matter, I found that beef, mutton and good fish – including crustaceans and oysters – were the mainstays of the traditional antipodean table. There were also rather more exotic delicacies. Fricassee of Kangaroo-Tail was one, a dish I imagine tasting something like a large fat ox-tail stew, although Australia House tells me kangaroo meat has now become a no-go area. These days it is only sold as pet-food. At the turn of the century, parrot pie was recommended, to be made with a dozen parakeets, each wrapped in a thin slice of beef. Budgie-fanciers, lock up your cages.

To return to the problem: I suggested an hors d'oeuvre of wichita grubs, with Kangaroo-Tail Soup for the faint-hearted, followed by a nicely roasted wallaby (rather like hare, I gather). If Australia House gives wallaby the thumbs down, too, then perhaps a down-under joke such as 'Australian Goose' might be suitable. This does not, inevitably, feature anything feathered. It is a leg of mutton, boned and stuffed with peas, onion and bacon. And of course, to crown the evening, a Pavlova, a confection of meringue, cream and fruit invented for the ballerina's visit to Sydney. The whole naturally to be washed down with a choice of Foster's famous lager, Australian Cabernet Sauvignon, or a nice refreshing mug of billy-can tea.

What I forgot to suggest to the enquiring colonials was the best Australian idea of all – a flash of culinary genius born of the availability of good raw materials and a life in the open air. It is the carpet-bagger's steak, still, says Australia House, known and loved today. 'Carpetbagger' was the sobriquet used to describe politicians and other seekers of worldly treasure who crowded into the defeated South of the United States of America to pick over the debris of the Civil War. Here it is, the first barbecue of spring, for our immigrant Australians, Clive and Germaine and Dame Edna.

CARPET-BAGGER'S STEAK

TO SERVE 4 AUSTRALIANS

1 thick rump steak (cut to weigh 2 lb)
A dozen oysters (2 dozen mussels
   would do at a pinch)
Juice of an onion

Juice of a lemon
2 tablespoons oil
Tabasco
Salt and pepper

Open the raw oysters or mussels. Cut a deep pocket in the steak and stuff it full of the shellfish. Season with tabasco, a squeeze of lemon, salt and pepper, and sew up the opening. Mix the onion juice, the rest of the lemon juice, oil and seasoning, and marinate the steak in the mixture for an hour or two. Grill the steak on a hot barbecue, basting with the marinade. It will take longer than an ordinary steak because of its thickness.

Serve with a tomato and onion salad, and genuine Australian dampers from a recipe recorded by Thomas Baines, artist to Dr Livingstone's first Zambesi expedition and later an antipodean explorer under the patronage of the Royal Geographical Society. These instructions come from his 1871 masterpiece, co-authored with W. B. Lord, *Shifts and Expedients of Camp Life*.

MR BAINES'S DAMPERS

TO SERVE 4 AS ABOVE

1 lb plain strong flour
Water

Salt

Pour the flour on to your pastry-board. (Mr Baines suggests a dried sheepskin as a suitable kneading-board.) Add a teaspoon of salt and make a well in the centre. Gradually pour into the flour-well from a bowl in your left hand enough water to be worked into a dough with your right hand (left-handed people will be used to this discrimination). Knead the dough thoroughly until it is thick, strong and adhesive. Form into a large ball and roll it flat into a pancake 2½ inches thick. Scoop the embers of your camp-fire aside and lay the damper on the hot hearth. Rake the coals back over it until the damper is deeply buried in them. In between one and two hours, says Mr Baines, it will be cooked to a turn, be a light rich brown, and a feast for a king.

20 April 1985

Chopping Up the Mutton

In spite of the length of my book *European Peasant Cookery* – all 596 pages of it – the writing was the easy part. It was the testing of the 500-odd recipes that was the hard labour. For the last year or two my family has patiently eaten its way, without leaving the safety of its own backyard, from the Bosporus to the Baltic, from the Rock of Gibraltar to the North Cape. The group was happy enough with the pastas and paellas of the Mediterranean, and the marinated fish and berry soups of Scandinavia met with universal approval. But a whole week spent perfecting a Saxon cabbage soup recipe brought more than a few rumbles of complaint, which could only be assuaged by a week among the delicious *daubes* and *gratins* of France.

For the testing of the chapter on lamb and mutton I negotiated the

114

purchase of a whole yearling lamb (technically mutton since it had passed its first anniversary), a plump little fellow from Hebridean pastures. About 40 lb of meat and bones, neatly jointed Scots fashion, appeared on my kitchen table. Since I have no deep freeze, all except the hams (which could be salted) had to be consumed by my family of six within the week. I pass on the experience for anyone whose freezer breaks down or who for any other reason is faced with a similar problem.

The offal is the most perishable. The Scots origin of the raw material dictated a haggis – which, I must confess, I made in a pudding basin, not in the stomach-bag (the household vetoed my idea of putting it to wash, well salted, in the washing machine on 'delicates'). The liver and kidneys were simmered in water until stiff and ready for grating through the cheese-grater. The grated meat, together with the suet round the kidneys, also grated, plus coarse oatmeal and a good seasoning of freshly ground black pepper and grated onions, was moistened with the stock from the cooked liver, and boiled in a covered pudding-basin for 3–4 hours. For the full instructions, see page 106. The sheep's head and trotters were not included in the package. Had they been, I would have simmered them with plenty of root vegetables and black pepper to make a sheep's-head broth, the shepherd's dish all over Europe.

One of the boned shoulders was made into a *pistache* – the famous French garlic-thickened stew. The other shoulder yielded a pyramid of Turkish *kebabs* for Sunday dinner – a meal when there are usually extra mouths to feed in my kitchen.

The two legs went into brine (1 oz salt to 1 pint clear water to cover) to tenderize and preserve them – a method still used in Scandinavia where salted and dried lamb is still, as it was in Britain until recently, a great delicacy. One leg was taken out the next week and roasted to be served with rowan jelly. The other was simmered with vegetables to yield a lamb pot-au-feu. The neck chops made a fine Irish stew. The cutlets were grilled and served with quartered lemons and a salad of tomatoes, onions and cucumbers in the Greek manner.

The breast of lamb is at its most delicious in Romania as a *tocana*, a one-pot dish from the Carpathian mountains of Transylvania. Carpathian shepherds still practise transhumance – moving their thousand-strong flocks straight down the modern motorway between the winter and summer pastures. At night men and animals take their ease and their nourishment. This is the stew which is prepared over the campfire.

TOCANA

TO SERVE 6 PEOPLE

2 lb breast of lamb off the bone
1 lb onions
Salt and black pepper
1½ pints water

2–3 bay leaves
2 lb potatoes
¼ pint sour cream or thick yoghurt
1 tablespoon vinegar

You will need a heavy casserole.

Cube the meat and trim off most of the fat (save it). Peel and slice the onions. Put the fat-trimmings to render in a heavy casserole or saucepan. Take out the scratchings and add the meat and the onions. Fry until well browned. Add the water, the salt, the pepper and the herbs. Bring to the boil and then turn down the heat. Leave to simmer for an hour.

Peel and slice the potatoes and add them to the stew. Simmer the stew for another 30 minutes. Take the lid off towards the end to allow the gravy to thicken by evaporation. When the potatoes are soft, stir in the cream and the vinegar, and remove the stew from the stove. Serve the *tocana* hot, with plenty of black bread.

Finish the meal with a nip of the water of life – in Romania it would be plum brandy (*tuica*), marc or calvados will do instead.

25 October 1986

Political Stew in the Camargue

Jean-Pierre is the horseman at the Pont des Bannes hotel in the Camargue, the huge marshy delta of the Rhône. He is also on the local council and a man of considerable influence in the area. French politics is full of passion, and Jean-Pierre is in there at the sharp end. The battle-lines are ancient: fisherman against hunter, farmer against cattleman. The tourists upset everyone's balance. Jean-Pierre, trailing his string of foreigners mounted on impeccably trained white ponies of the sturdy Camarguais race, is neither flesh nor fowl nor good red herring. Diversions for us visitors are his regular encounters with his constituents.

On the day I took my ride with Jean-Pierre luck brought us a disgruntled eel-fisherman. Apart from my husband and my sister-in-law, for both of whom I was of course answerable, my fellow-horsemen were a distinctly mixed bag. We included a very fat Italian

(whose horse looked as gloomy as Don Quixote's Rosinante), the Italian's beautiful dark-haired daughter and her suitor – a dusky gentleman in leather waistcoat, his well-oiled muscles decked with fine gold chains. The French contingent, three in number, were perfectly turned out for the *équitation*: all boots and spurs and John Wayne shirts. Two of them were in love, and the third was the hotelier of Roger Vergé, the famous chef. As might be imagined from his job, the hotelier was a person of considerable personal charm. Since his horse and mine were evidently as thick as thieves in the stables and insisted on travelling together, M. Vergé's hotelier and I spent much of the morning in each other's company. I learnt a great deal about the making of *rouille* and was gently nudging the conversation towards M. Vergé's version of a *bouillabaisse* when we happened upon the eel-man.

Jean-Pierre is a grass-roots politician. Grass roots in the Camargue are salty and tough as hobnailed boots. The eel-fisherman was not a contented man – and more than ready with his boots. The flood-gates of the *digues*, he explained, were not being used for the good of the fishermen. The water-levels were being kept low for the benefit of the *nidification* of the hunters' prey. He elaborated on the origins and paternity of the hunters. There were therefore no eels, no fish and no fortune for the fishermen, who were after all the original architects of the *digues*, back in the days of Henry IV. By this time the mosquitoes had spotted the large Italian. The French *amoureux* dismounted from their horses and turned their attentions to each other. Roger Vergé's hotelier's horse and mine (Babette, I think her name was) were similarly occupied. Furthermore, the fisherman explained, those *espèces* of rice farmers were taking all the water and making all the profit. Why, he enquired, were the spoils not more evenly divided? Why, for example, did Jean-Pierre not share the profits from the rental of horses to these good and no doubt rich and distinguished foreigners with those less fortunate, perhaps, but who gave the Camargue its unique flavour? At this point the discussion became too much even for Jean-Pierre's powers of diplomacy, and we were all instructed to remount immediately.

Jean-Pierre then set off at a gallop, enthusiastically pursued by all his horsemen – with the exception of the overweight Italian. Babette, her maternal instincts aroused by the plight of poor Rosinante, changed the company she wished to keep and landed me with the Italian for the rest of the trip. The mosquitoes were making so large a meal of him I didn't have the heart to talk to him about his native dishes.

Here is Jean-Pierre's favourite Camarguais stew.

ESTOUFFADE DE BŒUF CAMARGUAIS

WILL FEED 6 GRASS-ROOTS POLITICIANS

3 lb beef (for stewing)	*3 soup-spoons olive oil*
1 lb onions	*4 oz stoned black olives*
4 cloves garlic	*1 bottle good red wine*
1 lb tomatoes (or 1 tin)	*Thyme, rosemary, bay leaf*

Cube the meat. Peel and chop the onions and garlic. Heat the oil gently in a frying-pan and turn the meat in it to seal. Be careful not to over-heat the oil. Remove the meat and give the onions and garlic a gentle fry. Put the onions, garlic and oil in the bottom of a casserole (an earthenware *daube* if you have one, otherwise use a good sturdy one with a tight-fitting lid). Add the tomatoes, the wine, the olives and the herbs. Add a teaspoon of sugar and a few peppercorns. Cover and cook in a slow oven (300°F/gas 2) for an hour and a half.

Serve with rice and a nod to the farmers. Smoked eel as an hors d'oeuvre should please the fishermen.

22 June 1985

Trotters around the World

Pigs are more trouble than babies. Beatrix Potter was quite right when she scolded Aunt Pettitoes: 'Aunt Pettitoes, Aunt Pettitoes! you are a worthy person, but your family is not well brought up.' My own Pigling Bland was not at all well brought up. He had a shed at the bottom of the garden with a little stone-walled run to root in. When he was little he could only reach to the top of the wall with the

pink tip of his snout. By the time he was six months he could hurdle it with ease and trot up to the house to demand his food at the kitchen door. If he managed to get inside, he would skid round and round the kitchen table squealing and grunting until his blue feed-bucket was found and filled. Then he would follow it quite politely back to his sty. Poor old Pigling Bland. When he was a year old, he promoted himself to four self-service meals a day. By that time even the baby was down to three. I'd had enough.

Pigling was sent to market, figuratively speaking. The household pickled hams and stuffed sausages for days. Finally there was nothing left but the pettitoes.

PIG'S TROTTERS

4 pig's trotters
1 onion
2 tablespoons vinegar

Bay leaf
12 peppercorns
Salt

Scald the trotters and singe off any hair. A day or two in brine will improve their flavour. Pig's trotters have lots of little bones in them, rather like human hands. Since it takes several hours to boil them tender, they tend to drop to pieces in the cooking: to avoid this, tie them firmly and closely in pairs on either side of a little plank of wood the same length and width as the trotters. They can be cooked loose, but the danger of disintegration always remains.

Put the trotters into plenty of cold water in a large pot with the halved onion, vinegar, bay leaf, salt and the peppercorns. Bring to the boil and skim off the grey foam. Turn down the heat and then simmer for 5 hours – it could be in the slow oven of an Aga overnight.

When they are tender, allow them to cool down to a comfortable handling temperature. Slit each trotter in half. You may carefully remove the bones if you prefer.

This is the basic trotter recipe. It gives you a delicately flavoured, gelatinous meat. (In France, you would buy them at this stage, but further embellished by having been rolled in breadcrumbs ready for grilling.) Roll them in breadcrumbs yourself, trickle butter over, and crisp them under the grill. Serve them with English mustard or a mustard sauce. Or with a vinaigrette, spiced with chopped raw onion and capers.

Or *à la Sainte-Menehould* – the classic French recipe. The trotters are cooked, breadcrumbed, and grilled as above. The sauce is made with two chopped onions sautéd in butter, half a pint of white wine and two tablespoons of vinegar, reduced to a glaze with the onions. Add ½ pint of the cooking liquid, and thicken with an ounce of butter and an ounce of flour worked together. Flavour with pepper, chopped gherkins, herbs and a little mustard.

JIU TIAO/STUFFED TROTTERS

The Chinese stuff their trotters at the start of the process.

4 oz loin of pork	*1 clove garlic*
2 tablespoons soy	*Small piece of ginger*
2 tablespoons vinegar	*Five-spice powder and star anise*
1 oz sugar	*(if you can find it)*
4 pig's trotters	

Cut the pork into four long strips and put to marinate in the soy, the sugar and the vinegar.

Wash and singe the pig's trotters and put them into cold salted water. Bring to the boil. Take out the trotters and drain. Split them, leaving one side attached, and remove the larger bones.

Put a strip of marinated pork into the cavities left by the bones and tie the trotters up again with string. Peel and chop the garlic and the ginger. Put the trotters into a pan with the garlic and ginger and spices. Just cover all with water and add some more soy. Simmer for 5 hours. Untie the packets and serve the trotters with steamed spinach.

ZAMPONI CON LENTICCHIE

The Italians have a similar recipe; there was a lot of culinary give-and-take between them and the Chinese.

TO SERVE 4 PEOPLE

4 oz minced pork	*2 oz fat bacon*
1 clove finely chopped garlic	*1 onion*
Salt and pepper	*1 tablespoon olive oil*
1 teaspoon dried oregano	*½ lb lentils*

Treat the trotters as for *Jiu Tiao*, but stuff them with the minced pork mixed with the garlic, salt, pepper and oregano. Tie them up.

Put the lentils to soak in cold water. Dice the bacon and fry it gently in the oil in a stew-pan with the chopped onion. Put in the trotters, cover with cold water and simmer for four hours. Add the soaked lentils (more liquid may be necessary). Cook for another hour. Untie the trotters and serve them on a bed of the lentils.

12 October 1985

Pickled Beef as a Standby

Pickled beef is an excellent standby for any meal over Christmas (including breakfast) and makes a welcome change from all that poultry and ham. This is a dish to be served cold. It goes very well with your favourite potato dish – a *gratin*, a *galette*, or big floury baked potatoes.

Get at least a 5–6 lb piece of one of the cheaper cuts of beef. Flank is particularly good – well flavoured and with an even balance of meat and creamy fat. Buy the saltpetre (potassium nitrate, which, incidentally, is the chief ingredient in gunpowder) from the chemist. Saltpetre has been used in Britain since the Middle Ages to speed up the pickling process and give salted meat that appetizing pinkish colour. It is not essential, but if you do not use it the meat will turn out grey. The other ingredients can be had easily enough. I have adapted this recipe from my 1912 edition of Mrs Beeton. Here is her preliminary advice:

> *The Action of Salt on Meat.* Salt when applied to meat extracts the juices in large quantities. The salt and watery

juices form a saturated solution or brine, which is absorbed into the tissues of the meat, and being strongly antiseptic preserves it. In addition to the antiseptic action, salt contracts the fibres of the muscles, and excludes the air from the interior of the meat. The astringent action of the salt-petre or nitre is much greater than that of common salt, and if used too freely renders the meat to which it is applied very hard. In small quantities it intensifies the antiseptic action of salt and preserves the colour of meat, which the action of salt alone destroys.

SPICED BEEF

5–6 lb piece of beef   *2 oz rough salt (bay, sea or rock)*

Rub your meat all over with the salt. Allow the meat to take the salt and drain for 24 hours.

Pound together this mixture:

2 oz rough salt   *1 oz juniper berries*
½ oz saltpetre   *1 stick cinnamon*
3 oz brown sugar   *1 dozen cloves*
1 oz peppercorns

Lift the beef out of its brine and pat dry. Rub the meat all over with the spice mixture and lay it in an earthenware dish. Put in the larder to take the spices: 7–8 days should be sufficient. Keep it covered and turn it every day, rubbing it well with the spices and juice.

To Cook the Beef
1 large glass of red wine or port

When you are ready to cook the meat, take it out of the marinade, brush off the spices and pat it dry. Do not rinse it. Roll it and tie it up neatly with string. Put it into a deep casserole (one with a lid) and pour over a generous glass of good red wine or port. Seal the lid on firmly with a layer or two of foil or a paste of flour and water. The meat has to cook for a long time in its own steam, so none must be allowed to escape.

Cook in a very low oven (250°F/gas 1) for 4–5 hours. Leave to cool in its own liquid. Then take it out, wrap it in foil and press it between two plates with a 1 lb weight on top for 24 hours.

It will carve beautifully into very thin slices. Accompany with mustard and a horseradish cream. If you would like to serve it for a main meal, make a *Gratin dauphinois* – a highly controversial subject among Frenchmen, and whose composition arouses as much passion as the origin of lobster *à l'amoricaine*. Happily, the French are never averse to calling their experts idiots.

This is the way I like to make the dish.

Gratin dauphinois

TO SERVE 5–6 PEOPLE

2½ lb potatoes	*1 pint milk*
2 fat cloves garlic	*½ pint cream*
Salt and pepper	*½ oz flour*

Wash the potatoes first. Then peel and slice them on a 'mandoline' (that neat little French arrangement of guillotine-sharp knives mounted in a wooden board) or in an electric slicer.

Peel and slice the garlic finely. Layer the slices of potato with the garlic into a deep round casserole, seasoning with freshly ground pepper and salt as you pile up the layers. Some people like nutmeg in it. I just don't like nutmeg.

Bring the milk to the boil. Mix the cream with the flour (I normally try to keep my hand out of the flour-pot as much as possible, but this tiny quantity does make the difference between a curdled buttery mess and a delicious smooth cream bubbling gently round the potatoes).

Pour the boiling milk over the potatoes in the casserole and then pour in the cream and flour mixture. That's it. No eggs. No cheese. No butter.

Bake in a moderately hot oven (375°F/gas 5) for 45 minutes. Now slip a knife into the middle to see if the potatoes are soft. If not, continue to cook until they are done. Finally, turn the heat right up for five minutes, or slip the casserole under the grill to form a beautiful crisp golden crust.

14 December 1985

Pot Plan for a Weekend of Leisure

It has been a long hard winter and a pale imitation of spring. This year, June is no time to be boxed into the kitchen and at the weekend. Far better dust down your straw hat and settle down in the garden to watch the rosebuds open. Assuming a head-count of six for each meal from Friday evening to Sunday lunch, here is a catering master-plan to allow for a weekend counting butterflies. It needs but a little organization and a large cooking-pot.

All but the final preparations can be done on Friday morning. Your shopping-list should include:

1 whole salted ox-tongue weighing 3–4 lb

3 lb piece of stewing beef, rolled and tied (shin or brisket or both)

1 boiling hen (failing that, a 2½–3 lb roasting chicken)

1–2 pig's trotters, split and washed

Put the above ingredients into your largest stew-pan, plus a few pot-herbs, carrots and onions, parsley stalks and bay leaf, and cover all with cold water (if your chicken is a tender roaster, do not add it yet). Bring the potful to the boil, skim and then turn it down to a fast simmer. Cook steadily for 3 hours (the roasting chicken should go in halfway through the cooking time). After 3 hours, the meats will be tender and the stock strong and well flavoured. Remove all from the heat.

When the meats are cool enough to handle, take out the tongue, trim off the fatty bits, and skin it. Pack it neatly into a small pudding-basin and cover the top with a plate weighted with a 2 lb tin. Put it in the larder to await Sunday lunch.

Strain out the stock (there should be 5 or 6 pints) and put it aside. Also put aside for the pot-au-feu a whole fillet of the chicken breast and about a quarter of the beef. Remove the rest of chicken meat from the bones, cover and put it aside. Trim off the fat from the rest of the beef, pull the meat into shreds, moisten with a little stock and put it aside. Save the trotters. Now you have the basic ingredients for your weekend menus.

FRIDAY POT-AU-FEU

Start the cooking half an hour before you are ready to dine.

3 pints of the basic pot-au-feu stock
2 lb new potatoes well scrubbed
2–3 leeks or a bunch of spring
onions, washed and cut into
lengths

2 lb other vegetables (baby carrots,
baby turnips, whole green beans,
sliced cabbage, courgettes washed
and quartered lengthways, broccoli
– anything fresh which keeps its
shape after cooking)
The chicken breast and beef put aside
from the pot-au-feu

Bring the stock to the boil. Add the potatoes (and the turnips and carrots if you are using them). Simmer for ten minutes. Add the leeks or onions. Five minutes later add the green vegetables. Bring all back to the boil and simmer until all the vegetables are tender. Add the meats cut into chunks.

Serve in deep soup-plates and hand round a home-made mayonnaise with 2 crushed garlic cloves stirred into it. Hot bread to accompany. Complete the meal with a sorbet and fresh fruit.

SATURDAY LUNCH: BEEF AND PASTA VINAIGRETTE

Shredded beef from the pot-au-feu
6 oz short pasta (fusilli, the long thin
spirals, are best) cooked and
drained
½ cucumber cut into matchsticks
1 red and 1 green pepper de-seeded
and cut into matchsticks

1 bunch chives or spring onions,
chopped
A vinaigrette made with plenty of
mild mustard
A large handful of chopped fresh
herbs (basil, tarragon, parsley,
chervil)
Salt and pepper

Toss all together and serve at room temperature. Green salads, a bunch of scarlet radishes well washed but still in a posy, and cheese to accompany.

SATURDAY DINNER: CHICKEN GRATIN

The shredded chicken
1 pint well-flavoured cheese sauce

¼ pint double cream
2 oz grated cheese

Stir the shredded chicken into the sauce. Fold in the cream. Taste and adjust seasoning. Spread the mixture in a gratin-dish, sprinkle with grated cheese, and give it 20 minutes in a hot oven to heat through and gild the top. Serve with *risi e bisi* – rice *risotto* with plenty of fresh peas cooked in with it.

Asparagus to precede; finish with strawberries.

SUNDAY LUNCH: PRESSED TONGUE WITH CAPER AND MUSTARD SAUCE

Unmould the tongue, slice it and arrange it on a pretty dish. You can, if you wish, heat it through gently in a little of the stock. Sprinkle with plenty of chopped parsley.

Make the sauce with 1 pint hot pot-au-feu stock thickened with 2 oz butter worked with 2 oz flour. Stir in 2 tablespoons pickled capers (nasturtium buds will do instead), 1 tablespoon strong English mustard and 1 tablespoon vinegar. Serve the sauce hot in a jug. Accompany with the best from your garden or greengrocer: tiny French beans, new carrots or peas, and new potatoes. Finish with your favourite pudding.

31 May 1986

Venison off the Shoulder

Venison is excellent meat, not appreciated nearly enough in the south of Britain (the Scots have more of a taste for it), perhaps because it is often cooked too dry or not marinated. Most of our wild-killed deer are packed for export to the gastronomes of Germany, Austria, Holland and France, along with our native crop of wild mushrooms. A sorry loss on both counts.

Venison from deer farms is now available all the year round. The regulated seasons for wild deer shooting are not a little complicated to unravel – best consult one of the several published game-diaries to find out what meat (doe or stag) from what species will be available and when. As for the cooking of it, I love a venison stew best of all. But it must be dark and rich and pungent or you may as well have tame cattle and be done with it. The meat itself is so lean it needs plenty of extra fat.

The two shoulders of a small doe will yield around 12 lb of meat when off the bone. Although I prepared this recipe as a party-dish to feed 40 people it can be frozen in batches very successfully and used either reheated or to make excellent pies and pasties later in the year. At least 10 meals for 4 people: a bargain. It also solves the problem of what to do with the 2 shoulders of the deer when you have roasted the saddle and braised the haunch. (The French in fact prefer the shoulder meat, which they bone out, tie up and roast.)

The recipe is based on many a good 'all-in' venison stew I have enjoyed in a little Spanish *venta* on the way to the Andalusian hill-fortress of Castellar de la Frontera. The small restaurant is family-run and always well patronized. It fronts the road, its tables welcoming in the speckled emerald sunshine filtering down through the leaves of the surrounding cork-oaks. Its kitchen offices lean-to behind, half-hidden in the ancient deer-forest of Almoreima, until recently part of the largest privately owned estate in Europe. The venison, which is the house speciality, is allegedly farmed, but the presence of two elderly and clearly very tame old stags in an enclosure at the back fools no one. Not long ago Almoreima changed hands. Bought by the huge Spanish conglomerate RUMASA, which had plans to clear the forest and 'develop' the land, it was rescued by the government when RUMASA went spectacularly broke. Happily, there is still plenty of deer in the forest and venison in the *venta*.

VENTA VENISON

Start preparations the day before.

12 lb meat	½ pint olive oil
1 bottle full-bodied red wine	4 lb onions
6 bay leaves	1 lb dried mushrooms (chanterelles or
1 tablespoon juniper or allspice	cèpes) or 2 lb fresh mushrooms
berries	1 lb pork belly with skin
1 oz peppercorns	½ lb raw cured ham or ½ lb smoked
2 oz salt	bacon
6 cloves garlic	8 oz black olives
1 lb red peppers	1 slice stale bread

Cut the venison off the bone and into neat cubes about an inch square. Have the bones sawn in half so that you can get at the marrow. Put the cubed meat into a deep basin and pour over it the bottle of wine. Work in with your hands the bay leaves, the juniper or the allspice berries crushed with the peppercorns and the salt and add the six garlic cloves, peeled and roughly chopped. Leave to marinate overnight, with the bones on top. If you are using dried mushrooms, put them to soak overnight, too.

The next day, put half the oil into your largest stew-pan and heat it gently. De-seed and slice the peppers and put them to stew in the oil. Peel and chop the onions and add them to the peppers. Leave all to cook slowly.

Cube the pork belly, the ham and/or bacon. Heat a tablespoonful of the oil in a frying-pan and put the pieces to cook. When they are lightly golden and the fat well run, transfer them to the casserole where the vegetables are stewing.

Drain the venison, reserving the marinade and the bones. Adding more oil as you need it, fry the venison cubes in the hot fat in the pan. As they brown, transfer them to the casserole. When all has received its preliminary searing (including the fresh mushrooms, sliced, if you are using them) add the marinade to the meats and vegetables together with the dried mushrooms and their soaking water. Put the bones to cook in the steam on the top of the stew. Stew for 1 hour after it comes to the boil, or until the meat is tender. Pit the olives and pound them or process them with the bread. Stir the mixture into the dark juices 10 minutes before the end of cooking time to thicken them. Stir the marrow into the sauce before you serve it.

Delicious with a plain (undressed) watercress salad and home-made game chips.

18 January 1986

Fit for a Fan-Tail

It is very difficult to give away pigeons. They have that famous inclination to come home to roost. When I lived in Andalusia relations between my household and that of my Dutch neighbour, Mitte, became a little strained when the immaculate pair of white fan-tailed doves I had given her were found for the fourth night running roosting not in her well-provisioned dovecot, but in the eaves of their birth. They preferred, it seemed, to keep company in infinitely less luxurious accommodation with the rest of the two-dozen-strong flock which was eating me out of house and home. Had it not been for the birds' astonishing ability to read the thought 'pigeon pie' as it fluttered through my mind, they would all have been in the pot long since.

Mitte took the birds' decision personally. 'Allez Lisbet,' she said as she scrambled up the ladder and lunged at the miscreants. 'They are most ungrateful birds. Up in my house they have everything. Last night I despair. Instead of corn I give them my best Indonesian rice. It is a terrible thing they are doing not to stay in my house when they can eat my *Nasi goreng*.'

I could only apologize for the bird-brains, and agree. Mitte was a very good cook, and her *Nasi goreng with saté* was indeed an excellent reason to eat at her house. That these two dishes are now part of the Dutch national cuisine is due to Holland's own colonial pigeons coming home to roost. As the British inherited Indian and Hong Kong Chinese communities, the French their Vietnamese refugees, so the Dutch have their Indonesians.

Indonesian Food and Cookery by Sri Owen has just been reissued in a second edition by Prospect Books. A typical Indonesian meal features a selection of different dishes all served together – not unlike a hot-weather smorgasbord, and a very suitable arrangement for a summer barbecue. The recipes include Mitte's two favourite dishes.

NASI GORENG

The name, says Sri Owen, simply means 'fried rice'. This is her recipe for 4–6 people.

1 lb long-grain rice
4 shallots or 1 small onion, chopped
2 red chillies, de-seeded and chopped, or ½ teaspoon chilli powder and 1 teaspoon paprika
2 tablespoons vegetable oil or clarified butter or pork fat

Optional extras: shrimps, chopped bacon, finely chopped carrot or Chinese cabbage, little pieces of cooked meat or ham, chopped mushrooms

The rice should be plain-boiled at least two hours ahead and allowed to cool. This is the dish the Indonesians often make for breakfast, using left-over rice from the day before.

Heat the oil in a wok or frying-pan, and toss in the onions and chilli. Season with salt, soy sauce and tomato ketchup. Immediately throw in the rice. Stir all well as it heats. The optional extras should be heated separately and used as a garnish on top, not stirred in. The Indonesians eat their rice dishes with a spoon, or just their fingers (right hand only).

SATÉ KAMBING

The street-corner food of Indonesia. This quantity will feed 6 people.

2 lb lamb cut from the leg or shoulder

The marinade

2 shallots or ½ onion, sliced
1 clove garlic, crushed
2 tablespoons dark soy sauce
A pinch of hot chilli powder
1 teaspoon ground chilli powder

1 teaspoon ground ginger
2 tablespoons tamarind water or 1 tablespoon ginger
1 tablespoon olive or vegetable oil

The sauce (bumbu saté)

4 oz peanuts
1 tablespoon vegetable oil
2 shallots
1 clove garlic
1 tablespoon terasi

Chilli powder and salt to taste
1 tablespoon lemon juice
1 teaspoon brown sugar
½ pint water

Cut the meat into bite-sized pieces. Soak the pieces in the marinading mixture and leave them overnight if possible, certainly for a minimum of 2 hours. Thread the meat on to bamboo or thin wire skewers – about 5 pieces to each skewer. Grill them, turning once, for 10–15 minutes. If you are using a barbecue, less time will be needed.

Before you embark on the grilling, make the sauce. Fry the peanuts in a little oil and then grind them to a paste (in the liquidizer is easiest). Crush the shallots, garlic and *terasi* (a dark shrimp paste usually sold under its Malay name *Balacham*. Marmite is a possible substitute). Put them to fry for a few seconds in the rest of the oil. Add the water. As soon as the water boils, put in the ground peanuts, lemon juice and sugar, stirring well until the sauce thickens – which will take only a few minutes. Taste and salt if necessary. The sauce can be poured straight over the *saté* on its serving-dish, or handed separately. Accompany with as many little side-dishes of salad as you care to make.

7 June 1986

The French at Table

I have a friend who is a much respected botanist specializing in the flora of southern Spain. Such is her position of authority in her subject she is often prevailed upon to take visitors out on field-trips. A trim septuagenarian in brogues and a tweed skirt, equipped with a small digging tool and several capacious plastic bags for specimens, she shins up sheer rock-faces effortlessly, her followers puffing in her wake. On a dozen field-trips I have never known her unable to identify a plant to the satisfaction of an enquirer. 'It's easy,' she told me one day. 'If I don't know the plant, I just look at it and make up the logical Latin name. It keeps the peace.'

The same is true in the kitchen. Here is a quick French lexicon to cover your inventions – just prefix each designation with a translation of the main ingredient.

Alsacienne: generally northerly in feel, leaning heavily towards the German kitchen. As in *choucroûte à l'alsacienne*, a boiled dinner made with sauerkraut, bacon, fresh pork and slices of Strasbourg sausage. Foie gras and white Riesling are sometimes diagnostic ingredients.

Américaine/armoricaine: a contentious designation requiring tomatoes, sometimes garlic, and wine. I lean towards *américaine* meaning from the United States, rather than *armoricaine* as in pertaining to Brittany (the legendary Armorica). There are more tomatoes in the New World than ever ripened in the cold Atlantic breezes of Brittany. As in *homard à l'américaine* – lobster sautéd in oil, with tomatoes, white wine, garlic and onions, finished with butter.

Anglaise: anything of which the French are likely to disapprove. Plain boiled things. Things with white sauce. The only recipe they like in this group is *crème anglaise* – French for a pouring custard made properly with egg yolks. Happily, the French don't seem to have found out about the other yellow stuff we pour over our school dinners.

Bordelaise: a useful designation covering four possibilities. For *sauce bordelaise*, a lovely sauce made with wine enriched with marrow-bone fat, which can accompany a grilled steak. For a dish garnished with *cèpes* (those brown and yellow fungi which I recommend periodically). For a garnish of artichoke hearts and potatoes. Or for a dish sauced with a *mirepoix* base: finely chopped carrot, celery, and ham stewed gently in butter.

Bourguignonne: meat stewed with red wine, mushrooms, baby onions and bacon – as in *bœuf à la bourguignonne*. Burgundy has very good food indeed, and anything *bourguinon* is likely to be of the best: the fattest snails, the best crayfish, the sweetest beef, wonderful wines, excellent game and outstanding cooks. Append the designation to your richest and rarest invention.

Berrichonne: pertaining to Berry. Potato dishes as in *tarte berrichonne* are typical, as are chicken or meat stews thickened with blood. Otherwise a garnish *à la berrichonne* features bacon, chestnuts, onions and cabbage.

Chasseur: when the huntsman is in charge of the table. The Gallic sportsman in pursuit of the edible favours a garnish of mushrooms and onions sautéd in butter, and finished off with white wine. This can accompany meat, chicken, fish or eggs.

Flamande: the Flemish are the butt of French humour. Jokes about what is written on the bottom of a Flemish bottle ('open the other end') and other such subtleties have long been the high spot of the French child's repertoire. Anything *à la flamande* is predictably somewhat on the heavy side: pork belly, braised cabbage, boiled carrots and potatoes predominate.

Florentine: here come the Medicis. Catherine, wife to Henry II, arrived in Paris around 1540 and brought some of her culinary habits with her. One of these was perhaps (history has not been much concerned with such matters) spinach. She had a few less attractive characteristics, being the chief instigator of the St Bartholomew's Day Massacre of the Huguenots. *Florentine* involves spinach. Usually it is something white – fish, boiled or poached eggs – laid on a bed of spinach purée, covered with a cheese sauce and browned under the grill.

Jardinière: a useful portmanteau word, this, pertaining to the wife of the gardener. For anything with peas, baby carrots and turnips (scooped into little balls), new potatoes, baby beans both broad and long. Present the delicious little vegetables in small pyramids round the roasted meat or poultry. Rather English – experiment with Creamed Chicken Syrie Maugham (all white of course). Leg of Lamb Capability Brown might have possibilities.

133

Languedocienne: the Languedoc is my favourite part of France. Home of foie gras, confit d'oie and the stupendous *Cassoulet de Castelnaudary*, the dish to send strong men reeling. Wonderful thick soups and garbures. *A la languedocienne* indicates the presence of tomatoes, aubergines, garlic and/or *cèpes*.

Next week: French lexicon to be continued, revered editor permitting, including, among others, the exotic delights of *pistache* and *Rothschild*.

6 September 1986

Defining the Terms

The French lexicon of specialities is not always dictated by geography or ingredients: sometimes a note of Gallic gallantry creeps in. Diane de Poitiers, Grande Sénéchale of Normandy, as passionate a huntswoman as her namesake, and mistress to young Henry II, has just such a culinary claim to fame. The beautiful Diane had a sauce, composed largely of cream and pepper, named after her – delightfully appropriate ingredients to commemorate the older woman in the life of a king of France.

My maternal grandfather used to take my grandmother and me to the Mirabelle restaurant in Curzon Street on my allotted sorties from boarding school. It made a change from school dinners. My grandmother would always order liver and bacon. I, more romantically inclined, had Steak Diane. Later, when crossed in love (a not infrequent event), I would cook it for myself in consolation.

STEAK DIANE

SERVES 1 LONELY HEART

1 entrecôte steak, about ¼ inch thick
1 oz unsalted butter
½ teaspoon black peppercorns (fresh green peppercorns are even better)
1 teaspoon soy sauce
2–3 shakes from the Worcester-sauce bottle
2 tablespoons double cream

Before you begin, make a few sauté potatoes (well dusted with parsley) and a watercress salad.

Put a pretty plate to warm. Crush the peppercorns and press them into both sides of the steak.

Melt half the butter in a frying-pan. When the butter froths, put in the steak. Cook it on a high heat to your taste – I like it done for just 2 minutes on each side. Transfer the steak to the warmed plate. Add the rest of the ingredients to the delicious peppery bits in the pan. When all is hot and bubbling and well mixed, beat in the last bit of butter. Pour the sauce over the steak.

Consume immediately while it's hot, along with the better part of a bottle of good Burgundy. Start planning the next meal, this time for two; and, while you plan, consider the descriptions you might apply to it.

Pistache: mutton, lamb, partridge or pigeon cooked slowly with a great deal of garlic. Fifty cloves are the allotted portion to a shoulder of mutton. The garlic makes a delicious sticky sauce with a surprisingly mild flavour. Perfect for those who wish to be alone with each other.

Rothschild: the ultimate garnish – foie gras, partridge quenelles, cock's combs, truffles, freshwater crayfish. Basically in the style of Marie-Antoine Carême of revered memory. Stands in relation to the *financière* garnish as the manager of the High Street Barclays to a director of Rothschild's Bank.

A la poulette: a delightful sauce achieved by thickening cooking juices with egg yolks and cream. Whether the designation derives from the egg in its capacity as a potential chicken, or the '(fast) young lady' translated by my dictionary, I cannot be certain.

Lorraine: not many *nouvelle cuisine* inroads here. The people of Lorraine like good solid *potées* and soups, plenty of goose and pork, and of course their famous egg, cream and bacon tart. The style of

Lorraine features cabbage cooked with red wine, and dishes served German fashion with freshly grated horseradish.

Lyonnaise: the gastronomic capital of France breeds more Michelin stars per square mile than Pontypool turns out front-row Rugby internationals. Perhaps it's something in the waters of the Rhône or the bracing air of the Dauphiné. *Toques* off to M. Paul Bocuse, M. Point at nearby Vienne, Alain Chapel at Mionnay. Anything *lyonnaise* is likely to be good: potatoes and onions are diagnostic elements. And their Rugby is pretty *formidable*, too.

Provençale: lavender and butterflies, wistaria and whitewashed walls. Dishes *à la provençale* feature tomatoes, olives, garlic and olive oil, aubergines and anchovies, the herbs of the *maquis* – rosemary, thyme and sage. Everything, in short, that is sadly missing from our English summers.

Meunière: a great favourite with the British, this is in the style of the miller's wife whose hands are, naturally, constantly dipped in the flour-jar. Particularly suitable for flat fish: dust them with flour and then cook them in butter. Brown butter, parsley and lemon juice to finish. A good method for sweetbreads and brains if you like, as I do, these delicate neglected meats.

A la Milanaise: the French bow to the Italian gastronomic capital. When used to describe a garnish it should be spaghetti or macaroni tossed with ham, cheese and tomato. The Milanese method is chiefly applied to veal escalopes – which are egg-and-breadcrumbed and fried in butter (northern Italians alone cook in butter), with lemon quarters to accompany. Hungary and the Ukraine share this culinary habit: my other favourite restaurant dish, when school was out, was Chicken Kiev – particularly when the buttery balloon encased in the breadcrumbed chicken breast burst all over my hated school uniform. The Mirabelle waiter was a spoilsport and used to stick a fork in it before he served me. As for the Hungarians, as I discovered on my travels throughout Eastern Europe last autumn, Magyar cooks egg-and-breadcrumb most things, including their foie gras.

13 September 1986

The Reverend Sydney at Dinner

English cookery has of late been much maligned – largely, I fear, because it is often mistaken for English catering. There are still plenty of good cooks working in our home-grown tradition using the best of raw materials prepared with simplicity and honesty. Perfectly roasted meat with traditional accompaniments, a light hand with the puddings and pies, and above all a cupboard well stocked with home-made relishes such as ketchups, sauces and chutneys are peculiar to the English culinary habit.

The Reverend Sydney Smith, quintessential Englishman, was the author of much of our native wit and wisdom on gastronomy. It was he who described heaven in terms of foie gras and the sound of trumpets. The English habit of pouring gravy over everything met with less approval, as reported by his friend and chronicler, Lady Holland: 'Madame, I have been looking for a person who disliked gravy all my life; let us swear eternal friendship.'

The Reverend Sydney mused in 1837 on the matter of his countrymen's digestive systems from his vicarage at Combe Florey in Somerset. 'I am convinced,' said the Reverend, 'digestion is the great secret of life; and that character, talents, virtues, and qualities are powerfully affected by beef, mutton, pie-crust, and rich soups. I have often thought I could feed or starve men into many virtues and vices, and affect them more powerfully with my instruments of cookery than Timotheus could do formerly with his lyre.' The great clergyman might well have made use of the two recipes which follow.

SOMERSET SPLIT PEA SOUP

This recipe was collected and pronounced excellent by Florence White's English Folk Cookery Association in 1932. Quantities will serve 6.

1 lb split peas	1 teaspoon salt
2 oz lean bacon	½ teaspoon pepper
2 onions	½ teaspoon sugar
1 carrot	1 oz flour
1 turnip	1 oz butter
3 sticks of celery	To finish: 3–4 rashers streaky bacon,
Sprig of parsley	2–3 slices bread. Teaspoon
3 pints cold water	chopped mint, fresh or dried.

Put the peas in cold water to soak for a few hours, or overnight; the better the quality, the less time they need to soak.

Cube the bacon and put it to sweat in its own fat for a few moments in a large saucepan. Drain the soaked peas and put them in the saucepan along with the 3 pints of cold water. Bring all to the boil, skim and turn it down to simmer. Leave to cook over a gentle heat for 20 minutes while you prepare the vegetables.

Peel and chop the onions. Peel and dice the turnip and carrot. Wash and slice the celery. Chop the parsley. Add all the vegetables to the soup after the initial 20 minutes. Bring back to the boil and leave to simmer for another 40 minutes.

Mash the flour and butter together.

When the peas and vegetables are soft, take the soup off the heat and push all through a sieve, or liquidize it in the food processor. Return the soup to the saucepan and stir in the flour-and-butter mixture; this will bind the liquid and vegetable matter together. Bring all gently back to the boil, stirring to avoid lumps, and simmer for 5 minutes to thicken the soup. Sprinkle in the mint.

Dice the bacon and fry it crisp. Cube the bread and fry it in the bacon fat.

Serve the soup in a pretty tureen and hand the croûtons separately.

SHOULDER OF LAMB STUFFED WITH OYSTERS

Lamb will have to do for the mutton in these more delicate times. The recipe itself dates back to the Romans – great connoisseurs of oysters, and of British oysters in particular.

1 boned shoulder of lamb
6 oysters (½ lb mushrooms will do
  duty in lean times)
2 oz breadcrumbs
6 fillets of anchovies
2 rashers bacon

1 small bunch parsley
1 egg
Salt and pepper
1 oz butter
To finish: 1 lemon

Unroll the shoulder of lamb and lay it flat on the table.

Open the oysters carefully, saving the liquor. Roughly chop the slippery creatures.

Put the breadcrumbs to soak in the oyster liquor; if you haven't enough liquid, add a little milk. Crush the anchovies with a fork. Chop the bacon and the parsley. Beat the egg lightly. Mix all these stuffing ingredients together with the dipped oysters.

Spread the stuffing over the meat. Roll it up and tie it securely. Season with salt and freshly ground pepper.

Melt the butter in a casserole which will just accommodate the joint. Turn the meat in the hot fat until it is lightly browned. Lid tightly and transfer to the oven. The joint will need about 1½ hours at 375°F/gas 5 – more if it is a large piece of meat. Uncover for the last 10 minutes.

Serve with lemon quarters. If you are feeling extravagant, accompany with a sauce made with the other half of the dozen oysters chopped roughly and simmered for 3–4 minutes in cream and their own liquor spiked with Worcester sauce and cayenne pepper.

24 September 1986

Anatomy of a Feast

A disused sewer-pipe in Alice Springs is no place to hold an eighteenth-birthday party, even if the itinerant Aborigine family camped at the other end are willing to share their supper with you. So when my eldest son completed his twenty-first year last month,

now more comfortably housed as a Cambridge undergraduate, it seemed proper to celebrate it in style. The guests numbered twenty-four – the maximum I can possibly seat. I don't much like buffet suppers (too much standing and swaying as on British Rail), and the toasts and speeches essential to such an occasion need to be punctuated by standing up, sitting down, and falling off – for which chairs are indispensable. The dinner was therefore declared a four-course black-tie sit-down affair.

The young man has led a somewhat nomadic life, and the meal was planned to reflect his wanderings. Four years at an Andalusian school came first, so the guests were to be greeted with cold Manzanilla from Sanlúcar – home of the best Spanish sherries – and platters of *serrano* ham and *chorizo* (the spiced red dried sausage eaten as *tapas* all over Spain).

Then for the serious business of the dinner itself, beginning with *fruits de mer* for his year at school in France, accompanied by a young Muscadet. Following Escoffier's best of all advice, 'Faites simple', the *fruits de mer* were served plain: on ice with quarters of lemon, tabasco and thin slices of buttered brown bread.

3 dozen oysters
5 pints mussels (steamed open in a little Muscadet)
4 large crabs
3 lb freshwater crayfish

6 dozen piping-hot snails (prepared in-house; see page 26) to eat alternately with the oysters

Next, to mark the wanderer's return, good British roast game washed down with a vigorous Côtes du Rhône.

2 plump saddles of hare (bacon and
 butter, 60 minutes)
A brace of early pheasant (thin-cut
 smoked streaky bacon on breast, 55
 minutes)
1 fine fat black-cock (butter on breast,
 55 minutes in the oven)
A brace of grouse (bacon, 45
 minutes)
4 grey-legged partridge (bacon, 35
 minutes)

4 little teal (butter on breast, quarter
 of lemon within, 30 minutes)
2 snipe (not drawn, heads on, beaks
 used to skewer legs, bacon,
 20 minutes)
A dozen farmed quail (bacon outside,
 butter and a grape inside,
 20 minutes)

All drawn game (except the quail) had onion, bay leaf and butter inside. I have added 5–10 minutes to each cooking time to allow for an oven's tendency to cool down when overloaded. Bread sauce, game chips, rowan-and-apple jelly and bowls of watercress to mop up the juices from the birds. A purée of swede just for the earthy taste of it with the game. Simmering and reducing all day, a stockpot with shin of beef, onions and carrots. This, with the pounded livers of the birds, their cooking juices and a spoonful of rowan jelly, made excellent hot gravy. It also diverted the three cats and provided lunch next day for left-over guests.

Afterwards a chocolate birthday cake with a glass of sweet golden Beaume de Venise (Vidal Fleury).

RICH CHOCOLATE CAKE

8 eggs
8 oz caster sugar
8 oz bitter black chocolate

4 oz butter
2 tablespoons rum
8 oz ground almonds

Whisk the whole eggs with the caster sugar until thick and white (takes twice as long as you think). Melt the black chocolate and butter in the rum, then fold, alternating with the almonds, into the beaten egg and sugar. Pour the mixture into a large cake-tin lined with greaseproof paper. Bake for 25 minutes at 400°F/gas 6. This is a cake which should be under-cooked: let it shrink before you turn it out. Ice when absolutely cold with:

6 oz black chocolate
1 oz sweet butter

Small glass of rum
4 oz icing sugar

Melt the chocolate, butter and rum together gently. Allow to cool. Beat into the icing sugar.

Pink champagne (Chaudron Rosé) for toasts and attendant hazards. Finally English Stilton, French *chèvre*, Spanish grapes, and port – one wonderful bottle of Taylor's 53 stowed away for those who were still sober enough to recognize a decanter, Churchill Graham NV and strong Aussie billy-can coffee for the rear-guard.

And thus – give or take three hysterical cats and Pepe the borrowed Spanish butler prising open recalcitrant oysters and his own fingers – it came to pass. The arrival of the champagne galvanized all twenty-four into speeches – most of them emotional and some of them more than once. They were followed by twelve verses of 'John Peel' including the echoing bits with the horns. At that the cats and Pepe retired simultaneously into the comparative safety of the streets.

8 December 1984

Poultry and Game

The Princess and the Pheasant

Jason and his Argonauts, hacking their way through to the kingdom of Colchis, the Golden Fleece and the beautiful Princess Medea, bivouacked on the banks of the River Phasis, boundary between Europe and Asia. There the hungry wanderers feasted on a creature whose plumage equalled in brilliance the Fleece itself. They named the bird for the river, bundled the Fleece, the Princess and a few mating pairs into the luggage and brought the lot back to Greece. Medea never did settle down, but *Phasianus colchis* took to Europe's woods and fields like a duck to water.

The hen pheasant makes better eating than the cock, being smaller, tenderer and more delicately flavoured. Only young birds are worth roasting (the older birds make wonderful stews and pies). A young pheasant has a rounded first wing-feather – in older birds this will be pointed – and its beak will be pliable. Handle the bird as little as possible: game – which lives and feeds in the wild – has quite different resident bacteria from farmed animals. If left whole, apart from the inevitable shot-punctures, its flesh does not decompose as does a chicken's but, rather, dries and mummifies. This tenderizes the meat and develops its flavour. The feathers have oil in their bases which helps the process. Hang the bird, unplucked and undrawn, by its feet in a well-ventilated place away from flies. About a week is the normal hanging time, although this depends on the weather, the age of the bird and the taste of the cook. When it is ready, the tail-feathers will easily be pulled, and the beak will drip a little blood.

The pheasant is now ready to be plucked in whatever way you find convenient. I use two buckets, one full of warm water to rinse my hands, and the other to receive the feathers as I pluck. It is a tedious business. Any guest who arrives for the weekend with a ripe and feathered brace as a present should be thanked politely and sat down with the two buckets to take off the wrapping himself. Singe the little hairs off the plucked bird, slit the rear open and pull out the innards. Try to avoid puncturing the small bitter gland above the tail. Feel along the neck for the crop and remove it through a slit in the skin. Wipe the bird inside and out and clean off any dark blood-clots with a little salt. You will now have introduced civilization's deadly microbes, so the bird should be prepared and eaten without delay. Four people with modest appetites will be satisfied with one plump young pheasant prepared with bread sauce and game chips.

Put 4 oz of crumbled stale white bread, a bay leaf and half an onion stuck with 6 cloves to soak in half a pint of milk. Peel 2 lb of potatoes and slice them very thin – the French cutter called a mandoline is ideal for this, otherwise food processors usually have a special attachment which does the job. If you do it by hand, you will need a very sharp knife. Rinse the chips and wrap them up in a clean cloth to dry.

To roast the bird, tuck its wings under its back and skewer the legs through the body to keep them in place. Heat the oven to 350°F/ gas 4. Pheasant is inclined to be dry, so put in its body a piece of stale bread soaked in sherry, the other half of the onion, an ounce of butter and a bay leaf. Slip a small slice of butter between the skin and breast on each side and lay four rashers of smoked streaky bacon on top. All is now ready.

Allow 45–55 minutes' cooking time for the bird (slip the bacon off the breast and raise the heat for the last ten minutes to brown the skin). While the pheasant is roasting, bring the bread sauce gently to a simmer – it burns very easily – and heat the oil for the chips in a deep pan until it stops bubbling and gives off a faint blue haze. When the pheasant is cooked, take it out and allow it to rest for a few minutes while you fry the chips. Remove the onion, cloves and bay leaf from the bread sauce, beat in an ounce of butter, add salt and fresh-ground pepper. When the chips are crisp and golden, drain them on newspaper. Transfer the roast bird to a hot dish and pour a small glass of sherry into the roasting-tin. Over a high heat, scrape off all the brown sticky bits into the gravy. The alcohol will evaporate in a few seconds. As soon as it has, add the juices from inside the bird and half a cup of stock or water. Both the gravy and the bread sauce should be served very hot.

A dish fit for a princess, although it did not seem to do much for Medea's temper.

6 October 1984

The Game in Spain

The orange trees which shade the patios of Seville carry fruit far into the winter. The prettiest courtyard of all, the Patio de los Naranjos which flanks the Giralda tower next to the cathedral, bears the small sharp oranges which are the best variety for marmalade. The Sevillanos themselves use these bitter oranges as a seasoning to flavour the brine in which they pickle olives, and as a replacement for lemons to squeeze over their fried fish. Seville, in its heyday Spain's busiest seaport, exports both olives and oranges to Barcelona on the Catalan coast, whose climate is too cold for such sunny crops.

The wooded mountain slopes and fertile cornfields of Cataluña afford shelter to both red-legged and grey-legged partridges, and the Catalans put their imported oranges to good use. The Spanish huntsman does not like his game 'high' and plain-roasted in the English manner, and the game stews prepared in his kitchen are designed to add flavour and richness to birds of uncertain age and tenderness.

The partridge is the most widely appreciated feathered game of the Iberian peninsula. Chapman and Buck's *Unexplored Spain* (1910) devotes a chapter to 'Small Game'. Partridge is the first item on the agenda, and in La Mancha bags of 1,000 wild-bred birds a day are recorded:

Hardly will one enter a village *posada* or a peasant's lonely cot without observing one inevitable sign. Among the simple adornments of the whitewashed wall and as an integral item thereof hangs a caged redleg. And from the rafters above will be slung an antediluvian fowling-piece, probably a converted 'flinter', bearing upon its rusty single barrel some such inscription – inset in gold characters – as, 'Antequera, 1843'. These two articles, along with a cork-stoppered powder-horn and battered leathern shot-belt, constitute the stock-in-trade and most cherished treasures of our rustic friend, the Spanish *cazador* [hunter]. Possibly he also possesses a *pachon*, or heavily built native pointer; but the dog is chiefly used to find ground game or quail, since the redleg, ever alert and swift of foot, defies all pottering pursuit. Hence the *reclamo*, or call-bird, is almost universally preferred for that purpose.

Red-legged partridges abound throughout the length and breadth of wilder Spain – not, as at home, on the open corn-lands, but amidst the interminable scrub and brush-wood of the hills and dales, on the moory wastes, and palmetto-clad prairie. On the latter hares, quail, and lesser bustard vary the game.

Thither have resorted sportsmen of every degree – the lord of the land and the peasant, the farmer, the Padre Cura of the parish, or the local medico – all free to shoot, and each carrying the traitor *reclamo* in its narrow cage. The central idea is, of course, that the *reclamo*, by its siren song, shall call up to the gun any partridge within hearing. . . .

PARTRIDGE WITH ORANGES

TO SERVE 4–6 PEOPLE

6 partridges (old birds will do fine)
3 marmalade oranges or 1 lemon and
2 small thin-skinned oranges
4 oz raw ham (failing Spanish jamon
serrano, *use Italian* prosciutto,
or lean bacon)

4 tablespoons butter or lard
12 cloves garlic
2–3 sprigs thyme
1 glass white wine and 1 glass water
Salt and pepper

Wipe round the cavity of the partridges and trim off any stray feathers. Rinse one of the oranges, or the lemon, cut it into 6 pieces and tuck a piece inside each bird. Put the butter or lard to melt in a fire-proof casserole. Brown the birds all over.

Meanwhile cube the ham, peel the garlic cloves, wash the remaining oranges and cut them, skin and all, into rough chunks. Remove the birds and set them aside while you sauté the garlic and the ham lightly for a moment. Add the thyme, salt and pepper. Pour in the water and wine. Lid tightly and transfer to the oven (375°F/gas 5). Leave to cook until the birds are tender: 40–60 minutes depending on the age of the partridges. This recipe is also very good made with teal.

PARTRIDGE WITH OLIVES

TO SERVE 4–6 PEOPLE

6 partridges
½ lb tomatoes (or an 8 oz tin)
2 onions
2 tablespoons olive oil

1 glass white wine
4 oz black olives
2 bay leaves
Black pepper

To finish

2 tablespoons olive oil
4 slices bread

1 clove garlic

Wipe over the partridges. Chop the tomatoes, and peel and chop the onions. Put the oil to heat in a casserole which will just accommodate the birds. Put in the birds and turn them to brown them a little in the hot oil. Push the birds to one side, add the onions and allow them to soften but not to brown. Add the tomatoes, the wine, the bay leaves and a few turns from the pepper-grinder. Allow to bubble up, then turn the heat down and leave to simmer until tender – either on top of stove over a low heat, or in the oven at 350°F/gas 4 for 40–60 minutes.

1 November 1986

Fine Feathers

The Italians and the French have embarked on their seasonal slaughter of everything furred or feathered. Over here in EEC Albion, our position as Caesar's wife obliges us to discourage the inhabitants of the Outer Hebrides from laying in stocks of their favourite nibble: wind-dried gannet. Both the wind and the gannet are widely available in those parts, which cannot be said of ortolans in the vineyards. Nevertheless, a wise bookmaker would not offer odds on the old boiler brewing in a Hebridean fisherman's cock-a-leekie not having the webbed feet of an experienced salmon thief. The nearest I have been able to come to Roast Gannet or indeed a similarly prepared Cormorant is the news from *The Mull Home Companion* – who got it from the last islander to sink his teeth into so succulent a treat – that both these birds should be cleaned, skinned and boiled (to get rid of the fishy taste) for at least an hour before they are roasted with plenty of bacon and basting.

Sea-birds being but pie-in-the-sky, I went in search of a cock-a-leekie prepared with a barnyard fowl in the restaurants of Auld Reekie. Alas, there was nothing in Edinburgh last week between a £20 'Taste of Scotland Menu' at a posh joint in Stafford Street and a plate of haggis and neeps at £1.40 in a well-patronized cafeteria in George Street. Fortified by a couple of steaming ladlefuls of peppery oatmeal, liver and lights, I set out on my course of last resort: a tramp round the secondhand bookshops to find a copy of Mrs Margaret Dods's *The Cook and Housewife's Manual*. 'Margaret Dods' was the pseudonym of Mrs Isobel Christian Johnston, a hard-working novelist and journalist, and the mainstay of her editor-husband's publications in early nineteenth-century Edinburgh. Mrs Johnston had more in common than an editor-husband with her southern counterpart, Isabella Beeton, since she did for the Scots table in 1826 what Mrs Beeton did for the English in 1860. Her opinion on cock-a-leekie must be definitive.

There was a rumour when the book first appeared that the true author (at least of the introduction) was none other than Sir Walter Scott, partly because *The Cook and Housewife's Manual* purported to be the cookbook of the famous Cleikum Club from Scott's *St Ronan's Well*, but also because of the excellence and wit of the writing. Mrs Johnston herself was clearly no slouch at the repartee. Scott himself credits her with a fine example when she was taken by the Ettrick Shepherd, James Hogg, to visit a Fairy Well. The bard of Kilmeny, on handing her a cup of the water, delivered his line: 'Here, Mrs Johnston, any married woman who drinks a tumbler of this will have twins in a twelvemonth.' Replied Mrs Johnston: 'In that case, Mr Hogg, I shall only take half a tumbler.' The Cleikum Club was formed to assist the convalescence of the Nabob, Peregrin Touchwood, Esquire, whose appetite had failed and who was consequently afflicted with the fidgets – 'a malady to which bachelor gentlemen in easy circumstances, when turned of fifty, are thought to be peculiarly liable'.

Well, there was plenty of Mrs Beeton on offer in Edinburgh, but no Mistress Dods. Here, then, hot from the stacks of the London Library for the particular benefit of Italian and French fidgety bachelors, is the immortal lady, whoever she was, on the treatment of one of the few feathered natives of Scotland still on the menu. Bear in mind, if you please, that the very best Cleikum cock-a-leekie is made from the wiry sinews of the loser in a cockfight:

COCK-A-LEEKIE

Boil from four to six pounds of good shin-beef, well broken, till the liquor is very good. Strain it, and put to it a capon, or large fowl, trussed as for boiling, and when it boils, half the quantity of blanched leeks intended to be used, well cleaned, and cut in inch lengths, or longer. Skim this carefully. In a half-hour add the remaining part of the leeks and a seasoning of pepper and salt. The soup must be very thick of leeks, and the first part of them must be boiled down into the soup until it becomes a lubricious compound. Sometimes the capon is served in the tureen with the soup. This makes good leek-soup without the fowl. Some people thicken cock-a-leekie with the flour of oatmeal. Those who dislike so much of the leeks may substitute German greens, or spinage, for one-half of them, and we consider this an improvement, greens especially, if tender and long-boiled, and not too finely shred. Reject the coarse green of the leeks. Prunes and raisins used to be put into this soup. The practice is nearly obsolete.

Mistress Dods elaborates on the matter of the prunes. M. Talleyrand, before becoming Louis-Philippe's ambassador to the Court of St James, was anxious to authenticate the favourite dish of 'gentle King Jamie'. In the face of the controversy aroused by his questions, he suggested that prunes should be stewed in the broth and removed before the soup was sent to table: the perfect diplomat's compromise. He was sorely needed in Edinburgh last week. I have no doubt he could have talked someone into finding me a tureen with little webbed feet sticking out of it.

10 November 1984

A Bird in the Hand at Thanksgiving

The turkey has a foreign face. Only a fool would dispute it. Thus wrote (roughly translated) the Frenchman M. Brillat Savarin in 1800. The gentleman, author of the gastronome's handbook, *La Physiologie du goût*, was explaining the turkey's New World origins. Furthermore, he added, it was well known that the Jesuits had brought the delectable creature across the Atlantic in the first place, and indeed kept a profitable copyright on it for some time afterwards. In fact, in some parts of France the bird is called a Jesuit still, although the disrespectful may think the name owes more to physiognomy than to provenance.

Picture, then, the Pilgrim Fathers, stern and hungry in their Puritan black, leaping nimbly ashore from *Mayflower* on 22 November 1620, to be confronted by their first foreign face: complexion suffused with blue and scarlet, wattles a-quiver, feathers bristling, wrinkled throat throbbing with a noise like a dozen cross rattlesnakes. No fainthearts they, who could catch it, pluck it, roast it, and invite the neighbouring natives to dinner to share it.

Thanksgiving falls next week. As always in hundreds of

thousands of American homes, inside and outside the United States, its mainstay will be a turkey. I was invited to my first Thanksgiving dinner by an expatriate American lady named Mrs Norah Farouki. Norah was newly married to Mr Farouki. Mr Farouki, an Arab diplomat, forgot to mention (before she endowed him with all her considerable worldly goods) that he already had a brace of wives. As soon as Norah discovered she instigated a full and frank family discussion. Our Thanksgiving dinner was a double celebration: the safe deliverance of the Pilgrims and the rout of the first and second Mistresses Farouki. Persuaded it made good sense to get rid of them, Mr Farouki had just done so by the simple expedient of facing Mecca and pronouncing 'I divorce thee' three times per wife.

The third Mrs Farouki's turkey was a fine young hen bird from her yard, Jesuitically thin as becomes a bird which does its own foraging.

Norah put it to roast upside down in her little gas oven with a pat of butter and an onion for company. Then she made a pile of white breadcrumbs and mixed them with chopped fresh rosemary, sage and thyme. These she fried in the butter removed from the turkey half an hour before it was ready. Then she stuffed the cavity with the fried breadcrumbs and put the bird to finish cooking. The breadcrumbs stayed crisp, and the turkey was delicately flavoured with herbs and butter. It was excellent. There was also a small bowl of cranberry sauce. Before Norah stewed the berries with a little water and sugar, she bounced a couple of them on the table, explaining that a bouncing cranberry is a ripe cranberry.

The second course was pumpkin pie. To make it for six you will need half a small pumpkin (about 2 lb). Scrape out the woolly centre with the seeds. The seeds can be roasted in the oven with some salt: they are rather good to nibble – an expert seedsman can crack, chew and spit out the husk all in one smooth movement. Peel and cut the pumpkin into chunks and put it to stew in a very little water until soft. The Pilgrim Fathers would have baked it, wrapped in leaves, in its skin in the ashes of their driftwood fire. Line an 8 inch flan-tin with your favourite shortcrust pastry, prick it and bake it in the oven for 15 minutes at 350°F/gas 4. Let the softened pumpkin cool. Then purée it with half a pint of double cream, 4 tablespoonfuls of brown sugar, 3 tablespoonfuls of golden syrup or honey and 2 eggs. Spice it with powdered cinnamon, ginger and the little berries from the top of clove nails crumbled between your fingers. The Pilgrim Fathers and Mr Farouki would perforce have had to omit the addition of a small glass of rum. You should have no such inhibitions. Pour the mixture into the pastry-case and return it to the oven for an hour.

The pie we ate that day was the warm gold of Saharan sands, its scent as exotic as the souk in Goulemine. Mr Farouki, gloomy victim of Christian monogamy, brightened at its appearance. His cheer was short-lived. A few minutes later half a dozen burly close relations of the former Mistresses Farouki arrived at the door. They also wanted a frank family discussion.

24 November 1984

Lovely Leftovers

My middle daughter Poppy has an admirable, though not always appreciated, talent for putting her finger on the nub of things – semantically speaking. Some of her neater judgements have entered the family lexicon. One such she delivered at the age of six when contemplating a post-Christmas supper prepared with, I thought, great ingenuity. All to no avail. Her sharp eyes pierced the disguise of seasonings and sauce and she spotted the nub: the lurking turkey, the slivers of Christmas ham. 'Oh, good, Mum,' she said. 'Lovely leftovers again.'

Now for evermore defined, lovely leftovers it is. And very good they are, too. When you have had enough of the whole bird, strip off the remaining meat and make a good strong stock with the bones. Boil down until well concentrated. You then have the makings of White Soup – a most satisfactory Boxing Day supper. Finish the meal with a few mince pies.

WHITE SOUP

A MAIN-DISH SOUP FOR 6 PEOPLE

2 pints strong stock
2 lb potatoes
2 medium onions
1 lb root vegetables (carrots, leeks, parsnips)
Bay leaf

1 lb green vegetables (green beans, cabbage, peas – the freeze-dried sort are particularly suitable)
1 lb left-over turkey, chicken, ham, cut into large pieces
Salt and pepper

Bring the stock to the boil while you prepare the vegetables. Peel and slice the onion. Peel and cube the root vegetables. As soon as they are ready, add them to the stock along with the bay leaf and (if you are using them) the freeze-dried peas. Bring all to the boil and simmer gently for 20–30 minutes.

Meanwhile top-and-tail the green beans and/or slice the cabbage. Add to the soup ten minutes before the end. Add the cooked meat five minutes before the end. Salt and pepper to taste. If you have some fresh herbs, chop a teaspoonful and stir it in just before you are ready.

Serve the soup in roomy bowls. Accompany with either grated cheese, a bowl of well-garlicked mayonnaise or a *rouille* – that dramatic scarlet sauce of sweet red peppers pounded with bread-crumbs, garlic and a little chilli pepper which the Marseillais serve with a *bouillabaisse*.

DEVILLED TURKEY LEGS

TO WAKE THE JADED PALATE OF 4 EXHAUSTED REVELLERS

4 turkey joints – wings and/or legs
2 tablespoons French mustard
1 tablespoon Worcester sauce
1 teaspoon powdered ginger or minced fresh ginger

1 teaspoon cayenne pepper (if you like your devils hot) or a few drops of tabasco sauce
Salt and pepper

Cut each turkey leg into its two joints and strip off the skin. Score flesh of thicker joints with diagonal cuts.

Mix the other ingredients into a paste and rub it well into the

154

turkey legs. Leave to marinate overnight – or at least a couple of hours.

Dot the marinated turkey joints with butter and then sear them under the grill, turning once, until crisp and brown.

TURKEY GRATIN

TO SERVE 4 PEOPLE

1 lb cooked turkey and/or ham
3 oz butter
3 oz flour
1 pint strong stock
¼ pint double cream

½ teaspoon mustard
1 teaspoon paprika pepper (the mild kind)
Salt and pepper
4 oz grated cheese

Shred the meat and put aside. Melt the butter in a saucepan and stir in the flour. Fry gently until the mixture looks sandy but has not yet taken colour. Stir in the stock slowly, beating out the lumps. When the sauce has thickened and is well cooked, stir in the cream. Season with the mustard, paprika, salt and pepper. Stir in the meat. Stir in half the grated cheese. Spread the mixture in a gratin-dish, sprinkle the rest of the cheese over the top, dot with butter and then brown under the grill. Serve sizzling hot.

This mixture, without the cheese, with the meat minced smaller and the flour and butter doubled to give a very thick sauce, can be used to make *croquettes*. Let the mixture cool right down before you start rolling it into cork shapes and egg-and-breadcrumbing.

Kromeskis are the mixture as above, with the difference that each little croquette is rolled in a thin slice of streaky bacon, then dipped in a frying batter before being deep-fried.

BREAD SAUCE SAVOURY

The only recipe I have ever seen for left-over bread sauce, this is adapted from a wartime edition of *Farmer's Weekly*.

To half a pint of home-made bread sauce, add 4 oz of grated cheese, a spoonful of double cream and plenty of freshly ground black pepper. Mix thoroughly and put into well-buttered cocotte-dishes. Scatter some more grated cheese over the top and put a tiny piece of butter on each. Bake in a moderate oven until brown and bubbling.

POTTED STILTON

My favourite leftover. (I confess to liking this better than the Stilton itself.)

Take equal quantities of Stilton (the end-scrapings round the crust will do fine) and mix with equal quantities of sweet unsalted butter. Beat together until smooth with a little brandy and a few drops of tabasco or cayenne pepper. This can be done in the liquidizer, but you will then have to soften the butter until it is almost liquid. Pack into a jar and keep it covered in the fridge. Eat the potted cheese with hot toast. Delicious.

21 December 1985

Myths and Methods of Cockintryce

Of all medieval culinary oddities, the cockatrice, a dish named after a mythical serpent hatched from a cock's egg which could kill with a glance, is one of the most peculiar conceits. Instructions for the preparation of 'Cockintryce' were included in the Harleian manuscript of 1430:

> Take a Capoun, and skald hym, and draw hem clene, and smyte hem ato in the waste across; take a Pigge, and skald hym and draw hym in same maner, and smyte hem also in the waste; take nedyle and a threde, and sewe the fore partye of the Capoun to the after parti of the Pygge; and the after partye of the Capoun to the fore partye of the Pygge; and then stuffe hem as thou stuffest a Pigge; putte hem on a spete, and Roste hym; and when he is y-now, gild hem with yokys of Eroun [eggs], and pouder Gyngere and Safroun, thenne wyth the Jus of Persely withowte; and then serve it forth for a ryal mete.

In fact this produces two 'royal meats': a winged piglet and a four-legged chicken. The dish is probably a little robust for the modern epicure. It smacks of spare-part surgery. However, the cockatrice has a stable-companion which doesn't give the horses such a fright. This is a medieval *tour de force* which looks as good as it tastes, and makes a splendid centrepiece for a dinner-party. With patience you will find you can conjure two chickens out of one.

156

COCKATRICE

TO SERVE 8–10 PEOPLE

1 large chicken	1 lemon
2 fillets of chicken breast	Small carton double cream
1 lb minced pork	Small bunch tarragon
4 oz chicken livers	Salt and paprika
Small glass brandy	1 raw egg
4 oz butter	4 oz breadcrumbs
4 oz dried apricots	Salt and pepper
2 oz blanched almonds	4 rashers smoked bacon
2 small onions	1 lb puff pastry

First prepare the chicken by skinning it. This is not as difficult as it sounds: peel the skin off by starting at the neck end, carefully detaching the bits that stick with the point of a sharp knife. Negotiate the legs by cutting round the bone where the scaly skin ends and pulling the legs inwards. Leave the wings on the skin, just severing the joints at the carcass. At the end you will have a naked wingless chicken and an empty but winged chicken skin.

The skin is now ready to be stuffed with the forcemeat. Chop the chicken livers and mix thoroughly with the pork. Add the brandy and leave to marinate. Roughly chop the almonds. Grate the lemon's rind. Chop the onions small. Gently fry the onions in 1 oz of the butter. Chop the apricots roughly. Mix them, the grated lemon rind, the almonds, the onions and butter, and the beaten raw egg into the meat stuffing. Season. Lightly knead in the breadcrumbs. Moisten with the juice of half the lemon, and a little stock if the mixture is not soft enough. Cut a slit in each chicken breast and tuck in ½ oz of butter worked with a little chopped tarragon. Sew up all holes in the skin except the neck opening. Stuff the empty chicken skin with half the meat mixture, pushing it well into the legs and round the sides. Lay the two chicken fillets down the centre and pack in the rest of the stuffing. Sew up the neck opening and mould the sausage to look as much like a chicken as possible. Dot the breast with 1 oz of the remaining butter. Lay the rashers of bacon down the breast.

Now turn your attention to the skinned chicken. Cut the second onion in half and put the rest of the tarragon, the half-lemon and the onion inside the bird. Spread the last ounce of butter over the breast. Season inside and out. Roll out the pastry into a large circle. Put the pastry over the chicken and tuck it under the bird, dampening the edges to seal them as if the whole thing was a large pastry. Fold the pastry into the contours so that the chicken appears to have a new skin. Cut a breathing-hole in the top. Paint with a little beaten egg yolk.

Bake the two birds at 350°F/gas 4 for 1¼ hours, taking the bacon off the stuffed bird for the last 10 minutes to allow it to brown. Make a gravy to be handed separately: mix the juices in the pan with a little brandy and the cream, and reheat. Serve the birds side by side. The fruit and nuts in the stuffing – a very medieval taste – are enhanced by a fruity Moselle.

27 April 1985

Yorkshire Great Pie

The Yorkshire Christmas Pie must qualify as the grandest of all British regional recipes. The English in particular have always been good at pies, a mastery acknowledged by so partial an authority as M. Escoffier. The medieval Great Pie enclosed anything and everything: boned swans, bustards, peacocks, larks, partridges and all things beaked and feathered, meat, fish, prunes, raisins, and quantities of spices. It was one of the glories of the Elizabethan table.

By the eighteenth century the Great Pie survived in only its unsweetened form as the Yorkshire Christmas Pie, a kind of huge all-edible tuckbox sent by coach from the estates of Yorkshire to those relatives unfortunate enough to inhabit the capital, who might otherwise be unable to enjoy the bounties of the countryside.

The habit held until the middle of the nineteenth century. Then abruptly the magnificent gift was made redundant by progress. The Stockton and Darlington Railway was inaugurated in 1825, and a network of tracks spread across the land. Raw food, even fresh fish from the northern fisheries, could be transported swiftly to the south. There was still some risk in hot weather that the food would go bad *en route*, but by the end of the century the enterprising beef-butchers of Australia had successfully pioneered refrigerated transport. It proved to be the final death-knell to the enormous cabin-trunks full of baked birds and beasts which could survive a week's buffeting on the road.

When Hannah Glasse published her cookbook in 1747 the Pie was at the height of its glory. It contained a goose, a turkey (small), a chicken, a partridge and a pigeon, all opened down the back, boned and stuffed in order of size back into the goose and then into a sturdy pastry 'coffin'. The remaining space was filled with a jointed hare, whole woodcocks, moor game and any other feathered or furred creature that chance should provide. Four pounds of best butter to be poured in for good measure. However, when the first edition of Mrs Beeton appeared less than a century later in 1861, the Yorkshire Christmas Pie had vanished from the index, and probably from the English menu. *Sic transit gloria mundi*. Ever since then we have lived in a world of little veal-and-ham and pork pies.

Here is my own version of the medieval juggernaut. It makes a fine basis for a grouse-moor picnic and will feed at least a dozen exercise-sharpened appetites. A sturdy volunteer will be needed to lug it over the heather. Then, even if the birds elude capture and the total bag comes to one septuagenarian rabbit and a wandering London pigeon, at least the day will have had the appropriate flavour.

159

YORKSHIRE GREAT PIE

Filling

The pie should be prepared with as large a proportion of game as possible. It should include white meat – a small turkey or a large chicken. All feathered game – grouse, pheasant, partridge, pigeon, woodcock, snipe, are welcome. Venison, rabbit, hare and lean pork can also be used.

6 lb meats (weighed when off the bone)	1 oz juniper berries
	½ pint dry sherry
1 lb fresh firm pork fat	2 pig's trotters, blanched and split
1 oz salt	Bay leaves
½ oz ground black pepper	

Bone the turkey or capon by opening the bird down the back and paring the carcass away from the meat with a sharp knife. (See Cockatrice, page 157.) Lay the boned fowl meat-side up on the table and season with salt, pepper and crushed juniper berries. Sprinkle with a little of the sherry.

Strip the meat from its bones and chop roughly, keeping white and dark meat separate. Chop the pork fat very fine and mix it into the meats. Season as above and leave to marinate for an hour in a quarter of a pint of the sherry and seasoning. Slice any larger meat joints into fillets and put them to marinate with the rest.

Roast all the bones in a hot oven to brown them a little. Then put them into a large pan with the pig's trotters, some peppercorns and 2 bay leaves, and the brown papery skin of a couple of onions to give the stock colour (no onion flesh or the keeping qualities of the stock will be impaired). Cover with cold water, bring to the boil and skim off grey foam which rises. Simmer gently for 2–3 hours. Strain off 2 pints of the stock, add the remaining sherry and boil up until you have reduced the quantity to 1 pint. If the stock is not clear, pour it, hot, over a beaten egg white, bring nearly back to the boil and then remove from the heat and allow it to settle. Pour it through a fine sieve: you will find the egg white has collected all the impurities and it will strain out clear.

Meanwhile spread the boned fowl with a layer of dark meat, and then put in a core of white meat. Re-form the bird roughly. There is no need to sew it up. Leave all to rest while you make the pastry.

Hot-Water Crust

This is the pastry used to make a hand-raised pie crust – that is, a crust which holds its shape without being held in position by a tin. If the idea inhibits you, don't worry: a firm shortcrust pastry made with 2 lb flour, 1 lb fat will do fine.

2 lb plain flour	6 oz lard
1 teaspoon salt	½ pint milk and water mixed
6 oz butter	1 egg (to gild the top)

Mix the salt into the flour and pour into a warm bowl. Put the milk and water, butter and lard into a saucepan and bring to the boil. Pour the hot liquid into a well in the flour, mixing hard with a wooden spoon. (You may need a little less or a little more liquid, so have a kettle of boiling water available.) This operation is important, and the liquid must be poured and beaten in while still scalding – you may need an assistant to pour. You should now have a ball of slightly translucent dough. As soon as it is cool enough to handle, knead the dough thoroughly by hand. If you have a mixer, it can be beaten with the dough-hook immediately. Leave the dough to develop near the heat for half an hour. Do not allow it to get cold. If your dough is too cool, it will crumble when you work it. Too hot, and it will collapse down the sides of the tin. I use a 10 inch cake-tin with a detachable base (normally my wedding-cake tin) for this recipe since the pie is so large.

A pie-maker of the skilled school, making a classic round pie, takes a ball of the dough, slices a quarter off the top and hollows out the rest with his fist. Otherwise he moulds his crust round the outside of a wooden cylinder like a short fat single-handed rolling-pin. A glass preserving-jar or an earthenware straight-side pot will do as a mould. It should be floured first and the pastry allowed to cool before the mould is removed.

To return to the Yorkshire Great Pie: Keep a quarter of the pastry for the lid and put the rest in the middle of the tin. Push it over the base and then stroke it up the sides until you have a thick even crust.

Settle the stuffed fowl in the middle of the pie. Fill in the sides with the rolls of meat and the remaining boned feathered game. Pack all well in. There must be no gaps. Pour in as much reduced stock as will reach to within an inch of the top. Press out a lid and lay it over, cutting a hole in the middle for the steam. Decorate the pie with leaves and gild the top with a beaten egg. Bake for half an hour at 375°F/gas 5. Then turn the oven down and bake the pie for 2½ hours longer, at 300°F/gas 2 – a total of 3 hours. Test with a skewer into the meat through the steam-hole. When the juice runs clear, it is cooked. As soon as the pie is out of the oven, pour in the rest of the reduced stock, hot. Allow to cool – overnight is best to allow the jelly to set.

For pocket-sized Yorkshire pies, try making tiny ones with a quail doing duty as a diminutive goose. It is now possible to buy these little birds ready-boned from the quail farms.

As for the rest of the delicious game consommé: clarify it if necessary, season it well, heat it up and take it up on the moor in a Thermos. If you remember to include a bottle of vodka and one of tabasco in the picnic-basket, you will not go short of a fine hot Bullshot.

21 July 1985

An Amateur's Guide to Game

English cookery-books usually have plenty of good recipes for game. Sometimes they offer small but useful tips on the peculiarities of the business. Eliza Acton, conscious that she was writing for the housewife-amateur, rather than for the knowledgeable professional, goes into the subject in some detail. For the start of the season, here are some notes collected from her and from other sources, in particular Jane Grigson's excellent *English Food* (1974) and Dorothy Hartley's classic *Food in England* (1954).

Venison: Buck venison in season from June to Michaelmas. Doe venison: October to December. Red deer is the Scottish deer, the English roe is paler-fleshed and less gamey in flavour. Fallow deer meat is esteemed above all. Rub venison with pepper, particularly around the bones, and hang for 1–2 weeks. Venison should be dark in colour with white firm fat. Haunch of venison will take 3½–4½ hours to roast on the spit. Miss Hartley warns against making any kind of thick gravy to serve with it: the gravy should be clear and bright. Mrs Grigson stipulates 30 minutes to the pound if roasting.

Hare: in season September–March. Hang for a week, unpaunched and unskinned. Rub the inside with lemon and vinegar. Clean out blood-clots with salt. Take care to remove membrane skin from back and legs with a sharp knife. A large brown hare will feed 10 people, a smaller 'blue' hare 6–8. The saddle is excellent roasted (30–45 minutes) in a hot oven. Baste with salt and water. Roast saddle is good served with hot grated beetroot tossed in sour cream. Miss Hartley suggests basting an old hare with beer while you roast it.

162

Rabbit: open season. You can tell a young rabbit because its ears tear easily, and it has fat round its kidneys. Takes well to a mustard sauce or stewed with plenty of onions, says Eliza Acton. Miss Hartley quotes Andrew Boorde (sixteenth-century renegade monk, he of *A Dyetary of Helth* fame): 'Rabettes flesh is best of all wylde beestes, for it is temperate and doth nourissh and is syngulerly prazed of Physiche.'

Pheasant: in season from October to the end of January. Particularly good in November and December. Hang for 2 weeks in cold weather, a week to 10 days in warm. Do not forget to slit the back of the neck to remove crop. Put a piece of cold butter worked with lemon juice inside, and bacon on the breast. Roast in a hot oven for 45–55 minutes. Remove bacon, baste with butter and froth with flour just before the end of cooking time.

Partridge: 1 September–2 February. Young partridges have slender yellow feet which turn ash-grey with the first frost. Hang for a week. Pluck and draw. They are good stuffed with big black mushrooms sautéd in butter. Roast for 25–30 minutes. Mrs Grigson suggests a partridge casserole with bacon, cabbage and chestnuts.

Grouse: in season 12 August–10 December. Hang for 5–7 days. Eliza Acton says that moor game should not be drawn, but should be served on toast spread with trail (innards), minced with the drippings. Pluck grouse delicately – the skin is tender. Baste with butter when cooking. A young grouse will feed two people. Miss Hartley suggests that a sportsman's grouse should be hung for a fortnight, then roasted stuffed with butter and rowan berries, or better still with the little wild mountain raspberries. The juicy fruit, she says, melts almost away during cooking, but the melted, spicy, buttery juice is all the gravy required.

Woodcock and snipe: in season during the winter months. Not plentiful until after the frosts have set in. Hang for 5–8 days. Pluck gently and do not draw. Wipe with soft cloth, tuck head under wing and lay bill 'close along the breast'. Skewer through legs. Tie twice across and suspend them from an oven rack after you have floured them well. Baste with melted butter. Lay toast beneath after 15 minutes to catch the drippings from the trail. Cook for 20–25 minutes. Serve on the toast with the trail, mixed with a little brandy or lemon juice, spread on it. Brillat Savarin on woodcock: 'a bird well deserving of notice, but few know all its good points. It should be roasted under the eye of a sportsman, especially the sportsman who has killed it. . . .'

Wild duck and teal: hang for no more than 48 hours. Pluck and draw, remembering to take out the two fatty lumps above the vent. Eliza Acton recommends a bit of bread soaked in port inside. Roast in a quick oven, well basted with butter. Roast widgeon and teal for 20–5 minutes, mallard for 30. Serve with a purée of turnips, a purée of potatoes and a sharp salad.

10 August 1985

New Tricks with Old Birds

Young game birds are so delicious that it is hard to better the classic methods of roasting. With older birds, or as the shooting season advances and the annual novelty wears off, it is useful to have a few alternative tricks up your sleeve.

CIRCASSIAN PHEASANT

The pheasant, that popinjay foreigner and native of the Caucasus, takes well in middle-age to a Middle Eastern nut sauce. A very ancient Georgian dish.

TO SERVE 6 PEOPLE

2 pheasants past their youth
1 large onion
Stick of celery and 1 carrot
Bay leaf
Piece of lemon rind

Black peppercorns and salt
6 oz walnuts (could be almonds or hazelnuts)
2 oz white breadcrumbs

Wipe the pheasants. Put them in a closely fitting pan with the peeled and quartered onion, the celery and carrot chopped into lengths, and the lemon rind. Cover all with cold water and add the bay leaf, a few peppercorns and a little salt. Bring to the boil and skim off the grey foam which rises. Turn down the heat and put on a lid. Simmer the birds for an hour until they are tender, then remove them, joint them and keep them warm. Remove the vegetables and then reduce the stock by rapid boiling to a scant pint of liquid.

Meanwhile grind the nuts in the blender and mix them with the breadcrumbs. If you are using a liquidizer, moisten the mixture with some of the stock.

Stir the nut-and-breadcrumb mixture into the reduced stock and simmer until thick. Adjust the seasoning. Pour the sauce over the pheasant pieces.

To make the dish thoroughly Middle Eastern, mix 1 teaspoon of paprika with a couple of spoonfuls of oil and dribble a scarlet ribbon over the top. Serve with plain boiled white rice: 1 lb (dry weight) should be plenty.

SPANISH PARTRIDGE

The red-legged partridge, *Alectoris rufa*, is common to both Britain and Spain. An *Estofado de Perdiz* is a rich and thoroughly Spanish way with the birds, both young and old.

TO SERVE 6 PEOPLE

3 partridges
1 oz seasoned flour
2 Spanish onions (about 1 lb in weight)
1 red pepper and 1 green pepper
4 fat cloves garlic
1 thick slice of raw salted ham (Serrano or Parma, or a slice or two of back bacon)

Olive oil
6 black peppercorns
Salt
2 bay leaves and small sprig thyme
1 glass dry white wine or sherry
1 glass water

Halve the partridges, wipe them and dust them with the seasoned flour. Peel and roughly chop the onions. De-seed and chop the peppers. Peel and chop the garlic. Chop the ham or bacon.

Heat a layer of olive oil in the bottom of a casserole (the Spanish are always on the generous side with their oil). Fry the partridges gently to give them a little colour. Add the onions, peppers, garlic and ham and fry lightly. Add the bay leaves, thyme, peppercorns and the wine. Cover the casserole and cook in a medium oven for an hour. Check halfway through to see that the liquid has not evaporated too much, and top up with water if necessary. Taste for seasoning – a little sugar is sometimes needed if the wine is on the acid side.

For hearty appetites serve the dish with chips, cut thick and deep-fried in olive oil twice.

VINTNER'S PIGEONS

Many a French farmhouse still has a well-stocked dovecot. Such delicately nurtured young birds (squabs) are roasted with herbs in butter. Their cousins, plump and canny grain-thieves bagged in the field, are made of darker meat and sterner stuff. Barley makes an unusual nutty stuffing.

TO SERVE 4 PEOPLE

4 pigeons
¼ pint olive oil
8 oz pearl barley
Fresh herbs (tarragon, marjoram,
*   basil)*
2 cloves garlic

2 bay leaves
4 vine leaves (or tender cabbage
*   leaves)*
1 lb small green grapes (on the sour
*   side is best)*

Pluck, draw and wipe 4 plump pigeons and put them to marinate in the olive oil. Leave them there for at least 2 hours.

Meanwhile boil the pearl barley until soft. Drain. Chop the herbs and the garlic together and mix in with the barley while it is still warm. Season with salt and pepper.

Remove the pigeons from the oil marinade. Tuck half a bay leaf inside each. Stir 2 tablespoons of the oil into the barley and fill the cavity of each pigeon with this stuffing. Wrap each bird in a vine or cabbage leaf. Put the parcels into a casserole and trickle some more olive oil over them. Braise in a moderate oven until tender (40–60 minutes). Ten minutes before the end, pack the spaces between the birds with the green grapes, unpipped and unpeeled; they will heat and burst so that the juice forms a delicious gravy with the birds' juices. Serve on croûtons of bread fried in the rest of the marinade oil.

4 November 1985

Heaven

'Eating pâtés de foie gras to the sound of trumpets is my idea of heaven,' said the Reverend Sydney Smith, in the days when one was not held politically accountable for eating habits. Here, then, in response to the Labour Party's announcement that it would ban the importation of foie gras, is how to find your own. Not from Strasbourg, where the pickets might be out, but from the fiercely independent inhabitants of the Languedoc.

Gabriel winds his horn from October to January in the home of the Toulouse goose. Heaven and hell were always an issue in the land of the Cathars, which was not annexed by France until 1271. The natives had been giving their neighbours trouble for years: they

167

spoke a separate language, the *langue d'oc* (which still survives in the *patois*), instead of the *langue d'oïl* (now *oui*) adopted by the rest of France; their land was covetably fertile and produced an abundance of wine; but, above all, they didn't think much of the Church of Rome. Their very own protestant schism, Albigensian Catharism, was spreading like wildfire by the end of the twelfth century. It took the next fifty years and a combination of Simon de Montfort's bully-boys, an officially declared Crusade and a special Inquisition to bring the place to heel. All visible trace of the religion, including an extensive Cathar literature, was immediately destroyed. The victors then built the great redbrick fortress-cathedral of Sante Cecile at Albi as a warning to the Albigensians of the consequences of backsliding: its windows are high and narrow as arrow-slits, and the altar-screen depicts hell's torments and heaven's rewards with a vigour that would have delighted Hieronymus Bosch. Gabriel's group with the trumpets are, I believe, in the top right-hand corner. I'm still looking for the geese.

Their Inquisitors accused the Albigensians of fornication and riotous living – and, indeed, since the dualist religion declared the world the Devil's domain there may have been some truth in it. There is no doubt, however, that, Cathar or not, the Albigeois loves his food. Stout black-clad farmers' wives bear witness to this every autumn beneath the wooden rafters of the medieval covered market in nearby Revel. The fattening of geese and ducks for foie gras has long been a farmyard industry in these parts, and by November the market is in full swing. When I first saw the loaded tables one cold bright Saturday morning, the plump carcasses had been laid out on white-cloth-covered trestles for the inspection of the town: the merchandise may be gently prodded and squeezed by customers, but the bird must be bought whole and unopened. Purchasers take their chance on the size and quality of the *foie* within.

Madame Escrieu, matriarch of the tenant-farming family who

lived at the entrance to my cart-track, showed me the ropes. Since she had four sons, not one of whom weighed less than fourteen stone, Madame was something of an authority on fattening things up. Expertly her strong fingers kneaded the nether regions of a dozen fat ducks. Finally she nodded: two birds had been found acceptable. We took them over to the communal brass weighing machine to be priced. An expensive affair, but, as she explained, a magnificent investment for the winter: the foie gras to be put up in glass and stored for the festival feasts at Christmas and New Year, the rest to be made into a *confit* for the winter Sunday *cassoulet*.

Back on my kitchen table she examined the treasure. Perfection: huge (each nearly a quarter of the weight of the 8 lb duck) and pale cream in colour – just lightly tinged with pink. There was to be no fancy soaking of the foie gras in brandy, and no nonsense with truffles. Preparation must be innocent. Madame Escrieu accepted a small glass of the sinful *eau de vie* for herself.

MADAME ESCRIEU'S POTTED FOIE GRAS

1 fresh foie gras	*Pepper*
1 tablespoon salt	*2 glass preserving-jars*

Detach the foie from the cavity of the bird with care. Check the surface for bitter green stains or dark blood-vessels and gently remove. Sprinkle the foie with salt and leave overnight under a weighted plate. The following morning, drain, pat dry and wipe off any excess salt.

Sterilize the jars. Divide the foie into 1 lb pieces and grind a little pepper over. Then pack them into the jars. Close and place the jars in a pan of water. Boil steadily for 1 hour if the foie weighs 1 lb, and 1½ hours for a 2 lb foie. Through the glass you will see that the foie gras has turned a rosy pink and has sealed itself with its own golden butter.

The foie gras will keep, unopened and preferably refrigerated, for several months – if you can resist the temptation to eat it immediately with hot toast and a cold glass of the nearest thing to Château Yquem you can find. As for the trumpets, you will have to get a message to the Reverend Sydney.

17 November 1984

Christmas Goose

The goose, fattened on the gleanings of harvest stubble and served with the apples of autumn, is a far more ancient festive dish in Britain than the turkey. A young goose is a rosy-fleshed well-flavoured bird, heavy-boned and rich – quite different eating from those blowzy, pallid and overgrown fowl we now all order-early-for-Christmas.

A goose for roasting will weigh 9–10 lb. If you kill your own bird, it should hang for a week in a cool larder – less in warm weather. Allowing 3 lb of stuffing, it will feed 8–10 people.

The stuffing is a vital part of the cooking process. Naturally enough, all birds are hollow when drawn, and thus if the inside is unstuffed and ungreased the meat is bound to dry out as it is roasting. A juicy stuffing gives off a scented steam which is drawn through the bird by the heat of the oven, and serves the dual purpose of keeping the flesh moist and giving it flavour. Simple stuffings such as a piece of bread soaked in port, or an onion, or a piece of fat bacon are not meant to be eaten, but will still do their job.

Goose is a strong-flavoured bird and takes well to a robust stuffing. Sage and onion are the classic English solution. Victorian cookbooks often advise the blanching of the onions first in order to render the stuffing more delicate. Perhaps our modern onions are sweeter.

SAGE AND ONION STUFFING

2 lb onions	1 egg
10 fresh sage leaves	Milk to bind
2 oz butter	Salt and pepper
8 oz fresh breadcrumbs	

Peel and chop the onions finely. Chop the sage leaves. Melt the butter in a frying-pan and fry the onions for 5 minutes gently without browning them. Add the sage leaves for the final minute. (This is not in order to cook the onions and sage, but to allow them to flavour the butter.) Mix butter, onions and sage into the bread-crumbs. Beat the egg with an egg-cupful of milk and use it to bind the mixture. More milk may be required – the stuffing should be soft, but still stiff enough to hold together on a fork. Stuff the cavity of the bird.

If you would like a second stuffing, try making a 'Nek podyng' with sausage meat. It is an excellent dish, equally good made with a bread-based nut-enriched stuffing.

STUFFED GOOSE'S NECK

Make sure that you acquire the whole neck of the bird, complete with skin. (You will have to make a special point of this with your butcher.) Pull out the windpipe. You now have an empty flexible bag of skin on one side, and the long thin neck-bone on the other. Nick through the joints on the neck side to make it easier to carve. You can if you wish use the neck skin as a sausage casing on its own.

1 lb sausage meat or minced pork	Minced liver of the bird
2 oz breadcrumbs	Chopped fresh herbs
	Salt and pepper (generous)

Mix all the above thoroughly. Stuff the mixture into the neck and tie or sew up the ends. Prick in a few places. Put the neck pudding to cook beside the goose for the last half-hour or so.

APPLE STUFFING FOR GOOSE

A lighter though no less delicious way with the bird is to use an apple stuffing: a good recipe for an adult Christmas dinner.

1 teaspoon salt	*3 lb sharp apples*
1 teaspoon ground black pepper	*½ lb onions*
1 teaspoon crushed juniper berries	*2 oz butter*
1 measure gin	*2 oz raisins*

Mix the salt, pepper and juniper with the gin and rub this round the cavity of the bird.

Peel, core and roughly chop the apples. Peel and chop the onions. Melt the butter in a frying-pan and sweat the onions for a few minutes. Add the apples and caramelize them a little. Add the raisins and a little water if the mixture looks too dry. Stuff into the bird and sew it up.

TO ROAST THE GOOSE

Before you stuff the goose, feel inside the cavity and pull out the golden fat which lines it. Rub this over the breast of the bird, sprinkle with salt and pepper, then prick the skin all over without piercing the flesh.

Goose grease has a low melting-point (111°F) so the bird should be roasted in a moderate oven (350°F/gas 4) to allow the fat to run in its own time. (Duck fat, which melts at 126°F, needs a high heat to start it off.) Cover the breast and legs loosely with foil to prevent burning. Allow 20 minutes' cooking per pound weight. Pour off the fat – and there will be plenty – regularly during the cooking time. Remove foil and dust the goose with flour (old cookbooks call this 'frothing') 15 minutes before the end when you turn the oven up to crisp the skin. Leave to rest for 15 minutes before carving to allow the flesh to settle.

Save the melted fat and store it in small covered jars in a cool larder. Goose grease makes wonderful dripping which stays sweet for months, unless you care to put it to its ancient use as the main ingredient in embrocations and creams for the medicine-chest.

23 November 1985

Mad March Hare

In Tudor times pasty of red squirrel was accounted a fine dainty dish and a suitable entrée for a nobleman, while 'ragoo' of rabbit or a jugged hare was meat for the peasant who worked his land. With

the choice available, however, the poacher who scoured his lordship's hedgerows never failed to select a hare for his own pot. A *Civet of Hare* is a dish above class distinctions. This is the last chance to catch your hare this year. Mad March is nearly over and the boxing has begun. Seconds out.

A Civet, or Jug, or Stew or even a Royale of Hare needs a fine plump mature animal to do it justice. A leveret's meat is too pale and tender for such a dark rich dish. Hang the hare, unskinned and unpaunched (to avoid the danger of introducing civilized and alien microbes), for three or four days. Then draw it and skin it: cut the skin round all four paws first, then slit the back-leg fur up to the already-slit belly. Grip the loosened back-leg skin firmly and pull. The skin will come off like a glove. Keep the liver and all the blood you can collect. Chop off the head and the feet. Now examine your hare. You will see that the back and legs are encased in a fine white membrane. This must be stripped off or the meat will never be tender.

Wild mushrooms, thyme, good red wine, and smoked fat bacon all have an affinity with hare. This recipe includes all these good things, plus a couple of squares of Mexico-inspired chocolate to add depth to the sauce. You can cook it in one of those large stoneware jugs without lips still made in France and sold in Britain. It will then be truly and properly 'jugged'. It is not, however, essential to the nature of the dish. Jugging was only an old way of baking before domestic ovens were common. I usually make jugged hare in a large earthenware or enamel casserole with a lid.

JUGGED HARE

TO SERVE 6 PEOPLE

1 mature hare
1 bottle of the red Burgundy you will
 be drinking with it
4 cloves
6 peppercorns
Small bunch of thyme
2 heaped spoonfuls flour
Pepper and salt

¼ lb smoked streaky bacon
½ lb onions
4 cloves garlic
½ lb wild mushrooms (or big flat
 cultivated ones)
4 oz butter
2 squares bitter black chocolate
Small glass brandy

Chop the hare into a dozen joints. You will need a heavy knife and a mallet for the saddle. It is a good idea to marinate the meat in the red wine for a few hours. It is *essential* to marinate the hare if it has come from a butcher and you do not know if it has been properly hung (or it will taste like a mild little rabbit).

Cube the bacon and sweat it in a frying-pan until the fat runs. Take the joints out of the marinade and pat dry. While you are preparing the meat, put the marinade (with the sprig of thyme and the cloves and peppercorns) to boil and reduce by a third. Roll the hare pieces in the seasoned flour, then fry gently in the bacon fat. When the outside of the meat is sealed, put the joints in the casserole.

Roughly chop the onions and garlic. Slice the mushrooms. Melt the butter in the frying-pan and put in the onions and garlic to soften. Add the mushrooms and fry all gently for a moment. Tip the contents of the pan into the casserole. Pour a little of the red-wine marinade into the frying-pan and scrape all the little brown bits into it. Add to the casserole along with the rest of the marinade. Break the chocolate into pieces and stir it in.

Simmer the civet gently, in the oven or on top of the stove, for 2–3 hours, depending on the age of the hare. When it is tender it is time to thicken the sauce with the blood and the liver.

Warm the glass of brandy in a small saucepan and set light to it to burn up the alcohol. Stir in the liver, minced fine, and the blood. Heat the mixture gently but do not allow it to boil – blood curdles at boiling-point, like egg. Stir the brandy mixture into the juices in the casserole.

Serve with plenty of bread and good red wine. A watercress salad dressed with walnut oil and perhaps a few slivers of pickled lemon (see page 234) to accompany. A sharp damson tart with thick yellow cream or a caramelized apple tart to follow. Then you will certainly need a glass of calvados and a brisk walk in the March wind. Spring will not be far behind.

9 March 1985

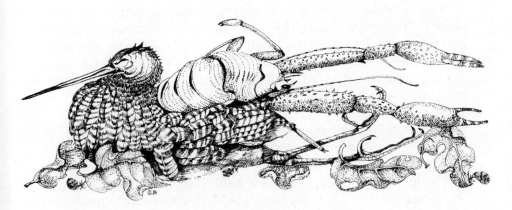

Wooster at Table

The English, say the French, take their dinner in the nursery. Culinarily speaking, that is – foreign visitors have always spoken highly of the grandeur of our table settings and the cleanliness of the napery in our larger mansions. The French, on the other hand, take the children so early into the grown-ups' dining-room that their underprivileged mites never develop a taste for cod and parsley sauce or jam roly-poly. In spite of the heroic efforts of Mrs Elizabeth David, we cannot altogether change our spots. The most cosmopolitan among us, worshippers for years in the gastronomic temples of Paris and Lyons, sneak back to the nursery to toast a reliable crumpet whenever Nanny isn't looking.

P. G. Wodehouse defined this ambivalence, this view that fancy cooking should ultimately be left to foreigners, via Bertram Wooster musing in *The Feudal Spirit* on the first dinner cooked at Brinkley Court by Aunt Dahlia's French chef, the great Anatole:

> . . . Anatole, that wizard of the pots and pans, had come through with one of his supremest efforts. He had provided the company with, if memory serves me correctly,
>
> Le Caviar Frais
> Le Consommé aux Pommes d'Amour

Les Sylphides à la crème d'Ecrevisses
Les Fried Smelts
Le Bird of some kind with chipped potatoes
Le Icecream.

Wise Anatole – nothing here to upset the apple cart at this early stage in his career. Apart, that is, from the brief flirtation with the crayfish-sauced wood-fairy. With the passage of time Anatole's menus develop and blossom. So much so that when after many a narrow escape Aunt Dahlia finally gambles her last negotiable collateral, the services of her chef, there is much to regret:

'Ice,' she repeated, and sighed dreamily. 'I think of those prawns in iced aspic of his, and I say to myself that I should be made to face a lifetime without Anatole's cooking. That Selle d'Agneau à la Grecque! That Mignonette de Poulet Rôti Petit Duc! Those Nonats de la Méditerranée au Fenouil! . . . Sweet suffering soupspoons!' she vociferated, if that's the word, anguish written on her every feature. 'I wonder what Tom will say when he hears Anatole is leaving!'

The *Larousse gastronomique* will have none of it, not even the Sylphides. Here, in memory of Anatole's youthful glory, is my suggestion for that mysterious delicacy with which Wodehouse's 'peerless disher-up' first enchanted his thoroughly English admirers.

LES SYLPHIDES À LA CRÈME D'ÉCREVISSES

The Sylphides' woodland connection is provided here by the game birds; since we are now right at the end of the season, they will be all the more appropriately elusive. Use chicken if you miss the deadline. Quantities given will feed 8 as an *amuse-gueule*.

The Sylphides

1 lb skinned, boned raw pheasant breast (or, better still, woodcock; failing that, any feathered game which has chanced your way)

2 egg whites
1 pint double cream
Salt and pepper

Mince and then pound up the meat into a fine paste. A food processor will do the job beautifully. Work in the egg whites to make

176

a smooth dough – the egg whites are there to *bind* the mixture, not specifically to lighten it. Put the mixture into a bowl resting in another bowl full of ice, and beat it thoroughly with a wooden spoon. Leave it to rest, covered, in its ice-bowl for 2 hours. Then beat it some more, this time gradually working in the cold cream, until you have a thick soft paste which will just hold its shape when dropped from a spoon. Add salt and pepper.

Bring a wide pan half-full of salted water to the boil and then turn down the heat until you have a discreet simmer. Drop egg-shaped spoonfuls of the mixture into the water and poach them gently, turning once, for 5–6 minutes until they are firm to the touch. Lift them out with a perforated spoon and put them on a clean cloth to drain. Put a large shallow dish to warm in the oven while you make the *crème d'écrevisses*.

The Sauce

4 oz cooked freshwater crayfish (or shrimps, faute de mieux)
1 pint double cream
Salt and paprika

Peel the crayfish, winkling out any scarlet roe and all the delicious juicy bits from the head. Chop the body meat.

Bring the cream gently to the boil and then add the chopped crayfish. Remove from the heat. Taste and add salt and paprika. Pour the sauce into the hot serving-dish and arrange the still-warm sylphides on the hot bed. Sprinkle the pink sauce with a little more paprika and put the dish back into the oven for a few moments to reheat.

If the cream is very thin, you may need to thicken it with an ounce or two of flour worked with the same quantity of butter, added when you bring it to the boil.

25 January 1986

Forty Garlic to the Chicken

The British roasting chicken is not the most appetizing sight in the supermarket cold cabinet. Sold as it is today, encased in clingfilm, each carcass stuffed with a sealed plastic envelope containing spares from some unidentified giblet-pool, the pallid offering does not inspire culinary confidence. It is of course most seductively cheap, this water-plumped odourless creature, featherless, headless, legless, without any of those identifying features by which the less 'advanced' world judges its table-poultry.

Should you find yourself by happy chance on the airy plain of Bresse – say, in Montrevel on market-day – you will find the true aristocrat of roasting fowl, the *poulet de Bresse* – or the even more highly rated *poularde*. The most esteemed chicken in France is corn-fattened until ready for the table. Its carcass is bathed in milk and powdered like an odalisque so that it goes to market pearly white. Local housewives examine their chosen bird with care. Its blue-tinged legs, wattles and combs are diagnostic features of the Bresse race which confirm the small lead seal of authenticity affixed by the proud poultry-farmer. In Bresse the bird needs no embellishment save roasting in a very hot oven, unbasted so that the skin crisps to a brilliant gold.

The less-than-perfect British bird needs far stronger management. The following recipe is a variation of the famous *poulet à l'ail* of Provence, the only treasure with which my daughter Poppy escaped from her 24-hour-nanny au-pairing stint in Paris. Her employer's best friend was a girl from Provence who would make this dish to her mother's recipe with the first new potatoes of spring. Poppy was enchanted by so vigorous a southern pleasure: after a long winter of trudging with her tiny charges between the cold bare park and the concrete-and-glass apartment-block where lived her upwardly mobile young employers, she was more than ready for it. Here is the recipe, just in time to celebrate the arrival of our own new potatoes.

Don't cut down or be inhibited by the quantity of garlic included. Roast garlic is the mildest of vegetables; it has a sweet and delicate flavour and can boast most of the virtues and none of the vices of the fierce bulb when eaten raw. One rub of raw garlic round a salad-bowl packs more punch than a dozen baked cloves.

POULET À L'AIL

This will feed 5–6, and you will need no other dish: it is the simplest and most delicious of one-pot meals.

1 roasting chicken, around 3 lb in
  weight
A bundle of fresh rosemary
1 oz butter
2 lb little new potatoes

1 wine-glass olive oil
40 cloves garlic, unpeeled; more if the
  chicken is large or the cloves small
Salt and pepper

You will need a baking-dish large enough to accommodate the whole chicken plus the potatoes and garlic.

Wipe the chicken outside and particularly inside (this will remind you to remove the bag of giblets – something I have on occasion omitted to remember). Stuff a few sprigs of rosemary into the bird, along with the nugget of butter, salt and pepper. Scrub the new potatoes, but leave them whole.

Sprinkle 2 tablespoons of oil into the baking-dish and then put in the chicken. Pack all round it the still-unpeeled cloves of garlic and the scrubbed new potatoes. Sprinkle all with salt and pepper. Pack the rosemary twigs around and above – the more the merrier. Pour the rest of the oil all over.

Put the chicken in a pre-heated oven to roast at 375°F/gas 5 for 10 minutes, then turn the oven down to 350°F/gas 4 for another 50 minutes. Allow about 20 minutes to the pound. Turn both the bird and the potatoes regularly so that all crisp evenly. Ten minutes before the end of the cooking time, pour off all excess oil.

Your guests will need plenty of fresh bread, ready-cut into thick slices, a large napkin apiece, and a water-bowl with a slice of lemon floated on the surface. This should warn the company that it is not about to be dainty. Put out the dish with a bundle of small scarlet radishes, carefully washed, but still left tied into a bunch with their leaves, flanked by a saucer of rough salt. Provide hot plates and plenty of wine in generous glasses. The wine should be cool and a little green – perhaps a chilled Muscadet.

Bring in the dish. The aromas should be wonderful: the sharp peppery scent of rosemary, the opulence of the olive oil and the pungent sweetness of the roasted garlic. Each diner helps himself to bread, a piece of chicken and as many of the little crisp new potatoes and whole cloves of garlic as he wishes. The garlic cloves should be popped from their jackets with the fingers, like creamy peas out of a pod. Or in the teeth straight into the mouth. The bread is there to mop up all the juices. Your guests will be well satisfied.

8 March 1986

Making the Most of the Grouse

An old grouse offers a challenge to the adventurous cook. In young grouse the primary flight-feathers are pointed, in older birds they are rounded. Test the youth of a plucked bird by bending the lower mandible of the beak; if it bends easily or breaks, the bird is a stripling, and roasting material. A young grouse will serve 1 or 2, but a plump old bird well handled can serve 3 or 4 diners.

GROUSE PUDDING

The dish has a long pedigree; grouse puddings were made in Saxon Britain. Snipe, woodcock, quail, partridge or even woodpigeon make excellent puddings to the same recipe. Quantities given will feed 6–8.

The Filling

A brace of old grouse
1 tablespoon chopped fresh herbs
  (thyme, parsley)
3–4 flat dark mushrooms, or any
  wild-gathered variety
Salt and pepper

1 glass red wine
1 fine-cut rump steak (about 4 oz)
1 pint good meat-stock or plain water

The Pastry

1½ lb flour
8 oz suet
1 level teaspoon salt

½ pint water (or 4 egg yolks plus
  enough water to make a soft
  dough)

Joint the grouse into neat pieces. Roll the joints in the finely chopped herbs, mix in the mushrooms (wiped and chopped roughly), add salt and plenty of freshly milled pepper, and put all to marinate in the red wine while you make the suet crust.

Mix the dry ingredients for the pastry in a bowl. Add the water judiciously and work all together with light fingers – you may need a little more or a little less liquid for a soft pliable dough. Roll out two-thirds of the pastry and use it to line a 3 pint pudding-basin. Roll out the remaining pastry for a lid, and put it aside.

Lay the slice of steak on the base of the pudding. Put in the pieces of grouse, mushrooms, marinade and all. Pour in the stock or water (you will need extra salt and a little chopped onion if you use plain water). Cover with the pastry lid. Seal the edges by damping and then crimping them together with a fork. Cut a hole in the top for the steam to escape. Either tie a pudding-cloth over, or cover with a double layer of tinfoil (make a pleat in the middle to allow for the expansion of the pudding). If you leave a handle of string tied right across the pudding, this makes it easier to lift it in and out of the hot water. Put the basin on an upturned saucer or pastry-cutter in a roomy saucepan, with enough boiling water to come two-thirds of the way up the sides of the basin. Leave the pudding to boil gently for 4 hours at least. Check every now and again that the water hasn't boiled away, and top up with *boiling* water – it is very important that the water should not come off the boil while the pudding cooks. Once cooked it can be successfully reheated by reboiling for another hour. Serve the pudding in its own bowl nestling in a clean white napkin. Accompany with lightly cooked runner beans or a dish of fresh broccoli spears.

GROUSE WITH WHISKY

ENOUGH FOR 6 AFTER A LONG DAY ON THE MOORS

2 plump old grouse	2–3 oz piece pork fat (or fat bacon)
4 oz butter	1 glass whisky
2 tablespoons French mild mustard	½ pint cream
Juice of 1 lemon	Salt and pepper

Wipe the birds inside and out. Make a paste with 3 oz of the butter, the mustard, the lemon juice, and plenty of freshly ground pepper. Rub the birds all over inside and out with this mixture. Cube the pork fat and put it in a casserole (just large enough to accommodate the brace of grouse). Melt all together until the fat runs. Add the birds and turn them to brown them a little. Lid the casserole tightly (seal with a flour-and-water paste if the fit is not close enough) and put it in a low oven (300°F/gas 2) to cook for an hour, until the birds are tender.

Take off the lid and pour the whisky over the hot birds. As soon as the whisky is warm, flame it to burn off the alcohol and concentrate the flavours. When the flames have died, take out the birds and joint them. Pour the cream into the juices in the casserole and bring all back to a simmer. Return the joints to the sauce. Simmer gently for 10 minutes. Taste and add salt.

Serve with a golden purée of well-mashed swede and potato whipped up with an egg yolk and plenty of butter.

SPATCHCOCKED GROUSE

A way to grill young birds, and an irresistible alternative to the usual roasting.

Split each bird down the back without cutting through the breast. Spread it, skin-side up like a flattened frog, on the chopping-board. Cut off the feet and double back each drumstick, poking the end joint into a slit which you have made in the base of each thigh. Double each pinion under each wing. Poor thing – it now looks like something the Inquisition proposes to interview. Run a couple of skewers crossways through each flattened bird to hold it in position. Brush with melted butter and coat with fresh (not dried) breadcrumbs mixed with chopped fresh herbs. Grill the birds for 15–20 minutes, turning them once and basting with more butter as they cook. Remove the skewers and serve the birds with all their delicious juices.

16ᵗʰ Aug. '89 – V. good.

16 August 1986

Sauce for the Tartars

The Tartars shared two characteristics at least with the early Scots: both were formidable fighters and both took their meals on the move. Whereas the Scotsman on the warpath would carry a bag of porridge-oats for his supper, pausing only to dip it in the nearest burn, the Tartar slipped a slab of steak under his horse's saddle so

that the pounding the meat received during the course of the day's marauding rendered it beautifully tender for the evening meal. Fast food for nomads inspired the Steak Tartar. Today it is more likely to be fast food for restaurateurs, not even requiring the services of a chef. A patty of chopped raw steak, crowned with a raw egg yolk and accompanied with capers, chopped onion and parsley makes a better instant dinner than most. Taken with a small glass of chilled vodka, it makes the perfect TV dinner for the armchair sportsman. The Lagradi restaurant in Budapest has added a third feature to the Tartar–Scots connection. They serve a *Finnan Haddock Tartar* as a delicious first course.

The Tartars' best-known culinary connection is a certain well-known sauce. However, *Tartar Sauce* in its home territory is not a caper- and gherkin-spiked mayonnaise as provided in tiny plastic tubs with fish and chips in motorway cafés. It is, as I had it served in the elegant art-nouveau Hotel Arani Bika in Debrecen, eastern Hungary, last autumn, a rather runny, sharp, creamy little sauce in which oil plays a very minor part. I must admit my Sauce Tartar came with breaded and deep-fried foie gras – not a dish widely available on the British motorway. On the way to my lunch I had passed flocks of the handsome grey and white geese cropping the grassy plain like cattle. In Hungary fresh foie gras is rather more available than the alternative, more expensive item on the menu that day – woodpigeon, served in the same way as the foie gras. The recipe is, as I discovered on my return home, a fine way to treat a brace of British pigeons which have been fattening on the gleanings of the autumn stubble.

SMOKED HADDOCK TARTAR

TO SERVE 4 PEOPLE AS A FIRST COURSE

*1 fine fat smoked haddock – the
  pale-smoked whole fish
1 small carton soured cream
1 onion*

*1 small bunch parsley
1 tablespoon capers
Paprika*

Skin, de-bone and flake the raw fish and toss it with the soured cream. Skin and finely chop the onion. Chop the parsley. Divide the haddock mixture between 4 small plates, arranging it in neat little patties. Sprinkle a pinch of paprika on each patty. Flank the haddock with small separate piles of chopped onion, chopped parsley and capers. Serve with hot toast.

WOODPIGEON SAUCE TARTAR

TO SERVE 4 PEOPLE

The Birds

*2 young pigeons
1 tablespoon flour
Salt and pepper
2 eggs
1 tablespoon milk*

*4–5 tablespoons home-made
  breadcrumbs (not those
  orange-dyed commercial ones)
Oil for frying*

The Sauce

*2 egg yolks
1 small carton soured cream
½ teaspoon salt
1 level teaspoon sugar*

*1 teaspoon mild mustard
Juice of ½ lemon
1 tablespoon oil
1 small glass white wine*

Pluck and clean the pigeons. Split them in two lengthways. Lay out three plates in a line: on the first spread out the flour seasoned with salt and pepper; put the eggs, lightly mixed together, in the second; on the third pile the breadcrumbs.

Put a pan of deep oil on to heat.

Roll each half-pigeon in the seasoned flour, then dip it in the egg, making sure all is covered; finish by coating thoroughly in the breadcrumbs.

When the oil is hazed with blue smoke, put in the pigeons. Leave them to fry gently for 20 minutes, turning them once, while you make the sauce.

Beat the egg yolks together in a bowl and place it over a pan of boiling water. Whisk in the soured cream, the salt, sugar, mustard and lemon juice. As the sauce starts to thicken, whisk in the oil gradually, followed by enough of the white wine to give the consistency of a pouring custard. Whisk until all is smooth. Do not allow the sauce to boil. If it does, add it to an extra egg yolk in the liquidizer and process till it amalgamates.

The pigeons should be cooked by now. Remove them from the oil and drain them on kitchen paper. Serve the crisp little birds on a hot plate, with quartered lemons and the sauce handed separately. A diced beetroot and apple salad dressing with yoghurt to accompany.

TARTAR FRITTERS

This Russian recipe serves 4–6. My children loved these fritters for their birthday-parties.

8 oz flour	*Oil for frying*
3 eggs	*1 small jar runny honey*
½ teaspoon salt	

Make a noodle dough by kneading the eggs with the flour and the salt. Work thoroughly till you have a soft firm dough. Cover and let the dough rest for 10 minutes. Roll it out and cut into thin noodle-like strips. Fry the noodles till golden in deep oil. Heat the honey and pour it over the drained fritters in a deep bowl.

11 October 1986

Puddings and Sweets

The Lost Peak of Mont Blanc

At tea-time the other day I went to Fortnum & Mason's Soda Fountain. Misty with memory, I sat at the bar and ordered my childhood pleasure: hot chocolate with whipped cream, and a Mont Blanc. The second is a wonderful confection of chewy meringue piled with buff-coloured spaghetti worms of sweetened chestnut purée, topped with a snowy peak of cream. What arrived was a powdery white commercial meringue decorated with a chestnut-flavoured whorl, accompanied by a glass of thin cocoa'd milk sprayed with froth from an aerosol container. I ate the excuses and left.

Back when things were done properly, tea at Fortnum's reconciled generations of boarding-school-bound children to their fate: the condemned man's last cigarette. It was my maternal grandmother, an absurdly young and frivolous beauty (bewilderingly unlike the usual grandmother), who took me there. Fortnum's was her natural habitat, and tea with her was a very special occasion. Slender in Balenciaga silk, she would order for herself a pot of Lapsang Suchong with lemon. I, lumpy in my brown school uniform, could order what I pleased. After a brief early flirtation with ice-cream sodas, what I pleased did not vary. It would be hot chocolate in a glass with a silver frame and handle: dark thick chocolate topped with whipped cream so heavy it did not melt into the scalding liquid but had to be scooped up with a special long-handled spoon. And of course the Mont Blanc. My grandmother would watch me warily as I ate my way through the whole impossible mixture. Then she would take me off to the train. Her parting gift was a white cardboard box tied up with string. Inside nestled a huge *mille-feuille* to stave off the rigours of the three-hour train journey to the Malvern Hills. I was gorged. The great cream-stuffed disc of iced pastry would arrive untouched, and have to be smuggled into school where no outside food was allowed. I would shut it up in the back of my dormitory cupboard under the hockey-boots. Occasionally I lifted the lid and broke off little sticky bits of pastry with my fingers. Finally the whole gooey mass would turn rancid and have to be smuggled back out again into the dustbin.

But back to the hot chocolate and the Mont Blanc. Here is how to create them as they used to be before Fortnum's discovered synthetics and aerosols. For hot chocolate for 4, pour a pint of milk into a saucepan and break into it 4 oz plain cooking chocolate, not cocoa powder. Warm it gently, stirring to avoid the chocolate sticking. Burnt chocolate smells horrible and tastes worse. Take it off just before it boils and pour into heat-resistant glasses. You will need ½ pint of double cream, whipped and lightly sweetened, to top this and the following recipe.

For the Mont Blanc, you start with some home-made meringues. Make these when you have a few whites left over from a mayonnaise, and then store them – meringues will keep almost indefinitely in an airtight tin. First, grease and dust with flour a couple of baking-trays, and turn the oven on low. Then add a pinch of salt to the separated egg whites and beat until they are very stiff. Fold in, spoon by spoon, a heaped tablespoonful of caster sugar for each egg white (about 2 oz of sugar per white). Work fast now or the mixture will soften. Take two tablespoons. Use one to scoop up a mound of the meringue, and the other to turn it out on to the tray. Sprinkle the ovals with caster sugar to keep the surface crisp. Bake the meringues in a very low oven, no more than 300°F/gas 1, for around 2 hours depending on size. If they ooze syrup or stick to the pan, your oven was too cool. If they are perfectly done, they will be a pale gold and slightly sticky inside.

For the chestnut purée, take a pound of chestnuts, slit their skins and either boil them for a few minutes or bake them so that both outer and inner skins can be slipped off. Without letting the chestnuts get cold and grey, put them to stew gently in sweetened milk until soft. Drain and rub through a wire sieve, letting the paste fall lightly on to the plate like a pile of fine vermicelli. It is this earthworm effect which is one of the chief charms of a Mont Blanc. Assemble the mountain: a meringue for the base, a pile of the chestnut threads for the rocky slopes, finally the whipped cream to crown the peak.

189

Anyone who has been returned to school without this consolation can make a passable midnight feast, the next best thing, with a small pot of Jersey cream and a tin of *purée de marrons sucrés* (it even comes in toothpaste tubes today). Mix and eat with a large spoon. It will at least give you an idea of the glory you missed.

27 October 1984

Revel of the Scarlet Tarts

The bakery in Revel near Toulouse opens early on a summer market-day. Visiting it became one of my children's chief delights during the school year they spent in the Languedoc. The local comprehensive had accepted them cheerfully and taught them philosophy and a whole new view of Napoleon, all in a thick southern patois. The four of them quickly learnt two important truths about life in France. The first, my children explained primly, is that the French are mad about sex. Their disapproval did not prevent them exploiting its potential. Every day my eldest daughter sold her seat on the school bus next to her long-suffering brother to the young lady who bid most bubble gum for the privilege of changing places. Her brother grumbled but went halves on the profits.

They learnt the second truth when the door of the bakery in Revel swung open: French food is wonderful. Into the market-square drifted the irresistible scent of warm strawberry tart. A long line of housewives formed immediately. We joined them just in time: the first strawberries had arrived. The baker's wife laid the flat open tarts on glass shelves stacked on the counter. The family's two small daughters, allowed to miss Saturday school on this special morning, were helping parcel them up. The tarts were 10 inches across, made with crumbly brown pastry filled with a *crème pâtissière* and crowned with scarlet fresh fruit. The tart we selected, so heavy with berries the cream was no longer visible, was packed carefully in a white cardboard box and tied with pink string. The youngest of my children was then delegated to carry the treasure home. Back on the kitchen table only its perfection saved it from being wolfed long before lunch. Such a tart must be eaten on the day it is bought, in fact as quickly as possible before the pastry loses its buttery crispness and the fruit its delicate flavour. As the summer passed the early

190

strawberry tarts were followed by a changing sequence of delights: there were raspberry tarts, blackcurrant tarts, mirabelle plum tarts and, in the winter, apple tarts patterned in concentric wheels tipped at the edges with caramelized sugar, even tarts made with dark rich prunes. But best of all were the first.

Living in France there was no need to make our own tarts, since their purchase was a major pleasure of market-day. Back in England this year the arrival of the strawberry season created a wave of nostalgia, and I dusted off my large flan-tin. The ideal baking-tin for a fruit tart has a removable base and low fluted sides which give the pastry a larger area to crisp on. Use your own favourite sweet shortcrust pastry. Otherwise, proportions of 4 oz flour to 3 oz butter and 1 tablespoonful caster sugar will fit an 8 inch tart-tin. Cut the cold butter into the flour and sugar with a knife, then finish by rubbing in with the tips of your fingers. Mix in a little cold water to form a dough ball. Flatten the ball and press it lightly over the base and into the corners of the tin. The pastry must be baked blind, that is, empty. I used to do this laboriously by lining the pastry with baking foil and dry beans. This recipe is nearly shortbread, so pricking with a fork is all that is necessary. Bake it in a hot oven (375°F/gas 5) for around 20 minutes until the pastry is dry and golden. As it bakes, make the custard cream. This is easiest to do in a liquidizer: mix together ½ pint of milk, 1 ounce of butter, 1 large egg, 2 tablespoons of sugar and 1 heaped tablespoonful of flour. Heat the liquidized mixture gently until it thickens, stirring all the time. The flour must be cooked, or it will taste starchy, and the eggs should not be over-cooked or they will scramble (though not very seriously, as with an egg-only custard). If the mixture does curdle or go lumpy, pour it quickly back in the liquidizer with a little cold milk and beat it up again. A shot of alcohol now – vodka, brandy or gin – gives it an adult edge and halts the cooking process. Cool the custard in a cold pudding-basin.

The final assembly is the most enjoyable part. The now-cooled pastry shell is spread with the cream. The strawberries are then hulled and halved and laid on it in a single layer of concentric circles. Finally, pour over the top a glazing of warmed thinned berry jam – it can be raspberry, or strawberry, or redcurrant, but it should be scarlet. The instant the warmed jam is poured over the ripe fruit all its delicious scents are released. This is the best moment to eat a Revel tart, before the Knave steals it.

8 June 1985

191

Sweets in the Queen Anne Style

Queen Anne liked her bonbons. The first queen of Great Britain and Ireland smiles plumply from her portraits, clearly well satisfied with the catering arrangements. Her confectioner, Mrs Mary Eales, confirmed the royal preferences when she published a collection of confectionery recipes, as prepared for her Majesty, in 1718, four years after her patroness's demise.

Mary Eales was a professional: her recipes have that authority and clarity which come only from long personal experience. She is not listed in the records as a member of the royal household, so it must be assumed she was an outside supplier – one of the earliest of the 'by appointment' tradesmen. Mrs Eales was not a creator of complicated set-pieces. She had access to the orchard and the sugar-barrel and made the best of both. Her strength lies in her delightful repertoire of recipes for the candying and conserving of English berries, fruits and flowers, including several for fruit clear-cakes – as far as I know, a vanished confection. Her master-recipe on the subject is for gooseberries, although she includes instructions for making clear-cakes with currants, raspberries, apricots, plums, pears, quinces, oranges and lemons.

GOOSEBERRY CLEAR-CAKES

Take a Gallon of white Goosberries, nose [that is, top-and-tail] and wash them; put to them as much water as will cover them almost all over, set them on an hot Fire, let them boil a Quarter of an Hour, or more, then run it thro' a Flannel Jelly-Bag;

To a Pint of Jelly have ready a Pound and half of fine Sugar, sifted thro' an Hair Sieve; set the Jelly over the Fire, let it just boil up, then shake in the Sugar, stirring it all the while the Sugar is putting in; then set it on the Fire again, let it scald 'till all the Sugar is well melted; then lay a thin strainer in a flat earthen Pan, pour in your Clear-Cake Jelly, and turn back the Strainer to take off the Scum;

Fill it into Pots, and set it in the Stove to dry; when it is candy'd on the Top, turn it out on Glass; and if your Pots are too big, cut it; and when it is very dry, turn it again and let it dry on the other Side; twice turning is enough. If any of the Cakes stick to the Glass, hold them over a little Fire, and they will come off;

Take Care the Jelly does not boil after the Sugar is in; A Gallon of Goosberries will make three Pints of Jelly; if more, 'twill not be strong enough.

Mrs Eales includes a recipe for sack-posset. Sack, the anglicized version of the French *sec*, was Spanish white wine, usually dry sherry. The royal mind was much preoccupied with things Spanish at the time. The War of the Spanish Succession dragged on from 1701 to 1714. It cost a fortune, largely provided by the American colonists. Queen Anne supported Charles of Austria's claim to the Spanish throne against the claims of Philip – Louis XIV of France's grandson. The first Duke of Marlborough, Anne's favourite general, brought the business to a satisfactory conclusion at the battle of Blenheim, and the Treaty of Utrecht settled the matter in the Austrian favour. As their share of the pickings the English acquired Gibraltar, which provided a clear trade route for the fruits of the Spanish sun, particularly the wines of Jerez.

A fino, a manzanilla or a montilla will do very well for this recipe, which must have been one of Queen Anne's favourites. It produces a wonderful thin alcoholic custard. Instead of a full quart of cream, 1 pint of milk and 1 pint of cream are adequate. The eggs were not the monsters we have today: 8 instead of 12 is about right. Use a blender.

TO MAKE SACK-POSSET OR SACK-CREAM

Take twelve Eggs, (the Whites of but six) beat them, and put to them a Pint of Sack and half a Pound of Sugar; set them on a fire, keeping them stirring 'till they turn white, and just begin to thicken;

At the same Time on another Fire have a Quart of Cream, boil and pour it into the eggs and Sack, give it a Stir round, and cover it a Quarter of an Hour before you eat it: The Eggs and Sack must be heated in the Bason you use [that is, work] it in, and the Cream must boil before you set on the Eggs.

7 September 1985

Pudding George's Special

Pudding George of Hanover, crowned George I of Great Britain and Ireland in 1714, never did manage to learn much English. He was content to leave the business of running his realm to a cabinet of the natives – an interesting innovation which appealed to his subjects.

The British were undemanding of their monarchs at the time. George fulfilled their single modest requirement: he was most certainly not a Frenchman. Thackeray, most English of Englishmen, provides the Hanoverian king's obituary: 'He took our loyalty for what it was worth; laid hands on what money he could; kept us assuredly from Popery and wooden shoes . . . better than a king out of St Germains, with the French king's orders in his pocket and a swarm of Jesuits in his train.'

George's heart lay in the royal larder – and he was not a man for French fantasies and sorbets. I have it on good authority (I would even admit to informed sources) that the pudding mixed in huge earthenware bowls every year in the kitchens of Sandringham follows Hanoverian George's recipe.

Here it is, as served to the Pudding King himself at 6 p.m. on 25 December in the year of his accession. Make it in time to ripen for Christmas.

CHRISTMAS PUDDING

This quantity serves two dozen revellers. It will make 3 puddings, each weighing in at around 3 lb.

1½ lb finely shredded suet	*1 lb dark brown sugar*
1 lb eggs, weighed in their shells	*1 lb brown breadcrumbs*
1 lb dried plums	*1 teaspoon mixed spice*
1 lb mixed peel	*Half a nutmeg, grated*
1 lb small raisins	*2 teaspoons salt*
1 lb currants	*½ pint milk*
1 lb flour	*Juice of one lemon*
	Large wine-glassful of brandy

Stone and halve the plums. Cut the peel in strips. Pick over and remove stones from raisins and currants. Sieve the flour.

Mix all the dry ingredients in a large bowl. Add the eggs beaten to a froth with the milk, brandy and lemon juice. Mix thoroughly. This is the moment when your own kitchen cabinet may stir the pudding and make a wish.

Leave the pudding to stand for at least 12 hours in a cool place. Butter three 3 lb pudding-basins and divide the mixture among them. Press the pudding well down. Cover with buttered grease-proof paper, pleated in the middle to allow for expansion of the mixture. Tie a clean cloth over all, stringing round and knotting on top to make a handle. (Baking foil will do, but is not so easy to lift in and out.)

Set the pudding, the bottom resting on a heatproof dish or metal ring, in a large pan of water to reach halfway up the side of the bowl. Boil for 8 hours – topping up regularly with boiling water.

You might like to make the classic round bag-pudding (quantities for 3 puddings as before). You will need large clean cloths and a colander. Flour the cloth and lay it in the base of the colander. Put in the pudding mixture and mound it over. Tie the cloth, corner to corner, over it. Pass the handle of a wooden spoon or a sturdy stick through the knots in the cloth and suspend the pudding in the boiling water. Cooking time as for the moulded pudding.

Store in a cool larder until Christmas morning; if you have made bag-puddings, suspend them from hooks. The puddings will need 2 hours' boiling before you serve them flamed with brandy (warm the brandy first).

Brandy butter is the best accompaniment. In fact there are those who believe that the whole point of the pudding is the brandy butter.

BRANDY BUTTER

FOR A 3 LB PUDDING WHICH WILL FEED 8 PEOPLE

½ lb unsalted butter
6 oz icing sugar

1 wine-glass brandy (or rum or whisky)

Cream the butter and then beat in the icing sugar. Continue to beat until light and fluffy as for a cake. Beat in as much brandy as the mixture will take without curdling. Pile into a bowl and refrigerate until solid.

LEFTOVERS

Lancashire makes a kind of Eccles cake with the leftovers. Crumble the pudding and pack it into a pastry case. Lay a lid over the top, turn it over and roll it lightly. Then cut slashes in the top, gild with egg and milk and sprinkle with sugar. Bake at 375°F/gas 5 for 30–40 minutes until the pastry is crisp and golden. Serve hot for tea.

Devon, rich in dairy products, has its own ideas. Cut the left-over pudding into wedges and put them in a pie-dish, criss-cross fashion like open brickwork. Make an egg custard mixture (say 1 pint of milk, or milk and cream, to 3 eggs) and pour over, so that it fills all the gaps. Put the pudding to bake in a slow oven (300°F/gas 2) for 40 minutes.

26 October 1985

Steamed Puddings for Grown-Ups

The secret of a light steamed pudding, says Mrs Venetia Parkes, my long-time companion-at-stove, is not to beat the daylights out of it when you mix it. What's required are quick fingers rather than muscle and brawn. Last winter Mrs Parkes abandoned crème caramel and chocolate roulade and got stuck into steamed puddings with a vengeance – and her versions are most certainly not for nursery supper. The current favourite is steamed jam pudding served with her own special and very adult version of custard-powder custard. Nanny would not approve.

STEAMED JAM PUDDING

TO SERVE 8 PEOPLE

8 oz flour
2 teaspoons baking powder
4 oz butter
4 oz sugar

2 eggs
¼ pint milk
1 lb jar of jam (damson is best)

Sift the flour with the baking powder. Rub the butter quickly into the flour with the tips of your fingers until the mixture looks like *very* coarse breadcrumbs. Or cut the butter in with a knife if your hands are too warm. Add the sugar. Beat the eggs and stir them in. Mix to a soft dropping consistency with the milk.

Put the whole pound of jam into a 2 pint pudding-basin and spread it up the sides and round the base. The basin need not be greased. Tip in the pudding mixture. Top with a circle of buttered greaseproof paper. Cover the basin with a double layer of aluminium foil well folded over the edges. Place the basin on a piece of wood or an upturned saucer in a large pan with a well-fitting lid.

Pour in boiling water to come just under halfway up the basin – any higher and you risk a soggy boiled pudding rather than a light steamed one. Bring the water back to the boil and then turn the heat down.

Keep at a steady simmer for 1½ hours, checking every 20 minutes or so that the pan has not boiled dry. Keep topping up with boiling water. Unmould on to a hot plate just before you are ready to serve the pudding; it is very good-natured and can be kept warm in its simmering water for as long as convenient.

Treacle can be substituted for the jam – use plenty to give a sticky, slightly caramelized coating to the pudding. Serve both puddings with:

CUSTARD

Make 1 pint custard-powder custard as specified on the packet. Stir in a carton of double cream and a full measure of brandy or whisky. Heat up again, but do not allow it to boil or the alcohol will evaporate and emasculate the mixture.

CASTLE PUDDINGS

These miniature puddings are excellent for a winter dinner-party, particularly to follow a main dish of fish. Light and rich, they are not steamed but baked. Their size makes them less daunting than a full-scale steamed pudding. The sauce would melt the chilblains off Jack Frost himself. Serve something very light and easily prepared as the first course – avocado, perhaps, or a few slices of Parma ham with pears or melon.

The Puddings

TO SERVE 12 PEOPLE

4 oz butter	8 oz flour
4 oz caster sugar	1 teaspoon baking powder
6 oz flour	Grated rind of two lemons
3 eggs	A little milk

Butter 12 dariole moulds or small cake-tins. Beat the butter and sugar together until light and fluffy. Beat in the eggs. Sieve the flour with the baking powder and fold it in. Stir in the grated lemon rind.

Stir in enough milk to soften the mixture so that it drops easily from the spoon.

Divide the mixture between the tins. They should not be more than half-full. Bake at 350°F/gas 4 for 20 minutes. The puddings should round up like little volcanoes. Decant on to a warm plate. Meanwhile make:

The Sauce

The juice of the 2 lemons (whose rind went into the puddings) mixed with same quantity of water.

1 teaspoon cornflour　　　　　　　　*Small glass of whisky*
2 oz sugar　　　　　　　　　　　　　*1 oz unsalted butter*

Dissolve the sugar in the lemon juice and water. Mix the cornflour with a teaspoon of cold water and stir it into the syrup. Cook gently to thicken. Take the pan off the heat and add the butter in small pieces, and then the whisky. Heat again. Pour some round the puddings on a serving-dish. Serve the rest hot in a jug.

BROWN BREAD PUDDING

A good old English bread-and-suet-pudding, sweet-scented and rich. Served with Mrs Parkes's custard there is nothing better for a cold day.

TO SERVE 8 PEOPLE

8 oz brown breadcrumbs　　　　　*1 teaspoon powdered nutmeg*
4 oz prepared suet　　　　　　　　*½ teaspoon powdered cloves*
6 oz dark brown sugar　　　　　　*2 eggs*
1 teaspoon powdered cinnamon　*Small glass of brandy*

Mix the breadcrumbs with the suet, sugar, cinnamon and nutmeg. Beat the eggs with the brandy and stir well into the breadcrumb mixture. If it is not quite moist, add a little water.

Put into a large buttered pudding-basin. Prepare as for *Steamed Jam Pudding*. Boil for 3 hours. Turn out and serve hot with a good custard, or brandy butter.

2 November 1985

Feeling like a Trifle

There are times when only a trifle will do. A proper trifle – I mean no nursery nonsense with packets of jelly and custard and eat-it-up-or-you-can't-get-down sort of travesty of a trifle. I have in mind a scarlet-berried, cream-crowned, custard-bathed, liquor-sodden, almond-sprinkled, crystallized-rose-petal-strewn Waterford-cut-glass-bowlful of trifle.

This trifle is a party trifle. It will serve 8–10 people. When the guests have gone home and it's four o'clock on a frozen winter's morning and the final crumbs of party debris have just been wiped off the table, you can sneak into the larder and eat the last spoonfuls of the trifle straight from the bowl. That is the real moment when only a trifle will do.

OLD-FASHIONED TRIFLE

Polish up your largest and prettiest glass bowl and then assemble the following ingredients. Make the trifle, up to the point when you decorate it, the day before you need it. This allows the flavours to mingle and develop.

For the Trifle

1 lb fresh or frozen raspberries
4 oz caster sugar
1 small spongecake or 6 trifle sponges
½ lb raspberry jam

1 glass medium dry sherry
4 oz macaroons or ratafias
3 whole peaches or 6 halves
1 liqueur-glass Drambuie
1½ pints creamy custard

For Decoration

1 oz crystallized violets
1 oz crystallized rose petals
2 oz blanched almonds

½ pint double cream
1 oz caster sugar
Liqueur-glass Drambuie

The Spongecakes
(These can be bought; there are even 'trifle sponges' on the market.)

4 eggs
4 oz caster sugar

4 oz plain flour

Beat the eggs and the sugar together with an electric beater until they are light, fluffy and *white*. Keep at it twice as long as you think is necessary. Then fold in the flour with a metal spoon. Do this quite firmly – the mixture needs to be 'tired'. Meanwhile, pre-heat the oven to 375°F/gas 5. Butter some small round patty-pans or a cake-tin (line this first). Bake for 15–20 minutes if the cakes are small, double the time for a larger one.

The Custard

(The French call this a *crème anglaise*. You can make it with the powdered mix as long as you use plenty of cream and liquor.)

1 pint milk	6 egg yolks
½ pint cream (double cream is twice as good as single)	1 oz caster sugar
	1 small glass Drambuie

Whisk all the ingredients except the Drambuie together in a heat-proof bowl. Stir over boiling water until the mixture thickens enough to coat the back of the spoon. (Should it curdle, put it in the liquidizer for a moment.) Then add the Drambuie and stir well in. I confess to cheating; I sometimes use 3 whole eggs and a tablespoon of flour instead of the yolks, put the whole lot in the liquidizer with the milk and cream and process until smooth. Then I stir it on a very low direct heat for longer than usual to ensure that the flour is cooked. If it goes lumpy, the liquidizer will solve the problem. Allow to cool before using.

Macaroons
(Can also be bought, but here's how.)

2 egg whites	Rice paper
6 oz ground almonds	10–15 blanched almonds
8 oz caster sugar	

Beat the egg whites lightly (not the full meringue treatment). Stir the almonds and sugar into the egg froth. Work well with your hands until the paste is smooth. Leave to settle for 15 minutes. Then roll about 20–30 little balls with the mixture. Line a baking-sheet with rice paper and dot with the macaroon balls, leaving space between. Flatten each ball with the back of a wooden spoon. Split the almonds and press one into the top of each biscuit. Bake in a moderate oven for 20 minutes at 350°F/gas 4.

Ratafias are made with the same mixture and method, but have an ounce or two of softened butter beaten into them. They should also be smaller and not crowned with the split almond.

To Assemble the Trifle
Sprinkle the raspberries with the caster sugar and set them aside for half an hour to form juice.

Split the spongecake(s) in two and spread one half with the raspberry jam. Sandwich with the other half.

Put the spongecakes in the bottom of the bowl and sprinkle them with the sherry.

Spread the raspberries and their juices over the top.

Cover with a layer of the ratafia biscuits and sprinkle them with the Drambuie.

Slice the peaches and lay them on top.

Pour the cooled custard over all.

Cover over with clingfilm and put in a cool place for 24 hours.

The following day, decorate the trifle with a layer of double cream whipped with the sugar and Drambuie. Scatter the crystallized petals and the blanched almonds over the top.

Sheer pleasure.

4 January 1986

Perfecting the Parfait

Ice-cream did not become widely popular in Britain until the early eighteenth century. The first English 'snow-pit' was installed in 1662 at the Palace of Greenwich, to the order of the newly Restored Charles II. The King may have tasted his first sorbet in Paris during his years of exile, perhaps in the parlour of an Italian ice-cream salesman, Signor Francisco Procopio, a Sicilian entrepreneur who had set up shop in Saint-Germain-des-Prés in 1660 as France's first *limonadier*.

The gentry of England followed the monarch's lead at their leisure. By the time Robert Kerr's blueprint for Victorian architects, *The Gentleman's House, or How to Plan English Residences from the Parsonage to the Palace,* was published in 1865, he found it natural to include plans for ice-houses as necessary offices of the country house. The more sophisticated ice-houses were underground bunkers, snugly floored and thickly roofed, dug close against the cellar's outside wall. Situated thus, there could be a door to allow access to the cook from within the house, and another to allow the estate's iceman to fill the pit with ice dragged up from the lake (created artificially if there lacked a natural water). A well-constructed ice-house packed with ice in mid-winter would remain below freezing-point throughout the summer. The ruins of these buildings, looking not unlike Second World War air-raid shelters, are still to be stumbled on in the grounds of many a rural residence. From the late seventeenth century onwards English cookery-books have included recipes for water-ices and cream-ices.

There are three basic steps in ice-cream making: the preparation of the mixture (which can be as simple as a flavoured syrup or sweetened cream), the freezing and beating to incorporate air, and the hardening. For a fine-grained light ice the mixture must be beaten as it freezes, a process which has encouraged the development of much patent machinery. The mixture to be frozen is put into a metal container, which is placed inside another container into which is layered crushed ice and salt. Salt has the same effect as sugar in lowering the temperature at which water freezes, so the sweeter the mixture the more salt is needed in the freezing-brine. The inner container is then churned either manually or, these days electrically, until the mixture has thickened. Then it is left undisturbed to harden.

On the other hand, I have made perfectly satisfactory ice-cream merely by freezing my chosen mixture in the ice compartment of the fridge. It is important to remember to take the ice-cream out and beat it two or three times as it thickens. In 1943 the *New York Times* reported that American airmen, nostalgic for maple-pecan and chocolate-chip, had an even more rough-and-ready method: they would sling a canful of the right stuff on the underside of a Flying Fortress. It would come home from a high-level bombing raid nicely shaken and frozen solid.

My favourite source for ice-cream mixtures is a slim volume which does much damage to the waistline: *Food for the Greedy* by Nancy Shaw, published in 1936. Mrs Shaw's *Parfait au thé* is particularly good served with brandy snaps.

PARFAIT AU THÉ

Make a syrup with 4 oz sugar boiled for 5 minutes in ½ pint water, and allow it to cool. Put 6 egg yolks into a basin, add to them ½ pint of the syrup and whisk over hot water until the consistency of cream. Take the basin off the hot water and add ¼ pint tea, which should be freshly made and fairly strong. Let the mixture cool, then whip ½ pint cream and stir it into the preparation. Pour into a prepared mould and bury it in ice and salt for 4 hours.

PISTACHIO PARFAIT

½ lb sugar
½ wine-glass water
Whites of 3 eggs
1 teaspoon vanilla essence
1 teaspoon almond essence

1 pint cream
A few drops of green colour
4 oz shelled chopped pistachio nuts

Boil the sugar and water together until the syrup will thread when dropped from the tip of a spoon.

Pour slowly, while beating constantly, on to the whites of the eggs beaten until stiff, and continue the beating until the mixture is stiff. Colour the cream a delicate green, and beat until stiff. Combine the mixtures, add the essences and nut meats, and freeze using 3 parts finely crushed ice to 1 part salt. Mould and pack in ice and salt. Remove from the mould, and surround with whipped cream, sweetened and flavoured with vanilla essence. Sprinkle with chopped pistachio nuts. Delicious.

GLACE À LA GRAPPE DE MUSCAT

Make a pint of rich custard by adding 4 yolks of eggs to 1 pint of milk. Put it on the fire in a double boiler, stirring constantly until the custard thickens and coats the spoon. Sweeten to taste. When cool, mix in 1 pint of lightly whipped cream and a little brandy. Put into a freezing machine and turn until it is frozen all through, then pack it into a bombe mould for 2–3 hours. Before serving, scoop out the centre and fill up with grapes that have been skinned and soaked in brandy. (Good with strawberries or raspberries, too.)

14 June 1986

Sweet Treats from the Nursery

It is usually the small pleasures that loom large in our childhood memories. Little things are the most important – even high drama such as war and its alarms does not have the immediacy of the demise of a pet or the loss of a teddy bear. My elder brother once fried his goldfish when he found it floating belly-up in its bowl one cold morning. He laid it carefully on toast and put it on our mother's breakfast-tray where it shone all gold and sunny like a perfect tiny kipper. Our mother was not at all pleased.

Most of my own early memories have a culinary turn to them. I remember sprinkling powdered ginger on melon in the dining-room of an ocean liner *en route* for Brazil – the unfamiliar peppery taste is much clearer in my mind than the ship itself. Then there was the piano in the nursery. I draped the baby grand with a blanket and played house underneath. I could never manage much more than 'chopsticks' on the keys, but I had a terrific kitchen in full operation beneath the sheltering mahogany: it didn't have any refrigeration, of course, and my experiments had a tendency to ferment rather quickly. The nursery had a tiny proper kitchen attached to it for our nanny to make nursery tea. She was a Scot and she produced wonderful pancakes and scones, soft-boiled eggs with toast soldiers, and sandwiches made with mustard and cress which we were allowed to grow ourselves on an old flannel. Sometimes by request she would make us her special biscuits. They were only Marie biscuits sandwiched together with pink icing sugar but they were delicious. Only Nanny knew the secret of the precise mix of icing sugar and water which would stick the biscuits together without making them soggy.

Her real speciality was puddings. In winter there would be various rice and semolina mixtures. Tapioca was the most interesting; it looked so much like frog-spawn it was almost possible there might be a hatch of tadpoles during the course of the meal. In the summer she would make us junkets and jellies with fruit set into it in kaleidoscope patterns. For special occasions she made a wonderful two-layer lemon pudding, where the solids set to a soft sharp jelly at the bottom and the rest of the mixture floated on top like a fluffy cloud. The times when Nanny made lemon mousse *and* icing-sugar biscuits were red-letter days indeed.

LEMON MOUSSE

TO SERVE 4–6 PEOPLE

1 large lemon or 2 small
1 rounded dessert-spoon powdered
  gelatine
3 small eggs

3 small extra yolks
4 oz caster sugar
¼ pint double cream

Grate the rind of the lemon and squeeze out the juice. Dissolve the gelatine in the lemon juice by warming the mixture gently in a small saucepan.

Put the whole eggs and yolks into a large basin with the sugar, and beat the mixture until it is white and frothy and doubled in volume – this is best done with an electric beater. Eggs and sugar always take twice as long as you expect to achieve the volume. Stir in the gelatine and beat the mixture some more.

Whip the cream until stiff and then fold it in. Pile the mixture into a clear glass bowl and leave it in a cool larder for a few hours to set.

VANILLA JUNKET

SMALL HELPINGS FOR 4 PEOPLE

1 pint milk
1 teaspoon rennet (this can still be
   bought from good chemists and
   grocers)
1 teaspoon caster sugar

1 drop vanilla essence (or a length of
   vanilla pod to infuse in the milk)
¼ pint thick cream
Nutmeg

Warm the milk to blood temperature (that is its natural temperature fresh from the cow: 98°F). Stir in the rennet, the sugar and the vanilla essence. Pour the mixture into either individual glasses or a large glass bowl. Leave to set at room temperature – this will take no more than a couple of hours. Float the cream over the top and grate on a little nutmeg. Wonderful with fresh strawberries or raspberries.

Nanny had a day out once a fortnight when she went to visit her mother in Aylesbury. To console us for her absence she would, when the soft fruit was in season, leave a Summer Pudding for our tea-time treat.

SUMMER PUDDING

TO SERVE 5–6 PEOPLE

½ lb redcurrants
½ lb blackcurrants
1 lb raspberries

4–5 oz sugar
Sliced day-old white bread

Strip the currants from their stalks, and put them in a saucepan with the sugar and the raspberries and a tablespoon of water. Simmer for 5 minutes, until the fruit is soft and has made plenty of juice. Cut the crusts off enough slices of bread to line a small pudding-bowl. The lining should be neatly done, the bread cut to size so that no gaps are left. Pour the hot fruit into the lined bowl, juice and all. Cover with a lid of more crustless sliced bread. Weight with a saucer and a 2 lb tin. Leave in a cool larder at least overnight for the juice to sog into the bread. Turn out on to a white plate, and serve with thick yellow cream.

12 July 1986

Layers of Summer in the Filo

A flour–water paste comes in many guises, as befits the human race's most primitive and available meal. Centuries of research and development have gone into perfecting its preparation. A. W. Kinglake, Victorian traveller besotted as were most of his travelling contemporaries with the romance of Arabia, watched his heroes preparing their desert meal.

> The Arabs adhere to those ancestral principles of bread-baking which have been sanctioned by the experience of ages. The very first baker of bread that ever lived must have done his work exactly as the Arab does at this day. He takes some meal and holds it out in the hollow of his hands, while his comrade pours over it a very few drops of water; he then mashes up the moistened flour into a paste, which he pulls into small pieces, and thrusts it into the embers. His way of baking exactly resembles the craft or mystery of roasting chestnuts as practised by children. . . .

It was in all likelihood (historians being vague on these important matters) the sophisticated cooks of India who first showed that Arab baker's ancestor how to roll out his simple paste until it was as fine as a cotton sari, then to spread the transparent sheets with ghee or oil, stuff them with nuts and honey or delicate little mixtures of meat and spices, and fry or bake the result into delicious pastries fit for the table of the Sultan of the Ottoman Empire. Frozen filo pastry is now, thanks in no small measure to our immigrant Cypriot population, quite widely available in Britain's supermarkets and delicatessens. Filo can be defrosted swiftly for use – half an hour in warm weather is ample. Those sheets which are required immediately can be taken off the roll; the rest refreezes well.

FILO MILLE-FEUILLE

Filo-plus-butter can be used to replace commercially prepared puff pastry – particularly for sweet pastries such as a *mille-feuille* in which the taste of butter is important. The following method can also be used to make pie-crusts and meat or fish *en croûte*. Remember that filo cooks faster than puff pastry.

1 packet filo pastry
3–4 oz butter
½ pint double cream

Icing sugar
½ lb raspberry, strawberry or
   redcurrant jam

You will need 8–10 layers of filo to achieve the usual thickness required for puff pastry. Melt 2–3 oz of butter in a small saucepan and provide yourself with a pastry-brush. Lay the first sheet of filo on to a buttered baking-tray. Lay a second sheet lightly over it and then brush it with melted butter. (Avoid using the milky deposit of whey at the bottom.) Lay on another sheet, and another on that. Then a layer of butter, and so on until you have used up half the filo. Light fingers all the way, so that as much air is left between the layers as possible. Repeat the operation on a second baking-tray with the rest of the filo.

Bake the two sheets of pastry in a moderate oven at 375°F/gas 5 for 15–20 minutes, until the leaves are well risen and golden brown. Transfer them carefully to a wire rack to cool.

Meanwhile, whip the cream. Sieve in a little icing sugar (very little – the jam is quite sweet enough already).

When you are ready for the dessert, spread one of the now-cooled sheets of pastry with the jam. Pile the sweetened whipped cream on top. Lay the second pastry-sheet over all. Dredge thickly with icing sugar. Eat the *mille-feuille* immediately – a lovely delicate pastry which waits for no man.

BERRY BUTTERFLIES

An airy pastry from the kitchen of Werner Matt, star chef at the Hilton in Vienna. This *nouvelle-cuisine*-inspired offspring of the Austrian passion for cream and pastry is really a lighter version of the *mille-feuille* recipe above. It is particularly suitable for our beautiful English summer berries.

TO SERVE 4–6 PEOPLE

1 packet filo pastry
½ pint whipping cream
1 heaped tablespoon thick yoghurt
Icing sugar

1 lb berries – raspberries,
   blackcurrants, redcurrants,
   blueberries, small strawberries
   (wild or the larger ones cut into
   small pieces), whatever your
   garden grows. Two or three
   different sorts is best.

Using a pastry-cutter with a 3 inch diameter, cut out 24–30 discs of single-layer filo pastry and lay as many of these medallions as will fit without overlapping on to a baking-tray (it is not necessary to grease the tray). Heat the oven to 350°F/gas 5. Put the pastry to bake in batches for the 3–4 minutes necessary to turn the delicate discs crisp and golden. When they are done, pile them on a wire rack to cool.

Meanwhile whip the cream and fold in the yoghurt. Sweeten it lightly. Pick over the berries. When you are ready for dessert, assemble the pastries directly on the individual plates. First lay down one disc of pastry, then a layer of cream and berries, then a pastry-disc, then a layer of cream and berries, and so on until you have a delicate little striped tower of alternating pastry, cream and berries. Dredge the top of each with icing sugar.

Eat the butterflies immediately. They are as ephemeral as their namesakes.

26 July 1986

Breads and Cakes

Bread for All Seasons

White jasmine, hayfields and new-baked bread are my favourite summer scents. Of these, only the bread can be reproduced in the cold of winter.

Making bread is not really cooking at all. It is a much more primitive pleasure – campfire-in-the-mouth-of-the-cave, survival-in-the-teeth-of-tigers stuff. There's a satisfaction in it, a feeling of beating the odds, of ancient millstones grinding. The original bread was a flat cake made of flour and water baked on hot stones or roasted over the coals on a forked stick: the most ancient 'made dish' in the world. Pliny the letter-writer, lecturing a friend on the hierarchy of Roman society, explained that he should know his place by the colour of his bread – the more lowly, the darker and more full of husk and weed. Beware, all upper-crust eaters of wholemeal buns.

Clear a good working-space on the table. Bread-making takes a deal of elbow-room. Mrs Beeton is content to quote Eliza Acton's recipe: Take a quartern (3½ lbs) of flour, some salt and nearly a quart of milk or milk and water, one ounce of fresh yeast (half if dried). Tip the flour into a large bowl – if the flour feels cold to the touch, put it in the lowest possible oven for half an hour to warm. All your utensils and ingredients should be around blood temperature, warm and comfortable for the yeast to thrive. Anything that would scald you will do the same to the little organisms. Mix the yeast into a cupful of warm milk and water: the yeast will miraculously liquefy into its bath. Dried yeast takes an extra 20 minutes to start working. Mix 2 teaspoons of salt into the warm flour and make a well in the middle with your hand. Add a pint of warm water to the yeast liquid and pour it into the well, sprinkling a handful of the flour over the top for the yeast's appetite. Cover and leave in a warm place for half an hour to set the sponge.

The mixture is now ready for kneading. Have beside you another pint of warm water. Draw the dry flour into the now bubbling well with your hand, adding more water as you need it to slake the flour, until it all sticks together in a soft thick mass. If the dough is too hard, it cannot expand properly. Tip it out on to the floured table and push and pummel it with your fingers and the heel of your hand, folding the dough back in on itself, pulling it out and giving it a thorough working until it is elastic. You will develop a lovely soothing rhythm which becomes quite addictive. When the dough is smooth and shiny, fold it into a cushion with the tucks underneath and replace it in the bowl. Cover the bowl with a clean damp cloth and put in a warm place for an hour to double in size. Experience will tell you where and how long; but I put mine in a cold oven with a tray of boiling water beneath. It is ready when it will hold the mark of a finger pushed into it. Now tip your beautiful puff-ball on to the floured table and punch it with your fist. This process is called knocking down. The idea is to distribute the carbon dioxide manufactured by the yeast evenly through the dough. Fold the edges over into the hole you have made with your fist, pulling and punching with your knuckles, and repeat several times. Cut the dough in half with a sharp knife and shape with your knuckles into two smaller cushions. The mixture has already begun to take on the delightful spongy resilience of fresh bread.

Leave the dough to expand while the oven heats to 425°F/gas 7. Grease and dust with flour two 2 lb bread-tins. (If you have no tins, bake your bread as oversize round buns on a greased baking-tray.) Take the two halves and press each gently into a tin, easing the dough into the corners with your knuckles. Allow them to rise until their bulk has doubled again and they fill the pans to the top. Now bake the loaves in the high heat for 15 minutes to seal the crust and finish the fermenting process, then turn the heat down a little to 400°F/gas 6 and bake for another 30 minutes. When the bread is cooked, it will fall easily out of the tin, and the base will sound hollow when you tap it. Dry the unmoulded loaves in the oven for five minutes, upside down. Take them out, rub the tops with butter paper for a shine and cool them on a wire rack. The aroma fills the house. Winter turns to summer. The tigers creep away.

25 May 1985

Manna at the Bishop's Table

Bishops bake the best bread. After ten days of short commons in Romania, which followed ten days of even shorter commons in Bulgaria, Bishop's Bread seemed nothing short of manna from heaven. When I set out in October on a gastronomic tour of Eastern Europe – punctuated, I planned, by a daily picnic lunch acquired in the local markets – nobody warned me that bread is rationed. Only the tourist hotels are exempt – their restaurant waiters recycle rock-hard little bread rolls indefinitely, lobbing them up and down the dining-room like Ottoman cannonballs at the siege of Cluj.

It is very difficult to make a picnic if you can't buy bread. In Eastern Europe ready money, even hard currency, is no help. What you need is coupons – and coupons I didn't have. The only alternatives for lunch, provincial eating-houses, were either shut or offered liquid refreshment only. Neither the local white alcohol, plum *tuica* (around 110 per cent proof), nor the weedy local beer is any substitute for the staff of life. My one attempt to beg, borrow or bribe a contraband yeast-cake *babka* from a cartload on its way to a peasant wedding in Transylvania might have been crowned with success had it not been for the last-minute intervention of the bridegroom's mother-in-law. So at midday for three weeks I subsisted on gleanings from the hotel breakfast-table garnished with a dwindling supply of paprika-crusted pemmican bought in the market in Istan-

214

bul (those were palmy days). Three weeks like that can leave a person hungry.

Hence my strong feelings for Bishop's Bread. A traveller in late nineteenth-century Romania had commended to me, via his memoirs, the market-square in Sibiu as fertile ground for picnic supplies. The gentleman promised a cornucopia of local produce on market-day. He listed smoked cheeses, mountain hams and mounds of beautiful vegetables – all brought into the town on picturesque carts drawn by teams of water-buffalo. Some remnant of past glories, I felt, must still remain. By a circuitous route (to be honest, the good offices of the British embassy in Bucharest) I secured an introduction to the wife of the Lutheran Bishop of Sibiu. Frau Klein, a sprightly great-grandmother, is, as might be expected from her name and faith, a Saxon. Not only do the Romanian Saxons have blond hair and blue eyes, and speak and educate their children in Saxon German, but they eat and drink in Saxon, too. They have done so in Sibiu and seven neighbouring villages for 800 years: an ancient island of northern virtue lapped for centuries by waves of unreliable southerners.

Frau Klein, being the bishop's wife, bakes a Saxon Bishop's Bread – for which I shall be eternally grateful, since the very evening I arrived in Sibiu she hospitably invited me to supper and served it at the end of the meal. Not even the arrival of a brace of water-buffalo and a whole sheepskin full of salty ewe's cheese in the market the following morning can dim the memory of this manna from a Lutheran heaven.

BISHOP'S BREAD

2 oz each of hazelnuts, walnuts and   *1 lemon*
almonds; or any nut combination,   *4 oz butter*
as long as the total quantity is 6 oz   *4 oz caster sugar*
2 oz each of dried figs, dates and glacé   *2 eggs*
cherries; or a total of 6 oz of   *4 oz self-raising flour*
whatever dried fruits you please

Skin and roughly chop the nuts as appropriate. Pick over the dried fruit. Halve the cherries and chop the dates and figs. Toss them in a little of the flour so that they do not sink in the cooking. Grate the lemon peel, then squeeze the lemon juice. Butter a 1 lb oblong bread-tin, lining the base with greaseproof paper.

Soften the butter in a warm bowl. Beat in the sugar. Go on beating until the mixture is fluffy and pale. Beat the eggs. It's funny how frequently the mixture splits: if it does so, stir in a spoonful of flour and carry on beating in the eggs. Fold in the rest of the flour. Stir in the lemon juice; there is a high proportion of fruit to go in, so the mixture must be on the soft side. You may even need a little milk as well.

Fold in the nuts and dried fruits. Drop the mixture into the baking-tin, building it up a little where it touches the sides so that you get a loaf-like cake which is not too high in the middle.

Bake in a moderate oven (350–75°F/gas 4–5) for 45 minutes, until the cake has shrunk from the sides of the tin, feels firm to your finger and has stopped hissing steam. (I find noises are important in the kitchen.)

A particularly good late-night cake – to be taken on a cold winter's midnight with a glass of mulled wine, perhaps after Christmas Mass.

17 December 1985

Wherein the Proof of the Cake

My Aunt Betty had a terrific wedding cake. I was only five at the time but I remember it vividly. It was a sugar Cinderella coach, driven by a sugar coachman and drawn by four prancing sugar horses. Through the windows could be seen the tiny bride in a tulle wedding dress of spun sugar decorated with pink sugar roses. Beside her sat her prim little sugar bridegroom. The coach was balanced on four beautiful sugar wheels with spokes. From the eaves swung four tiny sugar lanterns, each one glazed with scarlet

Cellophane. The moulding on the coachwork would have delighted Ludwig of Bavaria. It was magical.

The pastry chef responsible was a Frenchman, trained in the old school of Carême, architect in sugar extraordinary. Maître Carême himself served his apprenticeship making exquisite *pièces montées* for M. Talleyrand who, on leaving for the Congress of Vienna, declared to his employer, the gourmet Louis XVII: 'Sire, I have more need of casseroles than of written instructions.' For a time Carême's creations graced the table of the then Consul Napoleon, until he transferred his talents to the kitchens of the Prince Regent at Brighton, then to Tsar Alexander of Russia, and so on through the crowned heads of Europe, until he alighted on his final and perfect patron, the baron de Rothschild. His disciple, the creator of my Aunt Betty's wedding cake, was a young man on his way to the stars. He, too, was an artist in marzipan flowers and sugar fantasies. I believe he went on to the top of his profession, but this surely was his *chef d'œuvre*.

The ceremony of the cutting of the cake, the moment for the demolition of the masterpiece, arrived. I pushed my way at knee-level through striped trousers and silk stockings to the front of the audience. Together the real bride and groom plunged the knife into their miniature counterparts. I naturally expected a flock of singing larks to fly out, or at the very least a cascade of rose petals. Instead the beautiful coach was reduced in an instant to a plate of neat squares of perfectly ordinary cake, which swiftly disappeared among the guests. When the plate came round to me, I searched anxiously in the debris for a wisp of tulle, a sugar rose. There was nothing. Not even a scrap of scarlet from the tiny lantern. The cake, a kind of pale dry sponge, had crumbled to an edible heap of dust. All the pleasure had been in the wrapping.

This may explain my adult taste for cakes when all the pleasure is in the eating. There is one in particular which I serve as a pudding. It is the very antithesis of my aunt's wedding cake. Plain and un-adorned, it looks like a large flat puffy brown pancake, but it tastes wonderful.

ALMOND CAKE

TO SERVE 8–10 PEOPLE

6 eggs
8 oz sugar
8 oz ground almonds
2 lemons
2 ten-inch shallow cake-tins

Knob of butter
1 small glass whisky, Cointreau or
kirsch
Extra 2 oz sugar

Beat the eggs with the sugar until they are white and fluffy. This takes five minutes longer than you think is necessary and is easiest to do with a large electric beater like a Kenwood.

Grate the lemon rind on the fine grater. Squeeze the lemons of their juice. Grease the baking-tins with butter and line the bases with a circle of greased paper. Heat the oven to 375°F/gas 5.

Fold the ground almonds and the grated lemon peel gently but thoroughly with a metal spoon into the beaten egg and sugar. Fold in half the lemon juice at the same time. Turn the mixture into the two tins. Bake for 30–40 minutes until well risen but not dried out. Allow to rest before turning out. The cakes will shrink as all spongecakes do, but the almonds will keep them moist.

Meanwhile make a syrup with the rest of the lemon juice, an equal quantity of water and the sugar. Add the liqueur and pour the syrup all over the still-warm cakes.

Serve with a bowl of fresh fruit in juice – perhaps fresh pineapple in the winter or strawberries in the summer. The pudding needs no cream, but if you could just manage a sugar Cinderella coach with scarlet-windowed lanterns to balance delicately on the top it would be perfection indeed.

30 March 1985

The Easter Simnel in Full Fig

Buns marked with the Cross of Good Friday have now been on sale in certain supermarkets for at least two months, surely the longest Good Friday in history. Give a marketing man a molehill and you end up with a bun mountain. The Easter Simnel, a fruit cake baked with a layer of marzipan in the middle, is still relatively unexploited. The cake was particularly popular in the eighteenth and nineteenth centuries when young girls in domestic service were permitted to bake one to take home to their mothers on Mothering Sunday – a festival which falls on the fourth Sunday in Lent and was initially designed to honour the Mother Church in Jerusalem. The cake was then kept for three weeks to be eaten on Easter Sunday.

There are several theories about the origin of the name, the most mundane being that it comes from the old French–Latin word *simila*, meaning 'fine flour'. Another one, local to Shropshire, is that the cake was first made by an old couple called Simon and Nell who couldn't agree whether to boil it or bake it. They finally settled on a combination of the two, and the name was a similar compromise. My own favourite is that the cake originated with master-baker Simnel, father of the famous Lambert – pretender to the throne of Henry VII. As pretenders go, Lambert Simnel had a good run for his money. Funded by Margaret of Burgundy, his putative aunt, he managed to convince the Irish of his credentials and had himself crowned in Dublin as Edward VI. He then made his way to Britain with 2,000 German mercenaries to lay his claim there. The adventure was ended at Stoke Field in Nottinghamshire by Henry VII – victor, two years earlier, at the battle of Bosworth, and not a man likely to feel threatened by a stripling and a rabble of foreigners. The king disposed of the mercenaries and offered young Lambert a job in the royal kitchens, a position more suited to the lad's work-experience, which he accepted with alacrity. It seems quite proper that the name of Simnel should be commemorated in a cake whose origins are as mysterious as the pretender's own.

Simnel cake was originally made with dried figs – those familiar pagan fertility symbols. The almond paste balls used to decorate the top signified seeds for rebirth. They are now transformed into the eleven apostles who founded the Church. The Church of course has always had a way with such problems: the Easter egg underwent a similar conversion. Here is an ecumenical version which keeps the figs and crowns them with the apostles. If you can make it a few days before Easter, it will improve with the keeping.

ECUMENICAL SIMNEL CAKE

For the Almond Paste

12 oz ground almonds	*3 egg yolks, or 1 egg and 1 yolk*
12 oz icing and caster sugar mixed	

Knead the ingredients together thoroughly to make a stiff paste. Cut off a small piece to make the decorative balls and put aside. Divide the rest in half and roll out into two 8-inch circles. Do not use made-up 'marzipan icing' – it lacks the egg and will melt in the cooking.

For the Cake

2 oz whole almonds	*4 eggs*
6 oz chopped figs	*6 oz self-raising flour*
6 oz chopped stoned dates	*Grated peel and juice of 1 orange*
6 oz raisins	*½ teaspoon cinnamon*
4 oz crystallized peel	*½ teaspoon nutmeg*
6 oz butter	*Apricot jam*
6 oz soft brown sugar	

Grease and line with paper a deep round 8-inch cake-tin. Chop the almonds roughly and pick over the fruit, checking for little bits of stalk and pips. Sprinkle a tablespoonful of flour and toss the fruit in it (this helps prevent it sinking to the bottom of the cake). Beat the sugar and butter together until light and fluffy – the more you beat, the easier it is to incorporate the eggs without the mixture separating. Beat in the eggs one by one; if the mixture *does* curdle, stir in a spoonful of flour. Sieve the flour with the spices and fold them in. Fold in the fruit, nuts, spices and grated orange peel. Stir in enough orange juice to give a soft mixture which drops easily from the spoon. Spread half the cake mixture in the bottom of the tin and lay a circle of marzipan over it. Cover with rest of the cake mixture and bake for 2½–3 hours at 300–25°F/gas 2–3.

Allow the cake a few minutes to settle and then turn it out and peel off the paper. When it is cool, spread with apricot jam and lay the second layer of marzipan on the top. Decorate with eleven marzipan balls – Judas having disqualified himself by now. Put under a hot grill for a moment or two to gild the top.

6 April 1985

The Crokers of Saffron Walden

From the fourteenth century until the end of the eighteenth century the Crokers of Saffron Walden earned their living from the cultivation of the saffron crocus. *Crocus sativus* was probably originally cultivated by levantine crokers based on Corycus in southern Turkey. The Phoenicians introduced it to Europe: they had such a

taste for the spice they planted it wherever they went, and with particular success in Spain and Italy. The dried stamens – the operative part of the plant – reached Britain first in the saddle-packs of returning Knights of Jerusalem. These adventurous gastronomes also presented their countrymen with sugar cane and oranges – the raw material for marmalade.

By the fourteenth century the saffron crocus was well established as a profitable cash crop in the eastern counties of England. The croker's work was laborious: a quarter of a million flowers are needed to produce a pound of dried saffron. The sixteenth-century geographer Richard Hakluyt suggested the industry was so labour-intensive that its encouragement could go a long way towards solving the unemployment problem – a major preoccupation of his day as well as of our own. Someone should tackle the YOP-schemers and EEC grant-givers on the matter. The resulting saffron mountain would be not only romantic but also delightfully soporific: there is a report from a contemporary historian of Alexander the Great that the conqueror's army slumbered long in the scented air of the crocus-clad slopes of a mountain in Kashmir. Presumably any would-be ambushers were similarly afflicted.

John Evelyn seemed to think saffron a bit of a foreign habit:

> Nor here should I omit [the mentioning at least of] Saffron, of which German Housewives have a way of forming in Balls, by mingling it with a little Honey, which throughly dried, they reduce to Powder, and sprinkle it over their Sallets for a noble Cordial. Those of Spain and Italy, we know, generally make use of this Flower, mingling its golden Tincture with almost everything they eat.

Alas, by the practical nineteenth century East Anglian labour was otherwise employed. E. S. Dallas, author of *Kettner's Book of the Table* (1877), mourns the disappearance of the saffron industry:

> It is the elegiac muse that ought to write the account of saffron, for its glory is departed. The stigmas of this autumnal crocus were once all important in European cookery, and were supposed to possess the rarest virtues and attractions. . . . There was a time when England was known as merry England, and Lord Bacon in his *History of Life and Death* says 'The English are rendered sprightly by a liberal use of saffron in sweetmeats and broth'.

Saffron cakes are still baked in Devon and Cornwall, but there they now include sugar, raisins and spices. The original East Anglian saffron cake was not sweet. It was a rich bread dough in which a pungent infusion of saffron was the only flavouring.

SAFFRON BREAD

A pinch of saffron
½ pint water
¼ pint milk
2 lb strong white flour
1 teaspoon salt

1 oz fresh yeast (½ oz dried)
1 teaspoon sugar
2 oz butter
2 eggs

Put the saffron to soak in a little boiling water. Crush it with the back of a spoon or liquidize to release the brilliant yellow colour and warm flavour. The quality of the saffron and your own taste will dictate how much you need to use.

Warm the flour in a large bowl and mix in the salt. Dissolve the yeast in a cupful of the warm water with a teaspoon of sugar. Make a well in the flour and pour the yeast mixture in. Sprinkle a little flour over and leave for 20 minutes to set the sponge.

Melt the butter, beat the eggs. Strain the saffron liquid into the rest of the water and milk (warmed) and work it, with the eggs and butter, into the flour. Knead thoroughly until the dough is smooth and buttercup yellow. Use a little more flour if it is too wet. Leave to rise in a warm place (a seal of clingfilm over the bowl ensures a good damp warmth). After an hour or so, when the dough is well risen, knock the dough down again by kneading thoroughly. Shape into a round cushion. Put to rise for another half-hour on a baking-tray.

Brush the top with a little beaten egg or milk. Bake the bread in a moderate oven (400°F/gas 6) for 40 minutes. Delicious with butter and honey last thing at night. You might even dream of Alexander's sleeping army.

20 July 1985

Grandmother's Waterglass Cake

My paternal grandmother was born and bred in Edinburgh. Not only did she save string, she knotted stray lengths together and wound them on to a huge ball which she kept in the kitchen dresser. She also saved silver paper and aluminium bottle-tops, although I never did find out why.

Nothing frivolous was allowed in her kitchen, and it seemed to me, when my brother and I spent a school holiday with her, that nothing was ever thrown away. There was always a huge cauldron on the back of the stove into which she tossed stale bread, vegetable peelings, plate-scrapings – anything which could be boiled down into her thick pungent chicken-mash. Whatever that pot contained, it always smelt of old cabbage – like school corridors.

The recipients of this daily feast were her pride and joy. They were not, as might be expected, a flock of sober-feathered hard-laying egg-heads. They were the avian equivalent of a troupe of can-can dancers: a flock of fluffy brown flirts with scarlet combs and Folies Bergère backsides frilled with extravagant marmalade-gold feathers.

My grandmother took a steaming bucket of mash out to her girls morning and evening. She stood stern and tall in the roomy chicken-run, addressing her charges by name, knee-deep in the be-plumed and clucking chorus line. Sometimes I was allowed to fetch the eggs whose triumphant arrival had been announced *fortissimo* at intervals throughout the day. First the little wooden-flapped nest-boxes, each equipped with a china egg for encouragement, had to be inspected. One or two of the compartments usually housed a broody hen – there was one in particular called Mabel who could give a very nasty nip when you felt under her breast feathers for the fruits of her labours. Then I would climb the slatted wooden plank which served as the ladder up to the roost. There were always a few early-to-bed birds inside, fluffed up on their perches and keeping a single beady eye on me as I rustled through the straw looking for stray eggs, but the real triumph was to find an egg tucked behind a clump of grass or nestling under a bush in the big run outside.

Sometimes the eggs had double yolks of a glorious deep orange. These were put aside for our soft-boiled breakfast eggs, eaten with toast soldiers. If there was a glut, my grandmother painted the eggs with waterglass to preserve them, and packed them into a barrel which she stored in the cellar. When she made cakes with preserved eggs, she always cracked each one separately into a cup in case it had gone bad. Occasionally it had, and we would run from the kitchen before the smell overwhelmed us. There was one particularly delicious cake she made using waterglass eggs and the lemons which were newly back on the postwar market. Butter was still rationed at the time, so she substituted margarine. The cake was always wonderful and it became even better when she was able to use butter and fresh eggs, but we never got around to changing the name.

LEMON CAKE

The idea behind the cake is very simple. Weigh the eggs and take the same weight in sugar and butter and flour. Allow two eggs for every 3 people. Medium eggs weigh around 2 oz, so I give quantities assuming a 2 oz egg.

8 oz caster sugar	*1 teaspoon baking powder*
8 oz butter (or margarine)	*1 lemon*
4 eggs	*4 oz icing sugar*
8 oz flour	

Beat the sugar and butter together until they are white and fluffy. This always takes far longer than you expect. I used to beat it until my arms ached. If my grandmother was still not satisfied, I had to find my brother and make him take over. With today's electric mixers it has become much easier.

Sieve the flour with the baking powder. Grate the rind of the lemon. Line a rectangular baking-tin with greaseproof paper.

Beat the eggs into the sugar-and-butter mixture. If it curdles, stir in a spoonful of flour and continue to add the eggs. Fold in the flour and the grated lemon rind. The mixture should be soft enough to drop from the spoon. If not, add a little milk. Put the mixture into the cake-tin.

Bake at 350°F/gas 4 for 1 hour. Let it settle in the tin for 5 minutes, then turn it out on to a wire rack and let it cool.

Meanwhile squeeze the lemon and mix the juice with the icing sugar to make a sharp lemon icing. Spread this over the cake when it is cool. Serve the cake cut into squares.

19 October 1985

Making a Hole in the Mint

A garden in Northamptonshire for which once I was responsible had at one end of it an orchard with apples and plum trees. They fruited every year with embarrassing profligacy. However frantically I bottled and pickled and baked, I could never seem to keep up with the autumn fecundity.

Beyond the orchard half-hidden behind a thick screen of nettles, was another source of equal delight and embarrassment: an abandoned vegetable-patch. Since I was a weekend-only custodian, the vegetable-patch had perforce to remain abandoned. Although the previous incumbent, a farmer, had taken his greenhouse, his soft-fruit bushes and everything movable with him, a few stalwarts, long favourites of the English kitchen garden, had managed to survive and multiply among the weeds.

Mint-beds, parsley plants and rhubarb crowns, like old soldiers, never die. My household can manage a great deal of parsley, and the rhubarb leaves and flowering heads sprawling along the red-brick wall were decorative enough to justify their presence. It was the discharge of my responsibility to the burgeoning mint-patch which exercised me almost as much as the prodigal apples and plums. The more obvious uses – saucing the lamb, flavouring the peas and new potatoes, and decorating the odd glass of Pimm's – seemed to make no appreciable difference to the ever-spreading greenery. More drastic measures had to be found.

MOROCCAN MINT TEA

This goes through the mint-patch faster than anything. You will need a thick glass tumbler for each person, plus 4–5 sprigs of mint. Wash the mint. Put at least 1 heaped teaspoon of sugar in each tumbler – Arabs like their sweet things twice as sweet. Now there are several options open to you: either make a pot of weak tea, leaving it to stand for 2–3 minutes only, and then pour the tea over the mint leaves in each glass. Or add a few leaves of green tea and a long spoon to each glass, then pour boiling water over the leaves. Or make it with no tea, just the mint and, if you like, a slice of lemon. Deliciously refreshing.

ECCLES CAKES

Eccles cakes, today made with raisins, were originally made with mint leaves and fresh blackcurrants. They were called squashed-fly cakes by generations of English children including my own.

1 lb shortcrust or puff pastry   *A good handful mint leaves*
  (home-made with pure lard is best)   *4 oz sugar*
1 lb blackcurrants   *1–2 oz butter*

Make the pastry and leave it to rest. Strip the blackcurrants from their little branches and pick them over. Roughly chop the mint leaves. Put the currants and the mint into a bowl with the sugar, and mix all together thoroughly.

Roll out the pastry to a thickness of about ¼ inch. Cut out rounds with a 4 inch diameter. Put a teaspoon of the fruit mixture and a tiny piece of butter on each round. Gather the edges of the pastry together to enclose the filling. Turn the bundle over so the ends are underneath, and put them on a baking-sheet. Flatten each cake with the rolling-pin so that you can see a few bumps of dark berry through the pastry. Cut a cross in the top for the steam to escape.

Bake in a hot oven at 425°F/gas 7 for 10–15 minutes, until puffed and golden. Sprinkle the cakes with sugar.

These are wake-cakes for high days and holy days. Eat them warm and crisp, accompanied by a glass of ice-cold sweet white wine (Muscat de Beaume de Venise would be perfect) to round off a summer supper.

BILBERRY AND MINT TARTS

An old Lancashire trick which confirms the affinity of mint and berries, this recipe is recommended by Dorothy Hartley in *Food in England* (published first in 1954, but now happily reprinted by Macdonald) when making 'fruit between two skins'. First collect a pound or two of bilberries from the moors or the greengrocer. Then line your tart-tin(s) with your best shortcrust pastry. Spread in a layer of the fluffy white pulp of a baked apple or two. Cover all with a thick layer of bilberries – the juice runs in the cooking and the apple will absorb all the delicious dark liquid. Sprinkle with sugar and scatter the mint leaves over the top. Cover with a lid of pastry. Cut a hole in the top for escaping steam. Bake in a hot oven (400°F/gas 6) for 30–40 minutes. Serve sprinkled with more sugar, and hand round a bowl of thick cream.

9 August 1986

Chutneys, Jams and Pickles

Secrets

Macbeth's witches, practised purveyors of eye of newt and toe of frog, knew how to keep an audience guessing. Anyone could chuck in the old wool of bat. What they didn't list, of course, was the Secret Ingredient which actually made the whole thing work. The cauldron has simmered a long while since then and alchemy removed itself to the chemist's laboratory. Rather a pity, that – I would prefer toe of frog to Permitted Additive No. 315B any day.

Secret Ingredients usually manifest themselves by accident. They are often triggered by some culinary disaster, a shortage of a listed ingredient, or anything that stimulates a cook to invention. I have a habit of basting what I'm cooking with a glass of whatever I'm drinking – which has produced some unusual results in its time. It brings me to the matter of the ship's cook on the Greek magnate's yacht.

In the high old days when the Salle Privée in the Monte Carlo Casino played host to more royals than there are in a pack of cards, there were usually a few millionaires' yachts, too big to come into harbour, moored out in the roads. One of these belonged to a Greek tycoon then famous for his liaison with an opera singer. My grandfather was the Greek's companion-in-arms at the *chemin de fer* tables, and I (thirteen at the time) was bidden accompany my grandmother to dine with the two gamblers and the diva on the yacht. Left to my own devices on the floating palace before dinner, I went exploring and found the galley. The ship's cook was making the mayonnaise to accompany a mound of pink whiskery prawns. On the table beside him was what he described as a bottle of the Secret Ingredient. I haven't told on him until now, but here is:

230

GIN PALACE MAYONNAISE

Make your usual mayonnaise by hand, seasoning with lemon juice, salt, and a shake of tabasco. When the mayonnaise is really thick, add the galley-cook's Secret Ingredient: a shot from the gin-bottle. The juniper flavour is magnificent with shellfish.

TEA GRAVY

Tea is an interestingly versatile brew. I know of three tricks with it. The first was an accidental discovery. I like my gravy for a roast to be dark and rich in colour. Commercial gravy browning is likely to include Permitted Colouring C598 or whatever, Bovril is too harsh, soy sauce tastes of itself, and reliance solely on the little bits of caramelized meat in the bottom of the roasting-tin is risky. Nor will red wine do; it turns the mixture the shade of a bruised Victoria plum. The answer, believe me, is tea. Cold tea, hot tea, Lapsang Suchong, whatever you please, a quick slug of it into a pallid gravy works miracles.

BOSTON TEA

The second sleight-of-hand with tea is to use a good strong brew as the basis of a fruit punch – an American secret.

> 2 pints hot tea
> 1 pint fresh orange juice
> Juice of 3 lemons
> ½ pint boiling water
>
> 4 heaped spoons of sugar or honey
> Ginger ale

Mix all together while hot. Then chill. Serve iced, diluted with equal quantities ginger ale. Any and all experimentation is permissible – passion-fruit juice, grenadine, sprigs of mint – as long as the tea remains the base.

My third tea trick is a dye: a boil-up in a strong brew will turn anything, from boiled eggs to silk ribbons, a delicate shade of tan. There are moments in life when such knowledge can be extremely useful.

A few further Secret Ingredients have come my way. A tiny pinch of curry powder in the salad dressing is nearly as good as walnut oil. A single scented geranium leaf brewed in a fruit salad imparts a heady fragrance to the whole dish. And a brand-new one, on the wave of interest in Chinese cooking at home: ginger wine makes a good substitute for fresh ginger in a marinade or sauce.

Sometimes, nostalgic for Mediterranean markets, I make a big glass jar of preserved peppers to keep in the fridge. Just a spoonful can give a rich glow, both in taste and in colour, to a stew or a salad – but is best of all spooned straight on to a slice of hot fresh bread. The very sight of the scarlet flesh and golden oil will brighten the darkest winter day.

SCARLET PEPPER CONSERVE

2 lb scarlet capsicum peppers   *6 cloves garlic*
1 pint olive oil

The peppers can be peeled after being lightly roasted under the grill to loosen the skin. Sometimes I don't bother to peel them. Now slice them and de-seed them. Warm the oil in a pan and put in the peppers and whole cloves of garlic. Stew them *gently* (they should never fry) until soft (half an hour or so). Pack the whole lot into a jar.

All of which of course is secret. So read this in private. Then tear out the page, chew it up and swallow it.

2 February 1985

Hit for Six by Lemons

Auriol von Wachtel, expatriate Hungarian aristocrat (second-class, he felt bound to explain), was indirectly responsible for my introduction to the salt-cured lemon.

Auriol's nomadic life had provided him with a number of skills, the most marketable of which was an inventive hand with machinery. He was a sort of short round Roland Emmett, with a preference for short round devices. Soon after his arrival in our small community in southern Spain, a beautiful Englishwoman decided to build herself a romantic love-nest in the hills above us.

The view – of the Straits of Gibraltar with the ochre and blue hills

232

of Morocco beyond – was spectacular. The aristocratic (second-class) Auriol was given the job of overseeing the building. His brief was simple. Everything in the house was to be hexagonal: the rooms, the swimming-pool, even the tiles and plates. A hexagonal is close enough to a round square, and Auriol set to work with passion.

The local labour force was summoned, and the house rose swiftly. Within three months even the hexagonal flowerbeds were ready to be planted. Auriol himself provided the building's crowning glory. For the hexagonal dining-room he designed a wonderful clockwork levitating table – as six-sided as the wine-glasses specially made to grace it. The English lady cabled news of her imminent arrival and instructed that arrangements be made for an inaugural dinner.

The staff were installed the following day: a couple to act as housekeeper and butler, two young women to serve at table, and a magnificent Moroccan in a red fez. He was the chef, engaged so the owner could feast on Moroccan delicacies while admiring the view of the Moroccan mountains. Invitations were delivered by hand to all the neighbouring houses, and anticipation ran high as we arrived at the hexagonal palace. Auriol's masterpiece was tucked snugly into the dining-room floor, flush with the tiles: a hexagonal slab of polished black marble encircled by a shiny wood surround. When all the guests were gathered, the lady of the house called for our attention. She walked over to an elegant grandfather clock, and carefully set the hands to twelve. Instantly and apparently magically (in a stroke of genius Auriol had linked the hoist mechanism to the clock) the floor began to move upwards, accompanied by loud whirls and clicks. At table height it stopped, and the wooden bench surround began to ascend until it in turn reached seat-height. The guests applauded wildly. Auriol beamed and bowed.

It was an hour before midnight when we sat down to eat. The Moroccan chef had prepared a feast. There were laden platters of tiny pastries, each subtly spiced and filled with a delicate stuffing of meat, soft cheese or vegetables; little dishes of cold yoghurt mixed with chopped mint; a bowl of chilli and tomatoes for those who liked their food hot. The main course was borne in by the cook himself. Glowing with pride, he placed at the centre of the table a huge earthenware dish piled with golden roast chicken joints scattered with wedges of salted lemon. The aroma was heavenly – the scent of fresh blossom in a grove of lemon trees on a warm and starlit summer night.

At that moment the grandfather clock began to strike midnight. A few seconds later the guests became aware that the table and its delicious burden had started to descend towards the floor. Simultaneously the bench had begun to rise. Instantly panic set in among the diners, potential Toulouse-Lautrecs every one. Legs were whipped frantically from between the converging surfaces. Arms flailed among the flying chicken thighs and overturned glasses. In despair the chef, red fez bobbing, dived into the fray to try to rescue his masterpiece. Too late – the near-amputees were more concerned for their own skins than for his crackling, and the dish vanished in the stampede for safety.

Later in the week, when the memory of the disaster was fading, I went up to the house to ask for the lemon chicken recipe. The Moroccan chef, between streams of invective directed at the dastardly Auriol, told me the secret lay in the preparation of the lemons used to stuff the chickens, which were then simply rubbed with olive oil and roasted.

MOROCCAN SALTED LEMONS

You will need a large Kilner jar, which neatly contains six lemons, and a tablespoon of rough salt for each fruit. First soak the fresh lemons in cold water for four days, changing the water daily. Then quarter the fruit and layer it into the jar with the salt. Press the lemons down with a saucer and a weight so that the waterlogged pith and juice run with the salt to make a pickling brine. At the end of a week the lemons will be ready. They will keep for at least a month sealed in their jar in the refrigerator. The Moroccans use them in boiled as well as in roast chicken, and slivers of pickled lemon are delicious in salads.

I was, however, sworn never to disclose this information to the diminutive Magyar. So for the first, and I trust the last time, I have to hope somewhere there is someone (aristocrat, second-class) who doesn't read the *Field*.

9 February 1985

Shackleton's Stores

Pickled peaches and black cherry jam from Fortnum & Mason might seem an eccentric remedy for scurvy, but Ernest Henry Shackleton, ploughing through the ice of the Antarctic in 1915, found that it worked. It also made a change from seal stew and scrambled penguin's eggs.

The young naval officer's first job in the polar regions was as stores officer on Scott's 1902–4 'Discovery' expedition. Through no fault of Shackleton's, since it was Scott who did the shopping, the whole party suffered badly from the blackened gums and swollen joints of the old sailor's nightmare, scurvy. Trudging south through the blizzards on rations of a pound and a half of pemmican and biscuit a day, the men talked obsessively about food from the moment they woke and dreamt about it endlessly when they slept. There was considerable bitterness over Scott's ability to 'taste' the food in his dreams, while Dr Wilson spent his nights shouting at phantom waiters who wouldn't serve him. Shackleton, ever practical, wrote down his dream menu in his diary:

Duck crisp fried bread with salt and pepper
Thick bread soaked in golden syrup
Porterhouse steak and onions with plenty gravy
Huge salad of fruit and also greenstuff
Sirloin of beef with brown crisp fat soak bread in the gravy
Pastry three cornered tarts fresh but crisp. Jam hot inside. A pile of these with a bowl of cream.

Young Shackleton became determined never to make the same mistakes when ordering up stores for his own expeditions. He had not quite grasped that vitamin C was the problem – the vitamin was not identified for another twelve years – but he *did* know that fresh food was crucial, that preserved food must be of the highest quality, and that men needed a great deal of it to be able to function in arctic conditions. Scurvy had reappeared quite recently; British soldiers suffered from it in the Crimea and again in Mesopotamia during the First World War. The disease's links to a lack of fresh food had already been noted by the thirteenth century, and Hakluyt records the sixteenth-century mariner Sir Richard Hawkins taking oranges and lemons as an anti-scorbutic with him on his voyages. In 1803 the Navy made lemon juice a compulsory item in every crew's diet. This would have licked the problem, had the Navy's usual Mediterranean lemons not been replaced by West Indian lime juice. Limes are far less rich in the essential vitamin C. Shackleton's stores-inventory lists twenty-seven cases of lime juice, although quantities of other goodies more than made up for the deficiency: none of the members of his three expeditions suffered from scurvy. His list of provisions for the 1907 'Nimrod' expedition includes:

800 lb roast and boiled fowl and pâté	*1,000 lb Cheddar cheese*
1,000 lb York hams	*120 lb plum pudding*
1,400 lb Wiltshire bacon	*80 dozen assorted relishes and pickles*

– and so on, not forgetting a full 2,000 lb of jams and marmalades. Buried in the text are more details. One depot to which the explorers thankfully returned yielded a harvest of Carlsbad plums, fresh eggs, cakes, gingerbread and crystallized fruit. The Shackleton style became a legend. Arctic conditions are ideal for conserving stores, and all later expeditions used what was left by their predecessors.

Shackleton's magnificent leftovers were greeted with disbelieving delight. Robert Falcon Scott on his way to the Pole travelled the route taken by the 'Nimrod' expedition and made use of a Shackleton storehouse. One of his companions described the larder: huge slabs of chocolate, wholemeal biscuits that 'swelled like muffins on the red-hot stove', an inside wall built entirely of bottles of fruit. Poor ghost at the banquet – Scott never completed the return journey to Shackleton's feast.

Here, in memoriam, are:

SHACKLETON'S PICKLED PEACHES

4 lb perfect, scarcely ripe peaches
1 pint wine vinegar
2 lb brown sugar
3 cloves per peach

1 stick cinnamon
1 teaspoon allspice and pepper mixed
2 or 3 × 2 lb pickling-jars

Plunge the peaches into boiling water for a minute to loosen the skins. Peel them. Stud each peach with 3 cloves. Bring the vinegar and the sugar gently to the boil and add the spices. Simmer for 5 minutes and then slide the peaches gently into the syrup. Poach the fruit for 5–10 minutes, depending on the size of the peaches. Meanwhile put the jars to sterilize in a warm oven. Remove the peaches from the syrup and pack them into the sterilized jars. Continue to boil the syrup for another 10 minutes to thicken it, then pour it over the peaches – they must be well covered. Seal when cool. The peaches will be ready to eat in a month.

A wonderful pickle for cold meat, particularly ham or smoked chicken. I've never tried it with cold roast penguin.

16 February 1985

Offspring of a Vinegar Mother

Anyone for raspberry vinegar? Lady Jekyll, the *Times* cook of the twenties, when gay young things were exactly that and no more, suggests raspberry vinegar as 'a pleasant refresher, specially suitable for the young after lawn tennis or sports on hot days, but acceptable also to their elders when exhausted by church, depressed by gardening, or exasperated by shopping'. Oh, the pleasure of it all.

RASPBERRY VINEGAR CORDIAL

Take 1 lb raspberries to every pint of best white vinegar.
Let it stand for a fortnight in a covered jar in a cool larder.
Then strain without pressure, and to every pint put three
quarter lb white sugar. Boil 10 minutes, let cool, and bottle
in nice-shaped medium-sized bottles saved perhaps from
some present of foreign liqueurs or scent. A teaspoonful
stirred into a tumbler of water with a lump of ice, or
introduced to a very cold syphon, will taste like the elixir of
life on a hot day, and is as pretty as it is pleasant.

Lady Jekyll does not brief her readers on the making of the vinegar
itself. This is achieved with the assistance of a fungus, *Mycoderma
aceti*, which converts alcoholic liquid into a pure clear 'vin-aigre',
literally 'sour wine'. The fungus first appears as a fine oily slick on
the surface of wine, cider or beer – any alcohol can play host – and
flourishes in a temperature between 15° and 30°C. When it is fully
formed it becomes a thick sticky skin which can be pushed into
folds. This is the vinegar-mother, used in the same way as a yoghurt
starter. If you want to make your own vinegar, find someone with a
vinegar-mother and beg a little offspring. Italian delicatessens
sometimes keep them. You can then make wonderful vinegars by
adding wine or cider to your starter and keeping it within the correct
temperature range. (Warning: a friend of mine grew a vinegar-
mother and she says it took over the kitchen like a gigantic triffid.
She eventually buried it in the garden in the dead of night – and then
moved house.)

Mrs Beeton gives instructions for the making of a gooseberry vinegar which needs no mother, is made with gooseberries, water and brown sugar, but takes eighteen months to reach maturity. A long haul, but she says it is truly excellent.

Once your vinegar is a clear clean liquid, it may be drawn off and bottled up, either innocent or flavoured, or used to make pickles and chutneys. Delicious vinegars (either your own or shop-bought) can be made with a great variety of infusions, particularly while the herb garden is in full leaf. Boil the vinegar first, allow to cool and then pour into jars in which you have put sprigs of tarragon, thyme or rosemary. Leave to infuse for a month and they will be delicious in winter salads. Mrs Beeton suggests soaking a handful of tiny fresh red chillies in a pint of vinegar for two weeks, and using the strained liquor as an 'agreeable relish for fish'. Rather Chinese. Fresh ginger cut into matchsticks can be infused in vinegar for use when cooking Far Eastern dishes – particularly valuable when you cannot get fresh ginger. Grated horseradish (dig it in October/November) keeps well in vinegar all winter – stir it into whipped double cream seasoned with a little mustard for horseradish sauce. Chop fine the last of the summer's mint, pack it into jars with a little sugar, cover with vinegar and keep in a cool dark cupboard for an excellent mint sauce. If you make apple jelly in the autumn, stir a few teaspoons of the vinegared mint into a jar or two for mint jelly.

Here are three good store-room vinegars for winter salads and marinades.

ROSE VINEGAR

Infuse 3 ounces of rose petals in 2 pints good vinegar for 10 days. Strain and bottle.

RASPBERRY VINEGAR

Put 2 lb raspberries in a jar and cover with 2 pints good vinegar. Leave for 8 days, then strain off the vinegar without squeezing the raspberries. Bottle and keep in a cool dark larder.

CUCUMBER VINEGAR

3 cucumbers	1 tablespoon salt
2 pints vinegar	2 tablespoons black peppers
3 onions	¼ teaspoon cayenne pepper

Slice the cucumbers and pack them into a wide-mouthed jar. Cover with the vinegar. Slice the onions and add them, with the other ingredients, to the cucumbers. Let it stand for 4–5 days, boil it all up and, when cold, strain the liquor through muslin, and store away in sealed bottles. This vinegar, says Mrs B., is a very nice addition to gravies, hashes, etc., as well as a great improvement to salads, or to eat with cold meat.

Lady Jekyll finished her store-room recipes in style with a recommendation from an exalted source: 'In some such ways as these – and there are many, many more – can affection won be kept alive and tender, and have we not the highest authority for knowing that without love we are nothing?'

13 July 1985

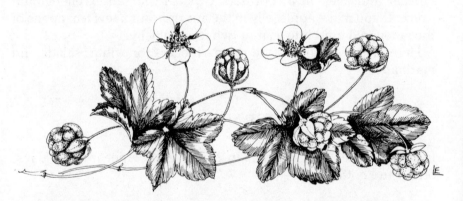

Berried Treasure of the Vikings

The end of August, advised the late Ethel B. Tweedie, is the appropriate time to visit the Land of the Midnight Sun for the berry harvest. For instance, take cloudberries. If you do any such thing, I discovered, you must expect to be battle-axed by an irate native with the blood of the Vikings hot in his veins and his winter larder on his mind. You may pinch a Viking's bilberries and snaffle his Arctic bramble, but you may not cull his cloudberries.

The Scandinavians are not normally mean with their moors. They can, after all, afford to be generous: half a million square miles – five times the area of the United Kingdom – is a lot of land for a population of 20 million. There is no law of trespass in Scandinavia. Unrestricted access is the rule. Townsmen and tourists are free to roam the mountains and valleys at will. With, that is, the exception of the cloudberry-patch. That is something quite other. Blows have been exchanged by normally mild-mannered good neighbours when faced with marauders during the ripening season at the end of August. Woe betide he who is found skulking with bulging knap-sack high on the hills in the twilight.

The cloudberry, *Rubus chamaemorus*, is listed in Fitter and Blamey's *Collins Guide to the Wild Flowers of Britain and Northern Europe* as a 'shy flowerer in Britain'. The fruit of the Vikings needs the twenty-four-hour sunshine within the Arctic Circle to set its reproductive processes aflame. Cloudberry blossom is a single, pearl-white, five-petalled flower – every bit as beautiful as a member of the rose family should be. It is a vulnerable plant, unprotected by the usual tangled mass of thorny stems. It grows low in the heather, and the thick palmate leaves make solid dark patches, clearly visible among the feathery fronds of the moorland vegetation. The fruit forms quickly after flowering. At first it looks like a large hard orange blackberry, striped with scarlet where the flesh is exposed to the sun by the separating sepals. Then, as the fruit ripens, it swells and grows paler. When it is fully ripe, the berry is a mass of sunny golden globelets – plump and fragrant and full of thick amber juice. The berries have one extraordinary property: they do not, as does other soft fruit, go bad. They have a built-in preserving agent. Cloudberry jam needs minimal sugar and very little cooking. It is possible to pick the berries straight into a storage-jar and keep them in a cool cellar all winter. They will still be miraculously fresh in the spring.

To return to the late Ethel B. Tweedie: the lady was an intrepid traveller in nineteenth-century Scandinavia. She found and sam-pled eleven species of edible berry and gave cloudberries top billing: 'The cloudberry grows in the extreme North in the morasses during August. It is a *most delicious* fruit with a pine tree flavour.'

I have a Norwegian friend with a small-holding 200 miles inside the Arctic Circle. Her farm runs from the mountain ridge above her steading to the lake-shore beneath. She harvests meadow hay for her cows, and the fish from the lake for her supper. But her most prized crop by far is the cloudberries on the moor which runs up to the ridge above the birch-wood behind her fields. Beneath her pretty wooden farmhouse she has a deep storage-cellar. In it she keeps her year's supply of potatoes, her rhubarb wine (clear and dry and packing a 15 per cent proof punch), bilberry cordials, bramble jellies and all her winter pleasures. Beyond, in a special secret place, is her shelf of cloudberry conserve, golden as the best caviare, hoarded against invaders. She brought a jar out for our supper. It was wonderful. The fruit is neither sharp nor sickly and has a thick rich texture. I could see what Ethel meant about the pine-tree flavour.

The problem is how to acquire this elusive treasure. Perhaps this year will be a good year for cloudberries on the northern moors of Britain. Or you might care to brave the Vikings and make a clandestine dash to the uplands of Scandinavia. There is one other possibility – although it is only an echo of the real thing. The Finns make and export under the state label, Lapponia, a liqueur made from cloudberries. The Scandinavians like their liqueurs on the sweet and sticky side, but the flavour of the berry in their Cloudberry Liqueur is still discernible. Should you be fortunate enough to find a handful of the ripe berries, restrain yourself from eating them (it requires resolve of steel), and slip them instead into a bottle of vodka or plain *eau de vie* such as the French sell for home-made fruit brandies. Keep the bottle hidden away securely until the long dark nights of January or February. Then open it and raise a glass of the pale gold nectar to the memory of Ethel B. Tweedie, who brought the good news from the Arctic tundra.

17 August 1985

The Raj Bequest of Chutneys

If your orchard is full of drunken red admirals, it may not be the fault of the Soviet navy. More likely *Vanessa atalanta* has discovered that your windfalls are fermenting. There is nothing a nectar-sipping butterfly likes better than an alcoholic plum. Red admirals are spectacular even when sober, with their beautiful black-velvet scarlet-slashed wings. Intoxicated, they lurch from fruit to fruit, aggressive as any bar-room alcoholic, quarrelling with the wasps. In their cups they are even capable of seeing off a hornet. But good times must come to an end. Now is the moment to make chutney before the entire crop falls to their excesses.

Chutney, a legacy from the Raj, is a corruption of the Hindi *chatni*. There is a whole lexicon of fresh chutneys prepared by Indian cooks to be served as relishes, as well as the more familiar preserve. I sometimes make a simple English version to serve as a counterpoint to a storecupboard chutney.

GREEN CHUTNEY

2 large sharp-flavoured apples
(cooking apples are fine)
1 small onion

1 handful fresh mint leaves
Juice of 1 lemon

Peel, core and chop the apples. Peel and chop the onion. Strip the mint leaves from their stalks and chop roughly. Put these ingredients in the liquidizer and add enough lemon juice to allow the mixture to be puréed. If you have no liquidizer, chop and pound by hand. Serve the chutney as a relish, very fresh.

The recipe the retired Indian Army major (*every* retired Indian Army major) brought home is the one which has established itself firmly in the British larder. It requires sweet, sour and hot flavourings. Vinegar provides the acidity, sugar and fruit (fresh or dried) the sweet, chillies and spices the heat. After that, anything goes. Apples, plums, damsons, apricots, marrow, tomatoes both ripe and unripe, blackberries, elderberries, gooseberries, carrots – all are grist to the chutney mill. Vinegar and sugar are both powerful preserving agents, and such a mixture is guaranteed to keep well and improve with the keeping. Once you have established a basic blend of the various elements to suit your taste, adapt it to the raw materials you have available.

Here is my version. It seems to come out more or less the same whatever fruit I use. I think I probably like more spice than most tastes approve, so those quantities can be reduced. The garlic can be omitted. Raisins, sultanas and onions can be added or subtracted.

RED ADMIRAL CHUTNEY

4 lb plums
3 lb apples
1 lb onions
1 lb raisins or sultanas
3–4 cloves garlic
4 oz fresh ginger (or 1 heaped
  teaspoon powdered)
1 dozen cloves (or 1 heaped teaspoon
  powdered)

2 oz whole black peppercorns
6 small red dried chillies or 1 flat
  teaspoon chilli powder
2 teaspoons salt
2 pints vinegar (malt or cider will do)
2 lb soft brown sugar

Stone the plums (no need to peel them) and chop them roughly. Peel and core the apples and chop them, too. Peel and chop the onions. Check the dried fruit for twigs and squeeze out their pips if necessary. Peel and chop up the garlic. If you are using fresh ginger, peel it and mince it fine. Pound the cloves and peppercorns together (in a mortar if you have one). De-seed and mince the chillies if you are using whole ones (don't rub your eyes afterwards – rinse your hands thoroughly. Chilli juice in the eyes is horrible).

Put all the ingredients except the sugar into a large thick-bottomed pan. The pan must be heavy and a good conductor of heat: chutney, like jam, has a nasty habit of sticking to the bottom and burning. Should this happen, don't attempt to stir it, just tip the whole mixture straight into a new pan, without scraping off the burnt bits.

Bring all to the boil and simmer until the fruit and vegetables are soft: 15–20 minutes. Then add the sugar and stir to dissolve. Bring the mixture back to the boil and cook the chutney gently until it is thick and dark. This will take about an hour. Turn up the heat to evaporate the moisture if the mixture looks too runny. Stir frequently to prevent sticking.

Meanwhile put your jars to sterilize in a warm oven. Pot the mixture while still warm. Cover when it has cooled with circles of waxed paper. Seal with Cellophane if you are not using a screw-top or Kilner jar. Keep in a dark cupboard so that the colour does not fade. Ready to eat when you are, but it improves with age. It's very useful around Christmas when there is all that cold turkey and ham lying about.

These quantities give around 10 lb of chutney: enough for a flotilla of admirals or a brigade of majors.

24 August 1985

Guilty in the Apple Orchard

There have been times in my life when I have been responsible for an apple orchard. As summer fades and the boughs bend under the weight of relentlessly ripening fruit the annual panic sets in. Even two or three healthy mature apple trees seem to produce more than my household can be expected to consume. These days not even the local lads are disposed to shin up for a spot of nocturnal scrumping. I expect South African Granny Smiths are too plentiful and cheap in the market to make it worth the effort.

Something has to be done, if only to appease Ceres or Proserpina or whoever is responsible for the fecundity of the earth. One year I gave up the unequal struggle and let the harvest lie rotting in the buttercups, only to be rewarded the following spring by a forest of vigorous saplings which gave the motor-mower terminal indigestion.

Here is a virtuous way of using an exuberance of apples. If you make apple pectin this year, you can set it aside and use it next year to set jams and jellies. You will have nine months in which to congratulate yourself on your thrift and foresight. Strawberry jam made with this apple pectin will be delicious – well set and fresh-flavoured.

APPLE PECTIN

Wipe and then roughly chop your apples – skin, core, pips and all. Put them in a large preserving-pan and cover them with water. Cook until the apples are quite soft. Strain through a jelly-bag, without stirring or squeezing the pulp.

You can make a large jelly-bag by upturning a stool and securing the four corners of a clean linen tea-towel to each of the legs. Place a large receptacle underneath to catch the drips, and tip the pulp into the middle of the tea-towel.

When you have processed all the apples, bring the juice back to the boil. Pour into heated sterilized screw-top glass jars. It doesn't matter if it is a little cloudy – that will clear when you make your jam.

Excellent herb jellies to eat with roast or cold meat can be made with it if nine months is too long to wait. Just add 1 lb sugar for each pint of apple pectin and bring it to the boil with the herb (finely chopped) of your choice: mint, thyme, rosemary, tarragon and ginger all make lovely jellies. Pour into small sterilized jars.

DRIED APPLES

Apples are a fruit which dries very successfully. These dried apple-rings are particularly good served after the cheese at dinner, perhaps with a bowl of unshelled fresh walnuts.

Peel, core and cut the apples into rings half an inch wide. A good drying-rack can be made with a wooden frame covered with wire netting, in which case lay the rings on it in a single layer. Or you can thread the rings on to a string. Put them to dry either in a warm airing cupboard or on the lowest possible oven setting. Store them in an airtight tin.

APPLE PIE

If you have a very small crop of apples or have to rely on the local fruiterer, an apple pie might be more suitable. As all our American cousins know, the best apple pies are made by Mum. Here is my mum's apple pie. I know it's the best because she makes it from her mum's recipe-book – and her mum was American.

Murberteig Pastry for Pies

¾ lb flour
½ lb butter
2 oz sugar

Yolks of 2 eggs
1 tablespoon brandy
4 tablespoons cold water

Cut the butter into the flour and then rub it in with tips of your fingers. When your mixture is like fine breadcrumbs, mix in the sugar.

Beat the egg yolks with the brandy and the water. Stir into the flour mixture. Press the mixture into a soft dough, again with the tips of your fingers. Everything must be kept as cool as possible. The palms of one's hands are too warm: using them will oil the dough and make it tough. Leave the pastry to settle down in a cool place for half an hour while you deal with the apples.

Chopped Apple Filling

4 large cooking apples
4 oz almonds
2 oz raisins
6 oz brown sugar

½ teaspoon cinnamon
Juice and grated rind of 1 lemon or
4 tablespoons white wine

Peel, core and chop apples. Blanch and chop the almonds. Put apples, almonds, raisins, sugar, cinnamon and juice or wine into a pan and stew all gently together for 5 minutes until the apples are soft and mushy. (At this stage the mixture would freeze very well, if you decided to do it in quantity.)

Roll out the pastry and line an 8-inch pie-dish.

Let the apples cool. Spread them over the pastry and dot the top with butter. Bake in a moderately hot oven (375°F/gas 5) for 30–40 minutes.

14 September 1985

Bulgar Skills in a Pickle

Life is real and earnest in modern Bulgaria. Collectively speaking, there are not many jovial faces around. This is not entirely surprising: a very saint might scowl if he had had an Ottoman Turk sitting

on his face for 500 years. Forty years behind the Iron Curtain has not brought the smile back. The national talent naturally lies in the greenest fingers in Eastern Europe, rather than in a recent and more-publicized skill with a poisoned umbrella. The Bulgars are excellent gardeners. So good are they that their neighbours, the Romanians, employed Bulgarians as gardeners whenever they could, and even called Romanian kitchen gardens 'bulgars'. In spite of State ownership of land, modern Bulgarian citizens find ways to conjure the fruits of the earth from the most unlikely common wasteland. Uncollectivized cabbages thrive along the verges of motorways. Non-State-owned stands of sweetcorn forest the central traffic islands.

Officially the Bulgarian kitchen is thoroughly collectivized: the State expects its citizens to take their main meal of the day at their place of work, and that is where all supplies of State food are directed. Short commons for the housewife who does not grow her own, but an excellent opportunity for an imaginative form of propaganda. Medieval rulers pioneered such propaganda when they gave their endless elaborate public banquets. Today's Bulgarian government has rather different objectives, and the Bulgarians, after their long national obscurity under the Ottoman yoke, have more reason than most to search out their ethnic origins in their country's food. The cult of the noble peasant is an essential ingredient of good communism, and Bulgarian culinary propagandists have come up with suitably ancient sources: the near-mythical Proto-Bulgars. These prehistoric folk heroes, their traditions and behaviour veiled by impenetrable historic fog, can be endowed with a national identity of the required purity.

248

Proto-Bulgarian diet provides an admirably earthy model. The careful Ottoman Turks are the main source of record for the new-style Bulgarian national awareness. Pre-Ottoman foodstuffs (untainted by conquest both foreign and capitalist) which were readily available in the native Bulgarian – or, indeed, Proto-Bulgarian – market-place were conveniently listed by the Turkish taxmen. The Bulgarian government can vouch for the Turks' accuracy: nothing makes a man so meticulous as a job in Customs and Excise. Noted and taxed in fifteenth-century Bulgarian markets was a variety of sturdy and officially acceptable peasant vegetables: cabbages, cucumbers, spinach, turnips, radishes, broad beans, peas, lentils, melons, onions and garlic.

The civilized Turks planted rice and the damask rose (attar for Turkish beauties and now the world's main source of rose perfume). Later came the introductions from the New World, powerful propaganda from Uncle Sam: maize, the haricot bean, the tomato, the capsicum pepper, the potato, the pumpkin – all now well tucked into the national kitchen-patch. They will not be easy to uproot. Perhaps a Proto-Bulgar gardening Leif Ericsson may yet be exhumed, complete with longship and magnetic compass-stone.

The Bulgarian national snack, the dish the lorry-drivers' pull-in can turn out at any hour of the day or night, is a plate of excellent home-pickled vegetables which include a few subversive New World elements. Bread and beer accompany, and the State factory supplies a pair of very nasty limp pink Frankfurter-type sausages of uncertain ethnic origin.

BULGARIAN PICKLES

The brine to make a gallon of pickles:

3 pints water   *4 oz salt*
1 pint white wine vinegar

Prepare a selection of 5–6 lb mixed vegetables trimmed into bite-sized pieces; choose among:

Carrots
Cauliflowers
Young turnips
Small pickling cucumbers
Red, yellow and green peppers
  (non-Proto-Bulgar ingredient)
Green beans

Bunch of dill
3 cloves garlic
3 small red chilli peppers (subversive
  non-Proto-Bulgar ingredient: add
  more if you like your pickles hot)

Peel and cut the carrots lengthways in quarters. Divide the cauliflower into florets. Peel and quarter the turnips. Wipe over the small pickling cucumbers leaving them whole (larger ones should be cut into quarters vertically and chopped into convenient lengths). Seed and quarter the peppers. Top and tail the beans.

Pack the vegetables with the dill, the halved peeled cloves of garlic and the whole chillies into sterilized jars. Bring the pickling ingredients, the water, the vinegar and the salt, to the boil together in a large saucepan. Pour the hot pickle over the vegetables. Cover, seal and store. Ready to eat in 4–6 weeks.

15 February 1986

Oranges and Lemons

Seville oranges, the small, sharp fruit used for the making of marmalade, have arrived in the shops from the banks of the Guadalquivir as they have done every spring, give or take the odd political hiccup, since the first commercial consignment was unloaded at Portsmouth in about 1289. Queen Eleanor, a Spaniard by birth, put in a successful bid at the time for fifteen lemons and seven oranges. Poor sun-nurtured princess shivering in the cold English winter.

Oranges and lemons were first brought to Britain in the luggage of Richard Coeur de Lion's returning Third Crusaders. Apart from the usual trouble with the Turks, the English had found the company of their fellow-Christian, Philip II of France, far from congenial. After spending the winter of 1191 squabbling in the scented shade of the orange groves and sugar-cane fields around Jaffa, only one thing was agreed by both parties: the Turks had the culinary edge over the Christians. Richard's knights packed the ingredients for marmalade in their saddlebags and took the short way home. Their king took the scenic route and ended up doing three years' solitary in a German gaol. Once back home, Philip II turned his military attention to his erstwhile ally and removed the English overseas possessions of Normandy, Anjou and Poitou. That left his fellow-Crusaders with nothing but the contents of their saddlebags, King John and a downhill slope to Runnymede. Each to his own.

Citrus fruits were not actually used to make the famous British breakfast treat for several centuries. *Marmelo* is Portuguese for 'quince' and its derivative was used to label a fruit butter made with quinces. The method pioneered by the Portuguese for their sweet-scented furry fruit – which was to brew up the pulp into a thick paste with sugar – was soon applied to plums and damsons, apples and medlars, strawberries and pears. In the Latin countries of Europe, fruit jams continue to be called marmalades, leading to bemused disappointment among modern British tourists and confusion among their hosts.

By the mid-eighteenth century the British were beginning to separate their marmalade from their jam. Instructions appear in household books for the making of a sweetmeat with oranges and lemons which contained the peel sliced into long strips. The concoction was still so thick that it had to be cut with a knife. It is difficult to unravel how so foreign a fruit came to be deeply embedded in the English culinary tradition. But there it is for all time, the acknowledged British breakfast essential, glowing amber on the larder shelf alongside its tea-time cousin, the equally foreign lemon curd. The time is ripe to make them both.

LEMON CURD

My absolute favourite spread – and everyone else's, it seems. The jars never last out the week in my household. This makes about 4 lb.

6 lemons	*8 eggs*
½ lb butter	
1½ lb sugar (granulated or	
preserving)	

Wash and grate the rinds of the lemons. Squeeze out the juice.
Put the juice and the grated lemon peel into a bowl with the butter

and the sugar. Set the bowl over a pan of simmering water and leave the ingredients to dissolve together gently. In another bowl, whisk the egg yolks and whites together. Pour in the melted sugar, butter and lemon, whisking steadily as you do so. Return the mixture to the bowl over the simmering water and continue to whisk as the mixture cooks and thickens. Don't let it boil.

When the curd has a slightly jellied, thickened look, it is done. This will take 20–30 minutes. It will thicken further as it cools and the butter solidifies. Pot as usual.

JELLIED MARMALADE

Rather an elegant marmalade, this. It doesn't look a bit home-made. Makes about 8 lb.

12 Seville oranges
3 sweet oranges
3 lemons
1 pint of water per lb of fruit after peeling (this quantity will weigh 4–5 lb)

1 lb preserving sugar to each pint of juice (have to hand 4–5 lb sugar)

Wash the fruit and pare off all the rind as finely as you can with a very sharp knife. Cut the rind into thin slivers and put aside. Weigh the fruit and then peel off and discard its white pith. Cut the flesh up roughly and put it in a large heavy pan with the water. Boil it steadily for half an hour, stirring every now and again.

Strain the pulp through a clean linen cloth pinned on the legs of an upturned stool. Measure the liquid and add 1 lb sugar for each pint of juice. Put the juice and sugar and the rinds back into the preserving-pan on the heat. Stir until the sugar melts. Turn up the heat and boil the mixture for 30–5 minutes until the jelly is at setting-point. Let it cool so that the rind sinks. Pot as usual.

1 March 1986

Pickling in the Still-Room

The earliest record of a still-room appears in the list of household offices for the Elizabethan mansion of Hengrave Hall in Suffolk. The first occupants of this peaceful backwater of the busy manor-house kitchen were the distillers of cordials and perfumes. To their duties were soon added those of preparing sweet preserves, jams, jellies, and fruit and flower vinegars for the storecupboard. By Victorian times, the golden age of the country house, the still-room had its own kitchen range for baking. It was virtually a second kitchen and accommodated a housekeeper and a still-room maid.

As the British expanded their empire, so the pace hotted up. New recipes with fancy Eastern ingredients – some of them using soy sauce and quantities of brand-new spices – joined the bright jars of berry jams on the still-room shelves. Recipes for peppery pickles and delicately spiced Indian chutneys began to appear in the cookery-books. Chutneys offered a perfect complement to the British taste for plain-cooked meat. Home cooks adapted them to the fruits available from their own gardens: a whole new repertoire of storehouse staples was popularized, and has remained popular ever since.

Here is a selection of these old-fashioned dainties.

PONTACK SAUCE

A fine old recipe contributed to Florence White's English Folk Cookery Association in 1931. Miss Sloane, whose storecupboard it graced, said that the sauce should be kept for seven years. The origin of the odd name is probably Pontack's hostelry of Lombard Street, a famous eating-house of Stuart days, from whence the recipe travelled to Leicester with Sir Charles Sedley of Wymondham. The London original was likely to have been made with claret, a speciality of Pontack's cellar. Elderberries are the country version. Wait until the fruiting heads turn downwards before harvesting elderberries.

1 pint ripe elderberries	1 small piece root ginger
¾ pint vinegar	40 peppercorns
½ teaspoon salt	12 cloves
½ teaspoon powdered mace	4 shallots or pickling onions

Pull the elderberries off their twiglets with a fork and measure out a pint of fruit. Put them in a preserving-pan with the vinegar. Leave overnight in a warm place; a warming-oven will do fine.

Strain off the liquid through a jelly-cloth without pressure. Pour it back into the pan. Crush the spices and peel, and roughly chop the shallots or onions. Add all to the liquid in the pan. Bring to the boil and let it bubble for 5 minutes. Leave overnight to cool. Strain, bottle and cork tightly. Ready in a month. Keeps for at least 7 years.

Delicious with cold game or with anything which requires Worcester sauce, including a *Bloody Mary*. Roast ortolans were the choice of Pontack's itself.

PICCALILLI

This pickle first appeared in print in 1769 – from *pickle* out of *chilli*. Make double quantities when the vegetable garden is at its best.

1 cauliflower	*12 peppercorns*
1 cucumber	*12 allspice berries*
½ lb onions	*1 teaspoon powdered ginger*
½ lb green beans	*1 teaspoon powdered turmeric*
1 small vegetable marrow	*1 flat tablespoon English mustard*
Salt and water	* powder*
1 pint vinegar	*1 flat tablespoon flour*
2 oz brown sugar	

Peel the vegetables as appropriate and cut them up into small pieces or florets. Lay them in a large dish and cover all with a brine: 1 oz salt to 1 pint water. Leave overnight. The following day, drain the vegetables. Mix the flour, the mustard powder and the turmeric with a couple of tablespoons of the vinegar – enough to make a runny paste. Boil up the rest of the vinegar with the sugar and the remaining spices, then allow the liquid to cool. Strain out the spices. Mix in the flour–turmeric–mustard paste and bring all gently back to the boil, stirring as the mixture thickens. Add the vegetables. Cook them in the pickle for 10–15 minutes, until the vegetables are done but still retain a bit of bite. Allow the pickles to cool. Bottle and seal. Ready in a few days.

GREEN TOMATO PICKLE

The full crop of tomatoes rarely has a chance to ripen in the English summer. This is an excellent pickle to make with the green fruit.

5 lb green tomatoes	*2 short sticks cinnamon*
Salt	*12 cloves*
1 quart vinegar	*12 peppercorns*
1 lb brown sugar	*1 lb apples*
½ lb onions	
1 teaspoon chilli pepper (cayenne)	

254

Pour boiling water over the tomatoes to loosen their skins. Peel and then slice them. Lay the slices in a dish in layers, sprinkling with salt as you do so. Leave them overnight.

The next day put the vinegar, the sugar, the onions peeled and chopped, and the roughly crushed spices into a roomy preserving-pan. Bring all to the boil. Meanwhile drain the tomatoes and peel, core and slice the apples, and add both to the vinegar mixture. Simmer all until soft. Taste and adjust the seasoning.

Allow to cool a little before ladling the mixture into sterilized jars. Seal tightly. Ready to use in a week. Keeps well.

2 August 1986

Hebridean Jellies

As elsewhere in these islands, spring in the Hebrides this year was late. When it came, it was colder than a new-sheared ewe. Later, and unlike the conditions imposed by freezing hurricanes on the rest of our shivering population, the sun shone throughout August. Instead of the usual soft summer rains, interspersed with those few clean-washed days of sparkling sunlight which compensate visitors to the Hebrides for their journey, day after day was dry and bright. The burns reduced to a trickle and the waterfalls narrowed to a single white thread twined through the dry rocks. Fishermen had no sport as the salmon waited impatiently at the river mouths for the spate, and the brown trout lay sluggish in the dwindling pools. However, the autumn colours were spectacular. Ling and the bell heather blazed royal purple against the copper of the turning bracken. The white blossoms of grass-of-Parnassus, most magical of flowers, starred each clump of sphagnum moss.

This year Gremlin Napier, supplier of larder stores – jellies, jams and chutneys – to the discerning gourmets of Mull, has had a spectacular harvest of rowan berries to collect. Gremlin, his nickname a reverse reference to his tall loose-limbed frame, combs the island hedgerows every autumn for the fruits he uses in his preserves. Each year he makes me a supply of rowan and apple jelly, the most delicious accompaniment to grouse and venison, to bring south. The hips and brambles are ripening well, but the sloes, usually among the most prolific of the berries of Mull, can manage but a handful on each tree. His sloe and crab-apple jelly – lovely on hot buttered breakfast scones – will have to wait for another, more generous autumn. Meanwhile, he has promised, in replacement, a dozen jars of his *Hedgerow Jelly*.

ROWAN AND APPLE JELLY

Pick the rowan before the birds strip the heads first. The berries can be stored in the deep freeze until you are ready to make your jelly – a useful trick, advises Gremlin, if you are putting up enough to last through the winter. The job of gathering berries is labour-intensive, and there is often not the opportunity to pick and cook at the same time. The recipe makes 7–8 lb of jelly.

3 lb rowan berries
3 lb Bramley apples
Approximately 6 pints water

Approximately 6 lb granulated or
preserving sugar

Roughly strip the berries off their stalks; it doesn't matter if some bits of stem are included at this stage. Chop up the apples – skin, pips and all. Put the fruit into a large preserving-pan and cover it to the depth of one finger with cold water. Bring all to the boil, turn down the heat and simmer until apples and berries are mushy – about 30 minutes will be enough. Mash the fruit a little as it cooks and keep stirring to avoid sticking.

Put the pulp to drip through a jelly-cloth overnight. I use a clean tea-towel firmly pinned by each corner on to a well-washed upturned stool. A large bowl beneath catches the juice. Don't squeeze or stir the pulp or the jelly will be cloudy.

The next day, measure the juice back into the pan. Stir in 1 lb sugar for every pint of liquid. Bring all gently to the boil, stirring constantly until the sugar is dissolved. Boil until setting-point is reached – that is, 220°F on the sugar thermometer. The test without a thermometer is a drop of the hot jelly on a cold saucer: setting-point has been reached when the liquid remains a drop without running. Pot in sterilized ½ lb jars. Cover with a circle of waxed paper when cool. Seal and store away from the light. This is a lovely jewel-clear jelly, like liquid garnets. Its bitter flavour is the perfect complement to a rich meat such as roast game or lamb.

HEDGEROW JELLY

One or more of the wild fruits are replaceable with their cultivated cousins, but try to keep the 'hedgerow' nature of the preserve as much as you can. All raw fruits for jams and jellies can be deep-frozen; there may be some slight loss of colour, but the flavour will remain true. Gremlin picks his Hebridean sloes as late as November.

5 lb crab apples (or, failing them, Bramleys)
1½ lb brambles (blackberries)
1¼ lb sloes (bullaces or damsons will do instead)
1 lb rowan berries (or elderberries)
½ lb hips (from the wild rose; I have never used cultivated ones, but I see no reason why they should not be good, too)

½ lb haws (from the hawthorn in the hedge)
Approximately 8 pints water
Approximately 8 lb granulated or preserving sugar

Chop up the apples – skin, pips and all. Check over the brambles and sloes and hull them if necessary. Strip the rowan from its branches. Trim the hips and haws. Proceed as for the rowan and apple jelly; this mix will take about an hour to cook to a pulp.

Pot in 1 lb jars; this quantity will make about 14 lb of jelly. Look ahead: a jar of Hedgerow Jelly makes a lovely Christmas present.

18 October 1986

Cheeses and Snacks

Roquefort in Springtime

The village of Roquefort perches on the side of a ravine overlooking the Causses, four stony limestone plateaux littered with boulders and scarred with deep ravines in the Massif Central of France. Good country for shepherds with few pockets of soil for arable farmers. Tough grasses and scrub support the large population of sheep whose milk is essential to the making of Roquefort cheese. By late April nine species of orchid share the high plains with more than a million grazing mouths. Although over-grazing must harm the flora, I have noticed that sheep and orchids seem to cohabit quite happily. From the valleys of southern Spain to the alvar plain of the Baltic island of Öland, sheep and orchids like the same dry thin soil and barren land. The sheep seem to nibble the orchid leaves when they first appear but leave the buds unscathed – and rarely touch the flowering stems.

So if you visit the heart of Roquefort country in the spring it need not only be for the cheese, although that would be excuse enough. I like Roquefort best of all the blue cheeses, better even than our own Stilton or the Italian Gorgonzola. Roquefort has the dry strong chalkiness of the Causses themselves – innocent food with an ancient pedigree. Its discovery has of course the obligatory legend. In the remote past a young shepherd from Roquefort drove his flock out one spring day on to the rocky wastes of the Causses to crop the new grass. For his midday meal he took a loaf of country bread and a *fromageon*, a fresh sheep's-milk cheese. His flock were hungry and the young spring lambs hard to follow. He left the bread, with the cheese leaning against it, beside a large boulder to eat on his return, and wandered far from the usual paths. Dusk fell, and the young man could not find the boulder which marked his meal. Some days later, by now extremely hungry on a diet of sheep's milk, wild berries and roots, he chanced on the spot again. By this time both the bread and the cheese, left in the spring damp and warmth, had grown a coating of greeny-blue mould. The young shepherd, far too hungry to be fastidious, brushed off the mould and downed his long-overdue meal. To his surprise, he found the cheese excellent. Thereafter he always ate his cheese blue. Word got around, and soon all the shepherds in the area were leaving their cheeses beside mouldy loaves to ripen.

Whatever its origins, Roquefort has a venerable fan-club. The Roman letter-writer Pliny recommended it in the first century AD. Charlemagne placed a yearly order for it. Casanova recalls his current light of love, 'leste comme une biche', setting it out for his pleasure in 1757. The cheese is matured in caves (guided tours available, 'vaut le voyage' as Michelin says) behind the town. The original caves were natural, but later man-made ones were gouged out as demand for the cheese grew. It is here that the crucial mould, *Penicillium roqueforti*, thrives. The mould is still grown on stale bread – a peasant bread kneaded with half wheat and half rye. The cheese is made exclusively of ewe's milk, which is heated and then set with a coagulant. After a couple of hours the curd is cut and the whey drained off. Then the curds are well salted and layered with a seasoning of blue bread mould into the nine-inch hoops in which the cheeses mature. The damp breezy limestone caves take care of the rest.

If you visit Roquefort in the early spring, carry a whole cheese away with you. Buy a bottle of Tavel, the excellent local rosé, a couple of fresh baguettes in the bakery on the way out, sweet butter and a bunch of radishes – and make your way down to the plain. Find a comfortable boulder to shelter you from the wind, and set your face to the spring sunshine. Fortunately, unlike the long-ago shepherd, you will not need to go hungry for several days before you can enjoy your picnic. As you eat, your eyes will grow accustomed to the shapes in the surrounding grass, and with any luck you should be able to pick out all nine orchids: *Orchis morio*, the green winged orchid; *militaris*, the soldier orchid; *purpurea*, the lady orchid (a sturdy female); *palustris*, a tall purple orchid much like the more familiar *laxiflora*; *ustulata*, which can be confused with *morio*; *Ophrys sphegodes*, the early spider orchid; *apifera*, the pink-petalled bee orchid; *insectifera*, the fly orchid; and the extraordinary man-orchid,

Aceras anthropophorum. You might even spot a clearing full of purple pasque flowers as well.

13 April 1985

Toasting the Nation's Rabbits

Whether or not toasted cheese is a rare-bit of the Welsh, Scottish or English variety (Dr Johnson's Dictionary gives a meaning of 'rare' as 'not fully subdued by the fire', but offers no rare-bit in 1755), or whether the dish acquired its alternative designation as a regional sub-species of *Lepus cuniculus* as a kind of chauvinist put-down in the spirit of those Belgian, Irish and Norwegian jokes which convulse their neighbouring nationals, is difficult to unravel.

This is not least because the earliest known written recipes for such rabbits appear in Hannah Glasse's *The Art of Cookery Made Plain and Easy*, published in 1747. She gives three such toasted cheese dishes: Welsh rabbit, Scotch rabbit, and the English variety, in which the toast is first soaked in wine.

By 1857 the first edition of Mrs Beeton's *Book of Household Management* has dropped the rabbits. She gives instead a pair of recipes for rare-bits. Perhaps the joke was wearing a little thin after a century and a half.

Recipe No. 1651: 'Toasted Cheese, or Scotch Rare-bit, composed simply of a few slices of rich cheese' melted together with seasonings of mustard and pepper: the surface to be browned with a salamander and the melted cheese to be sent to table in a bain-marie to keep it warm, accompanied by fingers of hot toast.

An alternative offered is to dish up the cheese already spread on its toast. The mixture can be improved, says the young Mrs Beeton, with a glass of porter or port wine – as in Hannah Glasse's English rabbit.

Recipe No. 1652: 'Toasted Cheese, or Welsh Rare-bit.' Cheshire or Gloucester cheese is stipulated. The bread is to be lightly toasted and then buttered and the cheese slices laid over. Toast again in a cheese-toaster: be careful to see that the cheese melts thoroughly without burning. Spread with mustard and send to table very hot.

By the 1912 edition *Household Management* had been considerably expanded and somewhat Frenchified. Recipe No. 1651 (Toasted Cheese or Scotch Rare-bit) now appears as the compromise No. 2810: 'Toasted Cheese (Fr. – Croûtes au Fromage).' The fondue-like recipe has disappeared, and the cheese is melted on the toast (in a Dutch oven – an early grill-toaster arrangement) before being sent to table.

In keeping with its new French elegance, the butter and mustard are to be mashed together with a pinch of cayenne and sandwiched between the slices of cheese before the toasting. The later edition then gives the next recipe, No. 2811, as 'Welsh Rabbit or Rarebit'. The joke has crept in again and we have our rabbit back.

In the face of such uncertainty I offer three culinary horse's mouths, an Englishwoman, a Welshwoman and a Scotswoman, as the ultimate authorities.

ENGLISH RAREBIT

This is Mrs Glasse's original version, as published in 1747.

Toast a slice of bread brown on both sides, then lay it in a place before the fire, pour a glass of red wine over it, and let

263

it soak the wine up; then cut some cheese very thin, and lay it very thick over the bread, and put it in a tin oven before the fire, and it will be toasted and brown'd presently. Serve it away hot.

WELSH RAREBIT

This is taken from Lady Llanover's *The First Principles of Good Cookery* which was published in 1867.

Welsh toasted cheese and the melted cheese of England are as different in the mode of preparation as the cheese itself; the one being only adapted to strong digestions, and the other being so easily digested that the Hermit frequently gave it to his invalid patients when they were recovering from illness. Cut a slice of the real Welsh cheese, made of sheep and cow's milk; toast it at the fire on both sides, but not so much as to drop; toast a piece of bread less than a quarter of an inch thick, to be quite crisp, and spread it very thinly with fresh cold butter on one side (it must not be saturated with butter); then lay the toasted cheese on the bread, and serve immediately on a very hot plate. The butter on the toast can of course be omitted if not liked, and it is more frequently eaten without butter.

SCOTS RAREBIT

Mrs Isobel Christian Johnston, alias Mistress Meg Dods (*The Field*, 10 November 1984), published this recipe in *The Cook and Housewife's Manual* (1826).

Pare the crust off a slice of bread cut smooth and of about a half-inch in thickness. Toast it, but do not let it winter or harden in the toasting. Butter it. Grate down mellow Stilton, Gouda, Cheshire, or good Dunlop cheese; and, if not fat, put to it some bits of fresh butter. Put this into a cheese toaster which has a hot-water reservoir and add to it a glassful of well flavoured brown-stout porter, a large teaspoonful of made mustard, and pepper (very finely ground) to taste. Stir the mixture till it is completely dissolved, brown it, and then, filling the reservoir with boiling water, serve the cheese with hot dry or buttered toasts on a separate dish.

8 February 1986

The Prince's Breakfast

The Elephant's Child's 'satiable curiosity about the crocodile's breakfast brought its own reward – a useful trunk, somewhat painfully acquired. A few days after the Royal Wedding I found my hooligan teenage daughters putting the same question to our neighbour's small grandson, although not about the crocodile.

The little boy had been a page on the great occasion, and the Wedding Breakfast menu, a closely guarded secret, was a matter of passionate public curiosity. The girls had abandoned earlier attempts to extract the information by charm and wiles, and were holding the lad by his feet over the edge of an ice-cold Hebridean trout stream. No Resistance hero could have been braver. He held on as long as he could endure, and then only yielded a single word.

'Kedgeree,' he gasped.

The torturers hauled him back on to the bank.

'With or without smoked salmon?' they demanded sternly.

Too late. The lad's lips were sealed. Not even the prospect of death by drowning would have got anything else out of him. He then took his revenge by hooking the only six fat brown trout left in the burn, and bearing them home for his supper. The ladies returned with three minnows.

So here in the brave young man's honour is a good and simple version of Kedgeree, legacy of the Queen Empress's India where it is made with lentils instead of fish.

KEDGEREE

TO SERVE 4 PEOPLE

½ lb rice
½ lb (2 cups) smoked haddock or
   smoked salmon

At least 4 oz butter
2 fresh eggs
Salt and pepper

Boil the rice in the way you like best. The final result must be dry and fluffy. The haddock only needs 5 minutes on top of the boiling rice to be perfectly cooked. The salmon will require no extra cooking. Boil the eggs hard, but do not over-boil (it is over-boiling which makes the yolk go green at the edges and smell of sulphur). One way to avoid this is to put the eggs into warm water and bring them to the boil. Then turn down the heat and simmer for five or six minutes, depending on the size of the eggs. Put them straight into cold water to loosen the shells. Shell and chop them.

Flake the fish. Melt the butter. Toss all the ingredients together, and season with salt and freshly milled pepper. All this can be done the night before. Reheat for breakfast for 15 minutes in a warm oven. There is a school of thought (to which I sometimes belong) which pours a quarter of a pint of boiling cream spiked with paprika over the whole dish. Kedgeree can be kept warm under covers, without spoiling, until the last sleepy breakfaster appears.

CHASSE

If on the other hand you prefer to be up with the hunters in the early morning, and would rather cook breakfast at the proper time, then Lady Jekyll, cookery correspondent of *The Times* in the 1920s, has the very answer.

> Collect 1 onion, 6 tomatoes, 3 potatoes, a slice of ham, some grated cheese, red pepper, and a pinch of allspice. Fry the onion lightly, add the skinned tomatoes and ham, both cut up small. When these are well browned in a buttered sauté pan, add a little water and the diced potatoes, and cook slowly till these are done. Before serving mix in grated cheese slightly flavoured with red pepper till the mixture is ropy. Pour on a hot dish, and serve with nicely poached eggs on the top. If preferred, omit the cheese.

This produces a rich and satisfying breakfast, particularly with the cheese. It has a comfortable bubble-and-squeak feel to it – with the added advantage of being a mixture of exactly the sort of things it is possible to find in the kitchen when you have run out of everything else.

BREAKFAST SCONES

The first thing I ever learnt to cook was breakfast scones, and it was an old lady from Aberdeen, Mrs Pocock, who taught me. The Scots have always made the best bakers.

½ lb flour	*½ teaspoon cream of tartar*
¼ teaspoon salt	*1 oz butter*
¼ teaspoon bicarbonate of soda	*⅓ pint sour milk*

Mix the first four ingredients together. The bicarbonate and cream of tartar can be replaced by self-raising flour with a little added baking powder, but the scones will not then be so light. Rub the butter into the flour with your fingertips. Knead into a soft dough with the milk. Roll out on a well-floured board and press out small rounds. If you were making them for tea, you would cut larger triangles instead. Mrs Pocock used to bake them on a hot griddle, but 10–15 minutes in a hot oven (400°F/gas 6) will do very well instead.

Breakfast like a king, lunch like a lord, dine like a pauper, always remembering that a royal breakfast can do wonders for your fishing skills.

26 January 1985

Buttering Up the Children

Modesty and cunning are not usually considered vital weapons in the cook's armoury. However, fifteen years of four birthdays and one Christmas each year taught me they are the qualities needed above all when catering for a children's party. Modesty first: if children don't like what you've made, no adult rules of manners will save your face. The whole offering will be left to moulder in the debris of streamers and cracker-paper. One standard item dropped early from my children's party menu was the sandwiches. I soon learnt the 'eat up your bread and butter before you have cake' routine went down like a lead balloon on party day. In their place I introduced combinations of bowls of potato crisps (I drew the line at vinegar-flavoured), twiglets, little cheese biscuits, small bowls of jelly-beans (not the coconut ones), chocolate cup-cakes, little triangles of processed cheese, popcorn, peanuts, and banana chips. All of them served naked and unashamed straight from the packet – for any cook, modesty indeed. As for the cake, children always seem to leave most of it, whatever you do. The cake should be disguised as a train, a teddy bear, or simply covered in Smarties – in my experience it has entertainment value only.

With the ground prepared and only treats on the table, comes the cunning. Today's jelly-bean queen is tomorrow's caviare connoisseur. The future of gastronomy is in their little hands. When your guests are all seated, happy and secure, in front of the shop-bought goodies – that's the moment to zap 'em. It's a culinary investment in the years ahead. Here is a tried selection of the small delicacies on which they can cut their milk molars, always remembering that with all the guile and skill in the world the whole lot may still get dumped in the litter.

PETS DE NONNE OR SOUFFLÉ FRITTERS

For the Chou Paste

4 oz butter   *5 oz plain flour*
½ pint water   *3 eggs*

Bring water and butter to the boil in a roomy saucepan. Off the heat, beat in the sieved flour. Dry the mixture over the heat, beating until the sides of the pan are left clean. Allow to cool a little and then beat in the eggs one by one. It will look like a curdled mayonnaise at first, but the paste will accept the eggs after a thorough working. When the paste is soft and shiny but still holds its shape, add salt and 2 oz of grated cheese to half the mixture, a tablespoonful of sugar to the rest. Take two teaspoons and scoop out little walnut-sized lumps. Fry them in hot oil until puffed and golden. Scatter the savoury ones with more grated cheese, and roll the sweet ones in cinnamon sugar. Serve immediately. Tell the children to look up *pets de nonne* in the dictionary: the translation always delights them. The same mixture can be used to make little éclairs and choux buns if baked in the oven at 400°F/gas 6 for 20 minutes. It also makes the basis for the most delicate of quenelles.

Further Tricks

Tiny *pizzas* made of circles of French bread baked with a trickle of olive oil for 10 minutes in the oven, then spread with tomatoes reduced with a little chopped garlic. Top with grated cheese, marjoram or thyme, a tiny piece of anchovy, and a black olive.

Miniature *Scotch eggs* made with quail's eggs and good sausage meat.

Mussels steamed open in their own juice. There might be a pearl in one.

Baby *croque-monsieur*: make ham and cheese sandwiches, quarter them and cut off the crusts. Fry in a mixture of oil and butter. Serve very hot on toothpicks.

Chinese *prawn crackers*. Packets of little dried discs are available from supermarkets – they only need to be deep-fried. (They're very good for grown-ups with a little red caviare and sour cream.)

Perfect *twice-fried chips*. Nothing to beat them if you use good oil and fry them crisp and golden.

On the subject of chips, my eldest daughter's godfather – a passionate gastronome – had an interesting way of discharging his culinary responsibility to the future. Once a month, on Sunday, he would take his own offspring and his godchildren, together with their various brothers and sisters, out to lunch. The mob could number a dozen, and all were sworn to secrecy. The children were sophisticated teenagers and the lunches long discontinued before I found out where they went and what they did. He took them to the London Zoo. They watched the seals' feeding-time and then retired to the Fellows' Restaurant. The young Mafiosi occupied the long central table and lunch was always the same: chips and ice-cream with chocolate sauce, served simultaneously and washed down with Coke. Any method of eating was allowed, including practising being seals. The Godfather himself sat at the head and contentedly drank Pimms. The children still insist they were the best parties ever.

15 December 1984

Hitch-Hiker's Guide to Fondue

The turning of the year sees the ski-slopes of Switzerland filling up with the annual British influx. From every ski-lift café wafts the spicy scent of glühwein and Switzerland's one true gift to the gastronome, cheese fondue. In London, palisades of skis fence off Victoria Station. A few people are already sporting those curious suntans which stop short at the wrist and neck, leaving acres of white flesh to the imagination. The Swiss look like this all the time, but since they are long on banking and short on jokes they are too busy to notice.

My good friend Danny-le-Suisse at seventeen was, conversely, short on banking and long on jokes, most of them in a thick patois. In his homeland the inhabitants tend to come a little short in stature, too, and Danny, six foot four and still growing, must have stuck out like a sore thumb. He arrived in my kitchen one year, unannounced and uninvited, after the snows had melted on his native mountains, explaining he had made *le auto-stop* all the way from Neuchâtel to southern Spain in order to visit his sister. The sister was working as a nanny for one of our neighbours, and there had been a little uncertainty over Danny's status and social position in her employers' household. He added he had left Neuchâtel and his beloved Madame Mère in order to make his fortune but, first, could he please borrow my kitchen to make his staple diet, semolina pudding? My household, deciding he would go far, gave him the freedom of the semolina and adopted him as an investment in the future.

The investment brought an immediate return. The following morning Danny hitch-hiked to the nearest town. Late that afternoon he returned with a large carrier-bag and summoned the household to watch him unpack it. Beaming happily, he took out a small glazed earthenware cooking-pot with a handle, a tiny alcohol-fuelled stove, a round peasant loaf from the local bakery, a couple of slender green bottles, and a paper bag containing two large pieces of cheese.

'This', he said as he picked up the pot, 'will serve as the *caclon*. And it is fortunate we have here wine of a quality approaching that of my native Neuchâtel. Here is my gift. I will show you how my mother makes a fondue.'

FONDUE DE NEUCHÂTEL

1 loaf day-old bread
1 clove garlic
½ lb Gruyère cheese (this is the one
   with only a few small holes)
½ lb Emmenthal cheese (the one with
   the large holes)

½ bottle dry white wine (Neuchâtel if
   you can find it)
1 teaspoon cornflour or potato starch
1 tiny glass kirsch

Lay the table for 4 with a fork and a glass each. You will be drinking the same dry white wine as you use in the mixture, and it should be very cold and plentiful. Cut the bread into comfortable bite-sized squares and put a plate of them in front of each place. Fill the spirit-lamp and set it in the centre. It is important to do this first, as once you embark on the fondue you will not be able to leave it.

Rub the *caclon* with the garlic to scent it. Madame Klein, being a purist, would then chop the two cheeses into tiny pieces, but the rest of us may be allowed to grate it. Pour all but a couple of spoonfuls of the wine, plus all the cheese, into the pot. Heat gently, stirring with a wire whisk, until the mixture boils. At this point it does not look very encouraging. The mixture smells strongly of alcohol, and the liquids and solids show no inclination to mix. Stir the cornflour into the remaining cold white wine and whisk the resulting milky liquid into the contents of the pot. Beat it all together over the heat. Continue to beat as it thickens. The haze of alcohol has cleared now, and it is time to add the kirsch. Continue to cook for five minutes. The fondue will now be thick and creamy, and all the alcohol will have evaporated. Take the dish to the table and keep it warm over the spirit-lamp.

All is ready. Each guest spears a hunk of bread on his fork and stirs it once round the pot to cover it with cheese. Delicious. Anyone who drops his bread into the fondue has to buy another bottle of wine. At the end a beautiful brown crust of toasted cheese is waiting to be discovered on the bottom of the *caclon*. This is the *dentelle* and is the best part of all.

Danny-le-Suisse is now a millionaire entrepreneur. He has business interests all over America and jets back and forth on Concorde with his beautiful girlfriend, a six-foot model. His passion for semolina has given way to a nice appreciation of oysters and caviare, in which, I am happy to report, my household sometimes shares. But he can still turn in a memorable fondue.

5 January 1985

271

A Taste of Oils from Tuscany

I have attended my first olive oil tasting. At this very moment a tide of superior Italian olive oil is lapping the shores of our sceptred isle. It is useless to take up the position urged on King Canute by his courtiers. This is no mere flash in the pan. The olive oil producers of Tuscany are determined such jamborees will become as much a part of the British way of life as wine-tastings.

I am very fond of olive oil. When it comes to an early-morning snack of hot fresh bread rubbed with a clove of garlic and blessed with a trickle of the green stuff, I am as game as the next man. However, the sight of eighteen tiny dishes of viscous liquid awaiting the taster's verdict is a little daunting. Particularly so if there are a dozen knowledgeable Italians discussing cold-pressing and acidity levels. I have no vocabulary suitable for their expectations in any language. The French are quite unequivocal about their olive oil: it is, in all its forms, quite obviously far better than anyone else's. The Spanish are perfectly simple – they fry things in it or throw it on their salads in as large quantities as they can afford. How the Greeks, who after all invented olive oil as they invented democracy and everything else, feel about it I do not know. They are probably content to rest on their laurels.

It is only the Italians who seem to be competitive: the tasting was, we were told, designed to find which of the various *mis-en-bouteille-au-château* oils appealed most strongly to the British palate. We were all requested to taste all eighteen oils (chunks of rather good bread being provided for the purpose) and then place them in order of merit. Oof. By the end of it I had taken on more oil than a Saudi supertanker. My powers of selection deserted me. I have a similar problem at wine-tastings, but that is only because I think it such a waste to spit out good wine.

I cannot list for you those Tuscan oils superior in quality to the others. I can only offer that some of them are a wonderful sticky leafy green, others golden as new honey. Some of them are clouded, some of them are clear. Some of them taste strongly of leaf, some of fruit. Some are delicate, some robust. The trouble is, I can't remember which was which. But I can tell you that if you want good olive oil, virgin olive oil from the first pressing, it will cost you as much as a decent bottle of wine. And it will be worth it.

The lighter oils make beautiful mayonnaise. Perfect for summer. The best and easiest lunch for the garden I know is a do-it-yourself club sandwich – served with your own olive oil mayonnaise, naturally.

CLUB SANDWICHES

Arrange in separate piles on a large platter: whole lettuce leaves, sliced tomatoes, sliced hard-boiled eggs, and slices of roast chicken (no bones or skin). At the last minute, fry some very fine-cut smoked streaky bacon until it is crisp, and toast two pieces of bread per head. (You may have to make more toast and bacon when it is needed, but they have to be hot and fresh.) Each guest then constructs his own sandwich, with a liberal basting of mayonnaise.

OLIVE OIL MAYONNAISE

One egg yolk will absorb about a quarter of a pint of olive oil and a tablespoonful of vinegar – enough for four sandwiches. It is essential to successful mayonnaise-making that both egg and oil should be at room temperature.

Put the egg yolk in a basin and season it with mustard, salt, pepper and a pinch of sugar. Beat with a wooden spoon to mix. Add the olive oil very slowly at first, mixing thoroughly so that the two substances emulsify. Quite soon you will see the sauce beginning to thicken. (If it does not thicken quickly, beat like crazy with a wire whisk. If the mixture still fails to emulsify, emergency first-aid is a

273

splash of boiling water. If you have no success even then, start again, more slowly this time, adding the curdled mayonnaise to a new egg yolk.) Once the egg has absorbed a quarter of the oil, you can speed up the rate at which you add it. Mix in the vinegar when it gets really thick. Then add more oil until it is as solid as you like. Stop when it looks very shiny – a sign it will take no more oil.

29 June 1985

Storecupboard and Cellar

Meals from the Storecupboard

Most cooks have a few dishes which are quickly prepared and easily available from their own particular household stores, and all cooks have different essential items in their larder. My own corner cupboard always contains tinned tomatoes, tomato paste, Basmati rice, sardines in oil, tunnyfish in brine, anchovies in oil, black olives, tinned sweetcorn, a tin or two of corned beef, pickled cucumbers and Chinese chilli sauce. Sometimes it contains very little else. However, with these few stores, plus whatever vegetables and eggs there are around, I can – if suitably soft-soaped – throw together an economical meal for a handful of hungry teenagers. None of these recipes should take more than half an hour from can-opener to table.

FAST FISHCAKES WITH TOMATO SAUCE

TO SERVE 4 PEOPLE

For the Fishcakes

2 lb potatoes
2 oz butter
1 tin sardines
1 tablespoon chopped fresh herbs
   (1 teaspoon dried)

Salt and pepper
2 eggs
Oil for frying

For the Sauce

1 medium tin tomatoes
1 tablespoon tomato paste
1 piece fresh ginger (optional)

½ onion
Chilli sauce to taste

Put a large pan of salted water on to boil before you do anything else. Peel the potatoes and cut them into even-sized chunks. Put them to cook until soft in the pan of boiling water; this will take about 20 minutes.

Meanwhile open the various tins. Peel and slice the ginger. Peel and slice the onion. Put all the sauce ingredients into the liquidizer and process them to a purée. Transfer this sauce to a small pan and put it to simmer gently at the back of the stove. Put on a simple vegetable to cook – shredded cabbage to be sweated in the water which clings to its leaves plus a knob of butter; or frozen peas; or beans. By this time the potatoes should be ready. Test them with the point of a knife. Drain them well and mash thoroughly with the butter. Beat in the contents of the tin of sardines (oil, bones and all), the herbs, a teaspoon of salt and plenty of freshly ground black pepper. Now beat in the eggs.

Pour oil to the depth of half a finger into the frying-pan. Heat the oil till you see a faint blue haze rise. Drop in spoonfuls of the fishcake mixture and fry till crisp underneath. Turn and fry the other side. Serve hot with the green vegetable and the tomato sauce handed separately.

RICE FRITTERS WITH PIMENTO SAUCE

TO SERVE 4 PEOPLE.

(This is a good recipe for left-over rice.)

For the Fritters

8 oz rice (uncooked weight)
3 eggs
2 tablespoons fresh chopped herbs
   (parsley, chives, marjoram)

Salt and pepper
Oil for frying

For the Sauce

1 medium tin pimentos
1 slice day-old bread

2–3 cloves garlic
3 tablespoons olive oil

Put a pan of salted water on to boil. Fast cooking, like old-fashioned childbirth, requires plenty of boiling water. When the water boils, throw in the rice. Give it a turn with a wooden spoon to separate the grains. Leave it to cook until soft – about 20 minutes. Meanwhile make the sauce. Open the tin of pimentos and drain out the liquid. Tear the bread into pieces. Peel the garlic. Put all the sauce ingre-

277

dients into the liquidizer and process thoroughly. That's all. It looks pretty in a plain white bowl.

Beat the eggs lightly together in a large bowl. Add the chopped herbs, ½ teaspoon salt and freshly milled black pepper. By now the rice should be soft. Drain it in a colander and run cold water through the grains. Shake well to dry. Mix the rice into the egg mixture.

Pour frying oil into a frying-pan to depth of half a finger and heat the oil until a faint blue haze rises. Drop in spoonfuls of the rice mixture and fry on each side until crisp.

Serve with the pimento sauce handed separately. Accompany with a salad of sliced tomatoes dressed with olive oil, black pepper and perhaps a little crumbled white cheese.

RICE AND TUNNYFISH SALAD

TO SERVE 4 PEOPLE

8 oz rice	Olive oil
4 oz tin tunnyfish	Wine vinegar
1 medium tin sweetcorn	Salt and pepper
2 pickled cucumbers (or ½ fresh cucumber)	12 black olives
1 mild onion (replace with pickled onions if you use fresh cucumber)	

Put on the usual pan of salted water to boil. When the pot boils, throw in the rice and cook it till soft – about 20 minutes. Meanwhile open all the tins. Drain the sweetcorn. Drain the tunnyfish and flake it lightly. Chop the pickled cucumbers; if you are using a fresh one, dice it into little cubes. Peel and chop the onion and add it to the rest of the salad. Put all these ingredients into a large china bowl and turn them together with a fork.

By this time the rice should be cooked. Drain it well in a colander and run cold water through it. Leave it to drain again. Add to the rest of the salad and toss well.

Dress with the oil and vinegar, a teaspoon of salt and plenty of freshly milled pepper. Scatter the olives over the top.

Accompany with a green salad or lightly cooked young green beans dressed with oil and wine vinegar and served warm.

4 October 1986

A Noble Lover's Last Meal

May Week and time for boats and balls and Byron's 'young barbarians all at play'. Miss Zuleika Dobson stirs in her leaves and opens her magnificent eyes.

Max Beerbohm's heroine, that 'radiant, irresistible member of the upper middle classes', hacked her way through the adoring undergraduate undergrowth in May Week *circa* 1910. Doomed by her beauty, the entire (fictional) male student population of Oxford threw itself into the river and drowned beneath the competing college oars.

The fourteenth Duke of Dorset, John Albert Edward Tanville-Tankerton, Earl of Grove, Earl of Chastermaine, Viscount Brewsby, Baron Petstrap and Wolock *et al.*, most brilliant undergraduate of his generation, most exquisite gallant, his hearth-poised feet arched as beautifully as, the narrator tells us, two glazed ox-tongues on a breakfast-table, shared one lovers' luncheon with the glorious Zuleika. The meal was frugal, considering the appetite engendered by the emotional state of the participants: a cold chicken and salad, a gooseberry tart, a Camembert. The gastronomic pace hotted up in inverse ratio to the progress of the romance. Here is the condemned lover's last meal, as provided by the duke's landlady, Mrs Batch. The duke's cooks – three French chefs, an Italian pastry-cook, a Spaniard for salads, an Englishwoman for roasts, an Abyssinian for coffee – are already in mourning at Tankerton (pronounced Tacton) Hall. The two black owls of the Tankertons have spent the previous night hooting (mournfully, of course) on the family battlements to herald the impending demise of their master.

MENU FOR AN OXFORD TRAGEDY

Cold Salmon

Let us do what we can for the unfortunate duke's commons. The cold salmon could be potted with sweet butter, a dish with a pedigree somewhat older than his Grace's.

Mix cooked and flaked salmon with an equal volume of melted butter, the two to be carefully seasoned with salt, freshly milled black pepper and nutmeg. Pack the fish into small pots and seal by pouring clarified butter over the top. Cool. It will keep in the fridge for a few days if necessary, but put an extra lid of tinfoil or

Cellophane film over it. Serve with quarters of lemon and brown toast.

Pigeon Pie (for 4)

A recipe from Bordeaux would go well with his Grace's French title, duc d'Etretat et de la Roche Guillaume, given to his father by Louis Napoleon for not cutting him in the Bois de Boulogne. In Bordeaux it would be made with the little migratory collared doves. British pigeons have had a hard thin winter; it may be necessary to use little rolls of beef escallops instead of the birds.

3 or 4 young pigeons	*1 bottle good red wine of Bordeaux*
1 oz flour	*6 juniper berries*
2 oz fat bacon	*Small bunch thyme*
1 oz butter	*Salt and pepper*
4 oz raw ham	*½ lb puff pastry*
1 onion	
8 oz mushrooms (cèpes would be even better)	

If you have access to plenty of pigeons, just use the breasts for this recipe. In that case, you will need the breasts of 6 birds for 4 people. Otherwise, quarter the pigeons. Flour them lightly.

Cube the bacon and sweat it in a frying-pan until the fat runs. Fry the pigeon pieces in the bacon fat to seize the outside, then put them and the bacon into the pie-dish. Dice the ham and onions and slice the mushrooms. Add the butter to the fat in the frying-pan. Fry the ham, the onion and the mushrooms lightly and add them to the pigeons. De-glaze the frying-pan with a glass of the red wine and add that to the meats. Put in the thyme and the juniper berries, crushed. Season with salt, pepper and nutmeg. Pour as much wine into the pie-dish as will reach two-thirds of the way up. Roll out the puff pastry to make a lid for the pie. Bake at 375°F/gas 5, for 45 minutes.

Custard Pudding

Also to be served warm. A Floating Island would be an elegant acknowledgement of the duke's watery end.

Beat the yolks of 4 eggs with 2 oz of sugar. Bring a pint of milk nearly to the boil, and then pour it over the egg-yolk mixture, whisking vigorously. Return the mixture to a gentle heat and stir until the custard thickens enough to coat the back of the spoon. Remove from the heat and stir in a quarter of a pint of cream. Add a spoonful of brandy to stiffen the sinews. Pour it into a wide bowl.

Whip the 4 whites of egg until they form peaks, then beat in 4 oz of sugar. Float spoonfuls of the meringue on to the surface of the custard so that they remain small white islands. Serve warm.

Champagne and port complete the menu. We leave the unrepentant Miss Dobson consulting her beryl-encrusted *Bradshaw's* for the train times to Cambridge.

25 April 1985

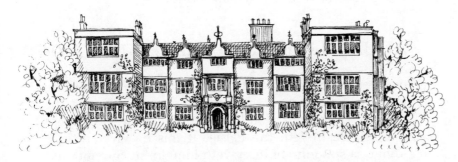

Sir Kenelm's Closet Open'd

Michaelmas to Candlemas, the time for mead and metheglin, great fires in the hearth and partridges fattening by the ant-heap. Keeping the home fires burning was the special accomplishment of the Eminently Learned Sir Kenelm Digby, Knight. Digby, depending on the authority, was either a romantic Renaissance scholar-cavalier or in John Evelyn's view an 'errant mountebank', whose Closet was Opened after his death in 1669. Skeletons had been falling out of it since his birth in 1603, so happily all that was left on the shelf by then was a magnificent and authoritative collection of recipes and instructions for the stocking of his cellar and the loading of his table.

The first skeleton tumbled out when the lad was but three years old: his father, the handsome unlucky Gunpowder Plotter, Sir Everard, was messily despatched by King James's executioner and his fortune confiscated. The family had always been high-risk: seven Digbys perished on Bosworth field. Fortunately, Lady Digby managed to hang on to her dowry, a house and some land at Gayhurst in Buckinghamshire. Among the neighbours was a young girl, a playmate for Kenelm although she was three years older, the beautiful motherless Venetia Stanley. The grand-daughter of the Earl of Northumberland, Venetia was 'a lady of far purer birth than fame'. Kenelm fell passionately in love with her – and was promptly sent off on the Grand Tour to get over his infatuation. He had already spent a year at Oxford, studying under the old mathematician Thomas Allen, a necromancer so powerful his servant reported spirits swarming on his stairs like bees. Allen thought highly enough of Digby to bequeath him his library (and probably the bees as well). Among the clear rose jellies and mushroom ketchups in the Opened Closet is a useful little potion that may well have come from Allen and should be invaluable during this season of surfeits (reports on its efficacy would be most welcome).

AQUA MIRABILIS (SIR KENELM'S WAY)

For preserving the Lungs, thickening the Blood, banishing heartburn, melancholy, Spleen, Rheum; preserving the Stomach, conserving Youth and good Colour. Preserveth Memory, destroyeth the Palsie. If this be given to one a-dying, a spoonful of it reviveth him; in the Summer use one spoonful a week fasting, in the Winter two spoonfuls.

Take Cubebs [a berry from Java, much like pepper], Gallingale [a mild ginger-root], Cardamus, Melliot-flowers [clover], Cloves, Mace, Ginger, Cinnamon, of each one dram bruised small, juice of Celandine one pint, juice of Spearmint half a pint, juice of Balm half a pint, Sugar one pound, flower of Cowslips, Rosemary, Borage, Bugloss, Marigold of each two drams, the best Sack [sherry] three pints, strong Angelica water one pint, red Rose-water half a pint; bruise the Spices and Flowers and steep them in the Sack and juices one night: the next morning distil it in an ordinary glass still, and first lay Harts-tongue leaves [a fern, *Scolopendrum vulgare*] in the bottom. Bottle and stopper it tight and store in the Closet.

The memory of Venetia did not fade as Kenelm travelled. He narrowly escaped the attentions of the Queen Mother of France, the libidinous Marie de Medici, who spotted him at a masked ball, by fleeing to Italy. A spell in Madrid to help his cousin in the arrangement of Prince Charles's proposed match with the Infanta found him flirting with a lovely Spanish girl, the sister of the Duke of Maqueda. He left her behind, but returned with several Spanish recipes, including very precise instructions for 'A plain but good Spanish Oglia' – a stupendous classic *Cocido Madrileño*, complete with capons, pigeons, beef, garlic and chickpeas. Meanwhile his light of love, the Lady Venetia, had removed to London and the attentions of, among others, the Earl of Dorset, by whom John Aubrey, who disapproved of her, says she had several children, and was in receipt of an annual income of £500. More than one other gentleman allegedly had her portrait – an accepted earnest of affection usually handed out with great discretion.

In recognition of Digby's embassy, King James decided to knight the young man. The monarch was nervous of steel, his mother having been frightened by a sword-fight in her bedroom during her confinement, and he nearly poked Kenelm's eye out when he averted the royal face from the sword at the crucial moment. Sir Kenelm then set about recapturing his Venetia. Duels were fought, seductions repelled, wandering portraits belligerently retrieved. Finally he married her in secret. The lovers were very happy for the eight years Venetia had left. Kenelm went adventuring as a privateer, and Venetia bore him a son, after which the marriage was made public. Her husband wrote a long allegorical memoir extolling her beauty and her virtue (although, always practical, he dwelt more on her chastity. after marriage than before). Ben Jonson eulogized her. Van Dyck painted her in many guises. When she died of consumption in 1633, gossips said she had been poisoned by the viper-water she drank for her complexion. Kenelm, prompted no doubt by the busy ghost of Dr Allen, opened her cranium and declared her to have very little brain left. Poor skeleton in the Closet. Her husband retreated in despair to Gresham College in London and threw himself into his scientific studies.

Eventually Sir Kenelm became a founder member of the Royal Society, and it was his interest in chemistry and medicine which made him such a fine and careful cook. His instructions and measurements are always clear and precise, as are his detailed observations of the husbandry of his friends. Since these included Bacon, Galileo, Descartes, William Harvey, Ben Jonson, Oliver Cromwell and Sir Thomas Browne, there was no shortage of originality or talent. The medicament for which he was most celebrated was his Powder of Sympathy – a magician's trick based on the ancient medical theory of sympathy and antipathy between paired objects. The decoction was very simple for the age (when moss from a murderer's skull was the easiest to procure of a dozen ingredients:) distilled vitriol to be dried in the sun during the dog-days. A bandage removed from the wound would be dipped in the powder and the wound would heal itself in sympathy. His recipe was hailed with great enthusiasm and kept in use for a hundred years.

For his flower cordials, quince jams and sweetmeats in honey, Sir Kenelm had the affectionate interest of three queens. To Henrietta Maria, wife of Charles I, who interceded for Digby when he was called to account as a Popish recusant by the Long Parliament in 1641, he credits the Countess of Penalva's Portuguese eggs. The recipe is for a fondant of egg yolks and sugar still made today as *Yemas*. He does not neglect the dairy and poultry-yard, and gives several highly technical recipes for clotted cream. His friend Lady Fanshaw has a very modern way with chickens:

> My Lady Fanshaw has her poultry in Coops so they cannot turn. She feeds them from two troughs. One contains three Barleys, one boiled in water, one in Milk and one in Ale with brown sugar. The other trough contains Water or Strong Ale. They will be very drunk and sleep; then wake and eat again. Let a candle stand all night over the Coop, and then they will eat much in the night. With this course they will be prodigiously fat in a fortnight.

His instruction 'To Boil Eggs' is elegant and, in its timing, exact:

> A certain and infallible method to boil new laid eggs to sup up, and yet that they have the white turned to milk, is thus: Break a very little hole, at the bigger end of the shell, and put it into the water whiles it boileth. Let it remain boiling, whiles your pulse beat 200 strokes. Then take it out immediately, and you will find it of an exact temper.

He's just as expert at frying fish:

> The best liquor to fry fish in, is to take Butter and Sallet-oyl, first well clarified together. This has not the unsavoury taste of Oyl alone, nor the blackness of Butter alone. It frieth Fish crisp, yellow and well-tasted.

Indeed it does. From a Jesuit who returned from China in 1664, Digby learnt that the newly arrived herbal drink of tea was ill-prepared in England.

In these Parts, he saith, we let the hot water remain too long soaking upon the tea, which makes it extract into itself the earthy parts of the herb. The water is to remain on it no longer than whiles you can say the Misere Psalm very leisurely.

Sir Kenelm died of the stone in 1665, the year of the Great Plague. He was buried beside his beautiful wife in Christ Church, Newgate, but the following year the ebony tomb of the lovers was consumed in the flames of the Great Fire. 'Living well is the best revenge' might well have been his motto. Here, neatly weighed as always (no strew-it-o'er-with-herbs from the master) is his parting shot at Christmas:

To Pickle an Old Fat Goose
Cut it down the back, and take out all the bones; lard it very well with green Bacon, and season it well with three quarters of an ounce of Pepper, half an ounce of Ginger, a quarter of an ounce of Cloves, and Salt as you judge proportionable, a pint of White-wine and some Butter. Put three or four Bay leaves under the meat, and bake it with brown bread, in an earthen pot close-covered, and the edges of the cover closed with Paste. Let it stand three or four days in the pickle; then eat.

Christmas 1984

Smoking Your Own

When a courageous eighteenth-century entrepreneur first packed a load of fresh salmon in ice for shipping to the southern markets, his venture was greeted with deep scepticism. The entrepreneur had the idea from an East India Company employee back home on leave. The East India hand observed that the Chinese transported their fish packed in snow, a method they had been using for centuries. Londoners were long accustomed to receiving their salmon salted, smoked, and dried into a hard plank about the size and configuration of a large pink cricket bat. Bad smells – and bad fishy smells in particular – were thought in medieval times to be responsible for epidemics (including the dreaded Plague), and the memory ling-

ered on. The entrepreneur's new method of refrigerated transport worked surprisingly well, and the brave fellow made his fortune.

The smoking of salmon, freed from the demands of the storage problem, subsequently evolved into the much more perishable modern delicacy. Preparation has nowadays largely passed into the hands of the professionals, but for those who catch their own it is well worth building a simple smoker and tackling the job yourself. Store smoked salmon in the refrigerator, or in the freezer if you mean to keep it for more than a few days. It is a lightly preserved foodstuff. I am indebted to Mr Jonathon Morshead for his method of smoking salmon, which he uses every year, his fortune as a fisherman permitting, with delectable results.

To prepare the fish: a salmon weighing 8–10 lb is the best size for home smoking. Scale the fish, behead, gut and remove the backbone, leaving two flat fillets with the skin on. If the salmon tops 15 lb, slash the skin (without going through to the flesh) to allow the salt to penetrate. A smooth wooden plank makes a good salting-board. Allow half a pound of ordinary salt per side of salmon. Sprinkle salt on the board and spread a layer of salt about an eighth of an inch thick on the flesh side of the salmon, with a thicker layer at the thick end of the fish. Leave the fish to take the salt, allowing it to drain as it does so, for 5–6 hours. When it is ready it will feel springy to the touch. The thicker the fish, the longer the salting. Wash thoroughly under running water to remove the surface salt (when you have done so, the surface should still taste salty). Tie a string round the top fin and the hard gill-joint. Hang the salted salmon in an airy room for about 12 hours until the outside of the fish feels dry to the touch.

To construct the smoker: an outhouse which still has a chimney in it makes an excellent smokehouse. Failing such luxury, use a corner of an open shed (good ventilation is important, but you do need to protect both fish and fire from rain). For the smoker itself, you will need an empty forty-gallon metal drum. Check to see that it contains no traces of dangerous chemicals before you embark on the project. Remove the base and the top of the drum, leaving you with a large wide iron tube. Cut a semicircle out of the base for the smoke to enter. Build a channel with bricks or a piece of wide piping leading into the smokehole, leaving the other end without a cover so that you can build the smoke-fire in it. This arrangement acts like a kind of large tobacco-pipe, except that the fire is at the stem end instead of in the bowl.

The fuel generally used for smoking is beech or oak sawdust. A timberyard can usually supply chain-saw dust for the purpose. Light a sawdust fire (you may need a little kindling) in the open mouth of the pipe-stem. When it is hot and smoking, push the smouldering sawdust into the covered part of the pipe. The draught will then draw the smoke through the pipe, into the drum and out, either up the chimney or into the open air. To keep the fire going, push at intervals a little more sawdust down the open pipe and into the embers.

The sides of salmon are strung on sticks which straddle the top of the drum so that the fish hang suspended in the up-draught of the smoke. It will take around 5–6 hours to smoke the two sides of an 8–10 lb salmon. On windy days the fish will be more quickly smoked. On a very still day, it can be left in the smoker overnight if necessary. You will soon learn how to tell when the salmon is ready: its surface will begin to look shiny and will sweat tiny beads of oil.

3 August 1985

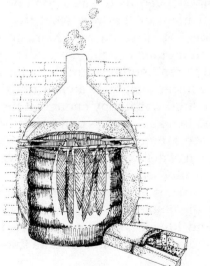

Taking the Waters

The trouble these days with spas and places to take the water is that nobody in them ever seems to look healthy. It was not always thus. In their heyday such places were seasonal resorts for the idle rich, many of whom suffered from little more than a surfeit of everything. All anyone really needed then was a good dose of bicarbonate of soda – and that more or less was what they got. Baden-Baden, Eugénie-les-Bains, Montecatini and Marienbad were all on my fashionable grandmother's circuit, and in my youth I was trailed round them. My grandmother went there for the clothes and the people, and she never took the waters seriously. My grandfather, who loved gambling, was happy enough at the gaming-tables and was only obliged to take one glass of the beastly mineral-laced dose at the pump once a morning. As for me, I was delighted by an endless succession of delicious meals which I was allowed to choose myself: ambrosia after school dinners.

Twenty years on, nostalgia drew me to make an overnight stop at Bad Gleichenberg in southern Austria, where once the Emperor Franz Joseph and his elegant Court disported themselves. Their ghosts must shudder in the cold corridors these days. The elderly inmates of the half-dozen faded Grand Hotels could not have tottered a Viennese waltz between them. The medical staff were in their late teens and inclined to take their pleasures at full volume via the jukebox in the dining-room – now converted into a cafeteria. Video games flash where sugar fantasies and diplomate puddings nightly trembled.

Just as connoisseurs of the once-fine art of football who still wish to enjoy the game find it cheaper and safer to do so in the peace of their own drawing-room, so those who like to take the waters do well to have their supplies home-delivered. Bottled waters are now available in ever-increasing numbers and diversity – and not all of them are medicinal. Some taste quite palatable: the rough rule of thumb is, as with most things in life, the nastier the stuff tastes the more it contains of that which is supposed to do you good. Some of the waters are flat and some are fizzy, and the brand-names of both are breeding like rabbits.

The key to mineral waters bottled in Europe, if you can unscramble the jargon, is given in the small print on the label.

'Mineral Water' indicates that the water contains mineral salts (presumably of a health-promoting nature) and has had no treatment apart from filtration and removal of iron. The water can come from a natural spring or a man-made borehole.

The designation 'Spring Water' assures the consumer that the water sprang naturally, unassisted by the hand of man, from the rock. No health claims attached.

'Naturally Carbonated' or 'Effervescent' or 'Sparkling' means what it says: the water has emerged from the ground in a fizzy toe-tickling state. The processors are, however, permitted to 'draw off' the fizz and put it back in at a later stage in order to make sure that all bottles are of a uniform fizziness.

'Carbonated' or 'Sparkling'. Here lie murkier depths. This definition merely indicates that the water (whatever water – it could be the legendary seven-times-recycled London tapwater) has been injected with ordinary carbon dioxide, just as for soda water or Coca-Cola.

Mineral content is analysed by boiling the water and measuring the dry residue or total dissolved solids (known to the trade as 'tds'). The water is then given a rating: lightly mineralized water has less than 500 milligrams per litre (mg/l). Medium mineralized can have up to 1,000 mg/l. Over 1,000 mg/l is rated high.

The pH factor, as every gardener knows, is the balance between alkalinity and acidity. A pH over 7 indicates an alkaline water; the

Italian San Pellegrino is in this group. A pH below 7 means an acid water; Perrier and Badoit both rank here.

'Carbonation Level' is an indicator of fizziness. German carbonated waters are particularly perky (perhaps to assist dumpling-laden German digestions) and are likely to have a carbonation level between 6 and 9 grams per litre. A lighter punch of 3 to 6 grams per litre goes into Perrier and San Pellegrino (to reflect the lighter menus of the French and Italians), while a gentle sparkle no higher than 3 grams per litre lightens Badoit (currently fashionable with the water-snobs) and Farrarelle. British Malvern water springs flat from the hillside and is not only bottled (by appointment) for the monarch, it is also supplied to Downing Street and the Houses of Parliament. The British voter-in-the-street, however, prefers his bottled water carbonated. As with their politicians, countries get the mineral waters they deserve.

22 February 1986

From a School of Spring-Cleaning

The Eastbourne School of Domestic Economy, a training establishment for young ladies in general and those aspiring to the hotel and catering trade in particular, had my custom for one formative teenage year. I came out equipped with an understanding of how to construct a mixed salad large enough to prevent scurvy in the crew of a small battleship; a comprehensive grasp of alternative methods of reconstituting dried eggs and dehydrated whale blubber (those were hard times in the British catering trade); biceps more than equal to the task of beating up enough white sauce to blanket half a stone of school cauliflower; and, last and most deeply rooted, a profound knowledge of the now-forgotten art of spring-cleaning. Some can lay claim to previous incarnations as Cleopatra or Marie-Antoinette. I know I am the reincarnation of a Victorian housemaid.

As the days lengthen and the hawthorn buds in the hedge, the first shafts of spring sunlight illuminate, inexorably, the failings of the last eleven months. March is nearly through, spring-cleaning time again. The Eastbourne School of Domestic Economy did not countenance commercial-brand household cleaners. No, indeed; Victorian housemaids made their own – and some of the tricks of the trade were both cheap and efficient. Time to shake out old memories and new dusters.

RECIPES FOR SPRING-CLEANING

Cleaning windows: Fill a bucket with warm water laced with a cupful of vinegar. Make a loose ball of old newspaper, dampen it in the water and vinegar, and use it to polish the glass. The *Daily Mirror* and the *Sun* seem to have the right newsprint and paper for this. *The Times* is hopeless. If you want to shine up a decanter, pour in a tablespoon of rough salt and a tablespoon of vinegar. Shake it around vigorously. Rinse out.

Instant silver-dip: Spread a layer of metal milk-bottle tops in the bottom of a plastic washing-up bowl. Sprinkle on a handful of household washing soda. Cover with water warm enough to dissolve the soda. Put in the silver to be cleaned. Magic. There must be some chemical reason why it works.

To clean rusty knives: Sprinkle out a pile of scouring powder and dip the end of a cork in it. Use it to scrub the blades with. Particularly useful for cleaning good non-stainless steel kitchen knives.

Furniture cream: Take 3 oz beeswax, ½ pint turpentine or white spirit, ½ pint warm water, 1 tablespoon ammonia. Melt the wax gently in a small pan. Pour in the turpentine and the water and mix all well together. Simmer gently for ten minutes. Leave it to cool a little and then stir in the ammonia. Bottle tightly and label clearly.

Feather quilts: Half-fill a bathtub with warm water and add a few handfuls of soap flakes – that is, not detergent, but old-fashioned soap flakes such as Lux. Put in the quilt and squeeze it gently and thoroughly until the water is dirty. Repeat. Rinse well in clean water, wring out well, and then hang up to dry in the spring sunshine. When it is dry, shake it well to fluff it up.

Burnt saucepans: Fill them with a strong solution of salt and water. Leave them to soak overnight. The following day, bring the water slowly to the boil. The burnt bits will come off easily.

Smoke stains: Smoked-blackened paint should be washed with warm water in which has been dissolved a little washing soda. Soap should not be used.

To clean a clock: Soak a wad of cottonwool in paraffin. Put it inside to line the base of the clock. Leave it there for 3–4 days. The paraffin fumes will loosen the dirt on the works, and the dust particles will fall on to the cottonwool. The works will be clean and sparkling.

To clean white fur: Put some ordinary plain flour to heat in the oven. When it is hot but not browned at all, sprinkle it over the fur, working it in with a clean cloth. Leave for a few hours, and then brush it out thoroughly. To clean a darker fur, use wholemeal flour and brush extra-thoroughly.

To wash old lace: Sew it into a fine cotton bag. Soak it overnight in clean salad oil. The next day boil it in soap and water for 15 minutes. Rinse thoroughly. Dissolve a couple of tablespoons of sugar in the last rinsing water. Take it out of the bag and pin it flat on to a clean towel to dry. The sugar will give it a little stiffness.

Ivory: Use lemon juice to clean ivory – most effective if made into a paste with sawdust, spread on the article and then allowed to dry. This has a gentle bleaching action.

Above all, remember to cover everything with dust sheets *before* you get going on the chimney. Marks will be deducted for deviation.

22 March 1986

Hot Orchids with Honey at Bedtime

Although all our native orchids are now on the list of protected species, their roots, dried and powdered, were until very recently a highly prized item of the British diet. As a nourishing bed-time drink, it might well have been the forerunner of milky mixtures like Horlicks and Bournvita. Now that the search is under way for new commercial crops to replace the annual contribution to the EEC's various surplus-mountains, perhaps the brew might be returned to the popularity it enjoyed in previous centuries. Although some species of orchid plants can be obtained from garden centres and specialist nurseries, the ground-orchid is notoriously difficult to propagate. *Orchis* and related genera are of an extremely volatile temperament, capable of disappearing underground for several years, popping up again a few yards away with a whole new family of plantlets, and (most problematic of all) needing a symbiolitic fungus for the seeds to germinate at all.

However, with the rapidly advancing techniques of bio-technology, where there is a market there is surely a way. Rippling meadows of orchids must at least have the aesthetic edge over screaming-yellow sheets of oil-seed rape. More practically, the tubers have a higher protein-content than fillet steak. Creamy-white salep powder can be bought from any spice merchant throughout the Balkans and the Middle East – the chief European source being Romania. All of the European *Orchis* species are used, and both the pyramid orchid, *Anacamptis pyramidalis* and the lesser butterfly orchid, *Plantanthera bifolia*, are also considered edible. The substance is quite expensive when bought by weight, but since very little is needed to make a meal it is much appreciated by the rural poor who can gather their own from the wild.

In Britain, too, salep was traditionally poor man's food. The roots of *Orchis mascula*, known to the country people as dog-stones, were preferred. As recently as 1954, Dorothy Hartley recorded in her book *Food in England* that she had been grateful for a bowl of 'salop' – served to her hot, thick and well sugared – in a seaman's cottage after a long wet crossing. The Irish, she continued, sup their salop from a teacup, and thicken the mixture with cream and egg yolk. The Scots, naturally enough, liked theirs with a shot from the whisky-bottle. Hannah Glasse mentions the substance as obtainable at a shilling an ounce in 1747; Victorian workmen drank it in their 'car-men's rests'.

Charles Lamb, in his *Essays of Elia*, enthusiastically recommends the very same drink for the refreshment of homeward-bound chimney-sweeps. Mr Lamb informs his reader that the wholesome and pleasant beverage is on offer at Mr Read's shop on the south side of Fleet Street.

> This saloop – the precocious herb-woman's darling – the delight of the early gardener, who transports his smoking cabbages by break of day from Hammersmith to Covent Garden's famed piazzas – the delight, and oh! I fear too often the envy of the unpennied sweep. Him shouldst thou haply encounter with his dim visage pendent over the grateful steam, regale him with a sumptuous basin (it will cost thee but three-halfpennies) and a slice of delicate bread and butter (an added half-penny) – so may thy culinary

fires, eased of the o'ercharged secretions from thy worse-placed hospitalities, curl up a lighter volume to the welkin – so may the descending soot never taint thy costly well-ingredienced soups – nor the odious cry, quick-reaching from street to street, of the fired chimney, invite the rattling engines from the adjacent parishes, to disturb for a casual scintillation thy peace and pocket!

Meanwhile, in anticipation of fresh home-grown supplies culti-vated and harvested in British fields, prevail upon a friend to purchase a few ounces for you in, say, the spice market of Istanbul. The drink is no more complicated to prepare than a mug of Ovaltine. Terrific for vegetarians, invalids, everyone who prefers unproces-sed food, and those optimistic souls still stocking up their nuclear-fallout shelters.

PLAIN SALEP

1 pint milk or water   *Powdered cinnamon or ginger*
1 teaspoon salep powder

Put the milk into a saucepan and stir in the salep. Heat gently and simmer until the mixture thickens into a runny jelly. Flavour with a pinch of powdered cinnamon or ginger. Sugar, honey, whisky, egg yolk or cream can be added as you see fit.

24 April 1986

Index